ECHOES *of* EMPIRE

ROBIN WARD

ECHOES *of* EMPIRE

Victoria

&

Its Remarkable Buildings

HARBOUR PUBLISHING

Published by: HARBOUR PUBLISHING
PO BOX 219 Madeira Park BC Canada VON 2HO

*Published with the assistance of the Canada Council and the
Government of British Columbia, Cultural Services Branch*

Typeset in Monotype Fournier by Robin Ward
Book Design: Robin Ward
Printed and bound in Canada

Picture credits ❦ BCARS: BRITISH COLUMBIA ARCHIVES &
RECORDS SERVICE ❦ RW: ROBIN WARD
FRONTISPIECE *One of two imperial lion sculptures that guard
the Neptune Steps at Hatley Park.* RW
RIGHT *Stained glass panel, Christ Church Cathedral.* RW
ENDPAPERS ❦ *British Admiralty chart of Esquimalt & Victoria
harbours, 1896—a revision of surveys by Capt. G. H. Richards,
first published in 1864.* BCARS CM/B798

CANADIAN CATALOGUING IN PUBLICATION DATA
Ward, Robin, 1950–
  Echoes of Empire
  Includes bibliographical references and index.
  ISBN 1-55017-122-4
  1. Historic buildings—British Columbia—Victoria.
2. Victoria (BC)—Buildings, structures, etc.—History. I. Title.
FC3846.7.W37 1996   971.1'28   C96-910513-4
F1089.5.V6W37 1996

Acknowledgements ❧ RESEARCH FOR THIS BOOK WAS GREATLY HELPED BY THE GENEROUS ASSISTANCE OF IAN BARBOUR, GENERAL MANAGER, THE EMPRESS HOTEL ❧ STAFF AT BC ARCHIVES & RECORDS SERVICE, VICTORIA AND VANCOUVER PUBLIC LIBRARY ❧ I ALSO WISH TO THANK MY WIFE, PORTA, AND EDITOR, MARY SCHENDLINGER, FOR THEIR ADVICE, PATIENCE AND ENCOURAGEMENT

Contents

Introduction xi

Historical Background xix

THE INNER HARBOUR

    Parliament Buildings 1

    Canadian Pacific Railway Steamship

        Terminal 10

    Empress Hotel 15

    Crystal Garden 21

    Union Club 24

    Church of Our Lord 28

    St. Ann's Academy 34

    St. Ann's Schoolhouse 37

    Helmcken House 43

    Thunderbird Park 47

    Royal British Columbia Museum 53

JAMES BAY

    Colonial Administration Buildings 61

    Pendray House 70

    Ogden Point 72

    Newcombe House 77

    Carr House 80

    Beacon Hill Park 83

FORT VICTORIA

    Fort Victoria 91

    James Douglas 98

    Bastion Square 107

    Matthew Baillie Begbie 111

    Songhees Indian Reserve 115

ON THE WATERFRONT

    Maritime Museum 125

    Wharf Street 132

    Amor de Cosmos 143

    Dominion Customs House 151

    Point Ellice House 154

THE OLD TOWN

    Government Street 161

    Weiler Building 165

    Rogers' Chocolates 167

    E. A. Morris Tobacconist 168

    Pemberton Holmes Building 171

    Temple Building 173

    Bank of British Columbia 178

    Bank of Montreal 180

    Munro's Books 182

    Driard Hotel 186

    Market Square 187

CHINATOWN

    Fan Tan Alley 191

    Chinese Benevolent Associations 194

    Chinese Imperial School 198

AROUND TOWN

    City Hall 205

    Victoria Public Market 208

    Maynard Studios 212

    Carnegie Library 217

    Hudson's Bay Company Department Store 219

Bay Street Armoury 222

Missionaries & Churches 226

Quadra Street Burial Ground 237

Christ Church Cathedral 238

ROCKLAND & OAK BAY

Rockland 245

Wilson House 247

Art Gallery of Greater Victoria 249

Craigdarroch Castle 257

Government House 265

Oak Bay 275

Uplands 281

Rattenbury Residence 284

Ross Bay Cemetery 288

OUT OF TOWN

Esquimalt & Nanaimo Railway 295

Captain Jacobsen House 297

Esquimalt Harbour 303

Her Majesty's Canadian Dockyard 312

St. Paul's Naval & Garrison Church 316

Fort Rodd 320

Fisgard Lighthouse 322

Craigflower Farmhouse 326

Hatley Park 333

Butchart Gardens 339

Epilogue 345

Bibliography 347

Index 351

Introduction

TO DESCRIBE VICTORIA, AND TO DO FULL JUSTICE TO HER
MANIFOLD CHARMS, WOULD REQUIRE THE PENCIL OF BOTH
POET AND ARTIST—*the* Colonist, *1891*

V ICTORIA, founded in 1843 by the Hudson's Bay Company, is known and admired by visitors and locals alike for its old-world charm and idyllic natural setting: by the sea, in sheltered waters, with verdant parks and gardens and views of snow-capped mountains on the horizon. Its cultural character is enquiring but unaggressive. There is an absence of heavy industry and commercial bustle. Victoria is a centre of learning and leisure with a lingering, somewhat eccentric, British air. In 1904 the local publicity bureau began to advertise the city as an "Outpost of Empire." Rudyard Kipling, writing in 1907, likened it to Bournemouth with the Himalayas in the background. But what sets Victoria apart from many other former colonial cities is its buildings. Victoria's nineteenth-century architecture—the most cohesive and best preserved in Canada—defines the city.

Charles Ross, Jr. and family, c. 1880. Ross's Scottish father, Hudson's Bay Company factor Charles Ross, was in charge of building Fort Victoria in 1843. His mother Isabella was half-Native. Charles Ross, Jr. had not been to Scotland but, like many of Victoria's second generation residents, he inherited and exaggerated the cultural identity of the old country that he never saw. BCARS F-05032

Victoria evolved into a tight little HBC trading and farming community of about six hundred Europeans, coexisting with a fluid Native population that often outnumbered whites during seasonal trading. This delicate balance was irreversibly upset in 1858, the year the Fraser River gold rush jolted the trading post into a boom town—the stopping-off point on the way to the gold fields for some twenty thousand prospectors from around the world. Residents who were, according to newspapers of the time, aghast at the "habitual drunkenness and disgusting language and the houses of ill-fame" that accompanied gold fever, took small comfort from the town's most imposing building of the time—a battlemented fortress-like jail. But rising above the shambles, ornate cornices hinted at grandeur to come. Bureaucrats, merchants, skilled tradesmen and well-bred sons and daughters of the empire set the tone of the town.

By the 1880s, industry and commerce had made the city the biggest and wealthiest in British Columbia. The Inner Harbour was lined with warehouses, shipyards and factories; the port—from which vessels sailed to Europe and Asia—was the busiest in the province. In 1891 the Board of Trade had 150 members. Victoria was the main supply centre for frontier communities, mining and logging camps and salmon canneries on the mainland and on Vancouver Island. Gas streetlights were lit in 1860 and water pipes laid in 1864; the first telephone in the city was tested in 1878; street lighting was electrified in 1889 and the the city's first electric tram line opened in 1890. An economic recession had followed the gold rush, but colonial administration and civic pride—the city became the capital of BC in 1868—saw Victoria ascend to a bourgeois fin-de-siècle apogee. In 1897 the magnificent new Parliament Buildings were illuminated for Queen Victoria's Diamond Jubilee. But the same year, the city's streetcar company was sold to London-based investors, and its main office was relocated to Vancouver—a sign that Victoria's metropolitan veneer was cracking.

The erosion had begun in 1887 when the first Canadian Pacific Railway passenger train from Montreal arrived at Vancouver. Victoria—which had been promised the railway terminus—found its big-city ambitions switched to a slower track. Vancouver became Canada's prime Pacific port and BC's principal industrial centre. By the turn of the century, Victoria, the home of British Columbia's pioneering aristocracy, was becoming a city of elderly gents and civil servants—a milieu that attracted a corps of British colonial officials lured by prospects of comfortable retirement in a clubable setting complete with English climate and Scottish coastal scenery. Their voices preserved echoes of an empire that had begun to expire elsewhere—and they were the inspiration for the city's revival as a tourist centre. Where Vancouver looked to the future, Victoria turned to the past.

And what a past—what people! Victoria's history—as an HBC trading post, Royal Navy station, gold rush town, seat of government and focus for colonial high society—features a remarkable cast of characters: HBC Chief Factor and Colonial Governor James Douglas, who ruled the colony with "a glove of velvet on a hand of steel"; his right hand man, "the hanging judge" Chief Justice Matthew Bailie Begbie; the honourable Dr. John Sebastian Helmcken, surgeon and diarist at Fort Victoria; Amor de Cosmos, the messianic newspaper editor who became premier of BC; John Fannin, the obsessive big game hunter and first curator of the provincial museum; Robert Dunsmuir, the miner's son who became the richest man in the province; Emily Carr, the artist who preferred painting Native totem poles to gossiping over afternoon tea—and, perhaps the most eccentric and colourful of them all, Francis Rattenbury, the petulant architect who gave late nineteenth-century Victoria its most enduring imperial monuments—the Parliament Buildings and the Empress Hotel. If ever a city owed its appearance to one man it is this one. Rattenbury's ghost looms large over the city just as his two most photographed buildings do.

Victoria had the perfect setting and temperament to act as provincial capital and gracious host. In the 1890s, steamers ferried railway travellers from the mainland and the CPR's Empress liners began regular sailings to Asia, making Victoria a port of call on the "All Red Route" around the British Empire. The Empress Hotel opened in 1908 and established an upper crust repute that reinforced the city's British personality. Victoria's urban fabric—which economic decline helped preserve—has since been embroidered enthusiastically, not to say relentlessly, as "a little bit of old England"—even if no English hotel could claim that a stray cougar was once cornered in its car park, as happened at the Empress in 1992. The surface imagery of the city that was named after Queen Victoria was, and still is, a convincing illusion. There are Tudor Revival villas, cricket grounds and rose gardens. Emily Carr thought Victoria "the most English-tasting bit" of the whole country. British-born residents outnumbered Canadian-born in BC until the First World War and it still shows: behind mock-Tudor facades on Fort Street, antique shops and antiquarian bookstores are littered with the bric-a-brac of the British Empire. The Parliamentary Library's copies of the *Times* of London and the *Cariboo Observer* evoke the era when frontier gossip was laced with comment about faraway diplomacy and imperial affairs. Royal Navy captains left imperial names on local maps—Albert Head, Sax Point, Coburg Peninsula, and Gotha Point cartographically complete the royal title of Queen Victoria's consort, Prince Albert of Sax–Coburg–Gotha. In 1862, on the day of the city's incorporation, an editorial in the appropriately titled local newspaper, the *British Colonist*, opined that Victoria was "The Queen City of the Pacific possessions of Her Majesty, Queen Victoria."

But there was more to the place than the surface current, as Rudyard Kipling sensed when he gazed across the Strait of Juan de Fuca to the Olympic Mountains. "Real estate agents recommend it as a little piece of England," he noted, "but no England is set in any such seas or so fully charged with the mystery of the larger ocean beyond." For Victoria's early immigrants, the anticipation and relief of landfall were heightened by the punishing passages they endured sailing from Europe or from the St. Lawrence River to cross Panama or sail around Cape Horn. One of the colony's first public works was Fisgard Lighthouse, built in 1860 at the entrance to Esquimalt Harbour. The name of Beacon Hill Park recalls navigation beacons that were once lit above the town. Fog banks, tides and tempests earned the exposed west coast the nickname "Graveyard of the Pacific." Salty winds still ruffle Victoria's edges—on the exposed braes of Beacon Hill Park, the trees grow at an angle planed by the stiff prevailing wind.

Protected by a treacherous coastline, located half a world away from the mother country, and perched just beyond a vast mainland wilderness, Victoria's unexpected beauty and tranquility were irresistible to early British settlers. James Douglas, who had explored the coast, was enchanted by the setting—he described it as "a perfect Eden"—and he led the HBC expedition in spring 1843 that built Fort Victoria. For HBC men, used to the bitter winters in the interior and the chilling rains on the north coast, it seemed a paradise. John Burroughs, an American writer on an expedition to Alaska in 1899, wrote: "We were in British waters on June 1st and set foot on British soil at Victoria . . . Even the climate is British—mist and a warm slow rain—with dense verdure and thick green turf dotted with the English daisy. Indeed, nature here seems quite as English as does the soberly-built town." But while the temperate climate may have reminded British settlers of home Victoria was never as English as the "old England" catchphrase implies: the notion was conjured up in 1918 by a San Franciscan, George Warren, Victoria's publicity commissioner, who had never seen the real thing, but recognized its appeal and employed it to revive the local economy. In the city centre, the nineteenth-century streetscapes, with their frontier copies of metropolitan architectural styles, are unmistakably North American. Even the British imperial blend of Rattenbury's Parliament Buildings is infused with a contemporary North American flavour—a cultural mixture rooted in the city's sudden growth in the late 1850s.

Nothing now remains of Fort Victoria nor, it would seem, of the Natives whom Douglas encountered when he landed in 1843. There are totem poles aplenty in the city today but they were not carved by the local Songhees Indians: the poles are mainly replicas based on styles that were created farther up the coast. The local Indians did leave their language on some street names and natural features, but they otherwise seem a phantom presence in a land that was once their own. Neither they nor the Chinese (Victoria's Chinatown is the oldest and was once the most populous in the country) had a role in George Warren's dream of re-creating "old England." For Warren—and the CPR, whose publicity polished the myth of Victoria as an imperial garden of Eden—history had little value unless it could be edited and repackaged to suit a different time and purpose. This misleading version of Victoria's past has been perpetuated so religiously that other voices are not easily heard, although today Victoria's heritage buildings and historic sites have all been scrupulously charted on plaques attached to their walls. These numerous signs seem a well-intentioned attempt to recover the past that Warren ignored, but their short summaries barely scratch the surface of the facades whose histories they are meant to illuminate. There is more to Victoria's past—and present attitudes to it—than the plaques are able to tell.

—*Robin Ward, Vancouver BC, August 1996*

Victoria was founded in March 1843 when a Hudson's Bay Company expedition led by James Douglas landed to build a fortified trading post. With its eighteen-foot high palisade and four octagonal bastions, equipped with nine-pounder cannons to defend its storehouses, barracks and officers' quarters, Fort Victoria was as much a military strongpoint as it was a fur trade post. It survived Indian attack but was defenceless against the effects of the gold rush of 1858. The fort was demolished shortly after this picture was taken from Wharf Street, c. 1860. BCARS A–04099

The Parliament Buildings were a convincing backdrop for imperial ceremony when Queen Victoria's memorial service was held in 1901. BCARS E–04093

Historical Background

From 1579, when the first European is said to have glimpsed the coast of British Columbia, to 1897, the year of Queen Victoria's Diamond Jubilee, when the Parliament Buildings were illuminated for the first time.

1579 ❦ ENGLISH MARINER SIR FRANCIS DRAKE *is thought to have penetrated the entrance to the Strait of Juan de Fuca on his round-the-world voyage of exploration.*

1774–79 ❦ SPANISH NAVIGATOR JUAN PEREZ, *in search of the Northwest Passage (the imagined short route from Europe to China) sails up the west coast as far as the Queen Charlotte Islands, anchoring at Nootka Sound to trade with Indians on his way back to Mexico. His compatriot, Juan Francisco de la Bodega y Quadra, ventures as far north as Alaska in 1775 and claims the coast north of California for Spain in 1779.*

1778 ❦ CAPTAIN JAMES COOK, *the British navigator, also seeking the Northwest Passage, lands at Nootka Sound on the west coast of Vancouver Island for repairs and fresh water. Cook finds the Natives eager to trade their sea otter coats for nails, buttons, iron and tin. Over the next fifty years more than 400 ships visit the coast to trade for sea otter pelts. Each pelt fetches $100 in Macao—two years' pay for the average seaman.*

1784–92 ❦ PUBLICATION OF COOK'S JOURNAL, *with its description of coastal wildlife, causes a flurry of trade with the Indians for sea otter pelts. Over 100 European and American vessels appear on the coast, undermining Spanish territorial claims.*

Captain la Perouse, a French navigator, sails down the coast from Alaska to Monterey in 1785–86; he and his two ships are lost en route from Macao to France in 1789. An international incident is provoked in 1789 when the Spanish arrest British traders at Nootka Sound and establish a small settlement. Franciscan padres from the Spanish ships attempt to introduce the Natives to Christianity.

1790 ❧ THE NOOTKA SOUND CONVENTION *gives Spain and Britain joint sovereignty of the Pacific coast north of San Francisco. A Spaniard, Manuel Quimper, anchors in Esquimalt Harbour and names it Puerto de Cordova, after the Viceroy of Mexico.*

1792 ❧ CAPTAIN GEORGE VANCOUVER, *previously Cook's lieutenant, charts Puget Sound and Burrard Inlet, and circumnavigates the island that will later bear his name. Off Point Grey (in present-day Vancouver), he encounters the Spanish ships of Dionisio Alcala Galiano and Cayetano Valdes, dispatched by Alejandro Malaspina, who had led a notable scientific voyage north in 1789. Vancouver later exchanges diplomatic courtesies with Bodega y Quadra at Nootka.*

1793 ❧ SCOTTISH EXPLORER ALEXANDER MACKENZIE *of the fur trading North West Company becomes the first European to reach the Pacific Ocean overland through the Rocky Mountains when he arrives at Bella Coola. Mackenzie learns from local Indians that Vancouver's ship was on the coast just over a month earlier. Vancouver returns to England in 1794.*

1795 ❧ THE TERRITORIAL DISPUTE *between London and Madrid is settled to British advantage and the Spanish abandon their settlement at Nootka Sound.*

1805 ❧ AMERICAN EXPLORERS LEWIS AND CLARK *reach the mouth of the Columbia River, the second successful overland expedition across the continental mountains north of Mexico.*

1808 ❧ SIMON FRASER *of the North West Company reaches the Pacific via the Fraser River. Reminded of family descriptions of Scotland, he names the territory New Caledonia.*

1811 ⚜ AMERICAN TRADERS *of the Pacific Fur Company establish Fort Astoria at the mouth of the Columbia River. The North West Company's David Thompson completes a survey of the river. The company captures Fort Astoria during the war of 1812 and renames it Fort George. It is handed back after the war.*

1818 ⚜ THE BOUNDARY *between Great Britain and the United States is extended to the Rocky Mountains along the 49th parallel. Both powers agree to "joint occupancy" of disputed territory west of the mountains. After the Napoleonic Wars, the British government is reluctant to provoke other powers. Boundary agreements are reached with the Spanish in California in 1819 and the Russians in Alaska in 1824. In negotiations with the United States, the British take a consistently moderate approach.*

1821 ⚜ THE NORTH WEST COMPANY *of Montreal and the Hudson's Bay Company of London, formerly fierce rivals in the fur trade, amalgamate. The HBC, whose name prevails, expands its trading interests west of the Rocky Mountains from the Columbia River to Russian Alaska and to the Sandwich Islands (Hawaii), aided by former NWC explorers and traders.*

1824–27 ⚜ HUDSON'S BAY COMPANY GOVERNOR *George Simpson orders the construction of Fort Vancouver on the north bank of the Columbia River, and Fort Langley on the Fraser River. Dr. John McLoughlin, chief factor at Fort Vancouver from 1824 to 1846, gains a virtual monopoly of the Oregon fur trade and extends the Hudson's Bay Company's Columbia Department between the Rockies and the Pacific from Russian Alaska to Spanish California. In 1827, the HBC brigantine* Cadboro *becomes the first European vessel to enter the Fraser River.*

1836–37 ⚜ THE PADDLE STEAMER BEAVER *is built in London for the Hudson's Bay Company. It is the first steamship on the west coast—and a symbol of the company's trading pre-eminence—*

when it arrives at Fort Vancouver. But British claims to Oregon Territory begin to be undermined by American settlement. Captain McNeill on the Beaver *surveys the southern tip of Vancouver Island.*

1837 ❦ QUEEN VICTORIA *succeeds to the British Crown, heralding the mid-nineteenth-century heyday of the British Empire.*

1838 ❦ GEORGE SIMPSON, *governor of the Hudson's Bay Company, visits St. Petersburg to settle a territorial dispute with the Russian-American fur company trading on the Alaska coast.*

1842 ❦ ANTICIPATING *an unfavourable resolution of the border issue with the United States, Simpson decides to relocate Fort Vancouver to the southern tip of Vancouver Island. John McLoughlin dispatches his assistant, James Douglas, on the company schooner* Cadboro *to find a suitable site for settlement.*

1843 ❦ DOUGLAS, *with lieutenants Charles Ross and Roderick Finlayson, lands on Vancouver Island to build Fort Victoria. Douglas's bastion, originally to have been called Adelaide (after William IV's consort), is briefly called Fort Albert (after Prince Albert, Queen Victoria's husband), but is changed in honour of the queen. Douglas returns to Fort Vancouver.*

1844–46 ❦ AS A NEGOTIATING TACTIC, *the United States claims the whole Pacific coast to Russian Alaska. The slogan "54–40 or Fight" (referring to the Alaska boundary) provokes the Oregon Crisis of 1844. HMS* Fisgard *and* Pandora *appear at Esquimalt to show the flag and chart local waters.*

1846 ❦ THE OREGON TREATY *establishes the border between British colonies west of the Rocky Mountains and the United States along the 49th parallel—not, as the Hudson's Bay Company had hoped, along the Columbia River. The British retain Vancouver Island but sovereignty over the Gulf Islands is unsettled.*

1846–47 ❦ LOSS OF THE LOWER COLUMBIA RIVER *to the United States prompts Douglas to send Alexander Anderson to explore the Fraser and Coquihalla rivers as potential routes for fur shipments from the interior to the coast to avoid American territory.*

1848 ❦ THE UNITED STATES *annexes California after the Mexican–American War. The California gold rush begins.*

1849 ❦ JAMES DOUGLAS *becomes chief factor of Fort Victoria. The Hudson's Bay Company, which had hoped to be given all Crown land west of the Rocky Mountains, is granted commercial rights to Vancouver Island. In London, the company's self-interest and autocratic administration are increasingly criticized as a hindrance to colonial settlement.*

1850 ❦ THE CROWN COLONY OF VANCOUVER ISLAND *is founded with its capital at Victoria. Richard Blanshard, the first Royal governor of Vancouver Island, arrives in Victoria. Gold is found on the Queen Charlotte Islands but the deposits are not worth the risk of encounters with hostile Haida Indians. Douglas signs the first of fifteen treaties with Natives on Vancouver Island.*

1851 ❦ A PROVISIONAL COUNCIL *(James Douglas and two colleagues) is established in Victoria. Douglas succeeds Blanshard as governor. The industrial and cultural achievements of the British Empire are featured at the Great Exhibition at the Crystal Palace, London.*

1852–53 ❦ THE HUDSON'S BAY COMPANY *begins mining coal at Nanaimo, with miners from Britain. The company's ship* Otter, *the second steamship on the coast, arrives from London.*

1854–56 ❦ DURING THE CRIMEAN WAR, *the British Admiralty, planning raids on Russia's Siberian ports, asks Governor James Douglas for coal, provisions and a temporary hospital at Esquimalt. Governor Douglas suggests to London that he annex Russian Alaska. Permission for an expedition is not granted; the tsar later sells Alaska to the United States. An American customs officer is sent to the San Juan Islands where the Hudson's Bay Company*

has established a territorial claim with a farm and fishing station.
1856 ❧ THE EUROPEAN POPULATION *on Vancouver Island num-*
bers around 450 people—all Hudson's Bay Company employees
and settlers—some of whom petition for a legislative assembly,
duly approved by the Colonial Office in London and elected,
despite Douglas's displeasure. Only property owners (there were
about 40) are enfranchised.
1857 ❧ GOLD IS FOUND *on the North Thompson River.*
1858 ❧ NEWS *that gold has been discovered reaches San Francisco.*
The first of over 20,000 miners and camp followers sail to Victoria,
the main supply centre for the mainland gold fields, causing a surge
of speculation and development that undermines the Hudson's Bay
Company's monopoly. Douglas imposes colonial authority by issu-
ing licences, enforcing the rule of law and travelling to the gold
fields. A parliamentary bill to create the colony of New Caledonia
is introduced in the House of Commons, London to establish the
new Crown Colony—named British Columbia by Queen Victoria
to avoid confusion with the French South Pacific possession,
Nouvelle Calédonie, and to cock a snook at the American Columbia
territory. Douglas is appointed governor of the new colony and he
retains his post as governor of the Colony of Vancouver Island.
London sends 150 Royal Engineers to plan for settlement and devel-
opment. Matthew Baillie Begbie arrives from London as the main-
land colony's first chief justice. The Sisters of St. Ann from Quebec
disembark at Victoria.
1859 ❧ COLONEL RICHARD MOODY, *Royal Engineers, selects*
Queensborough (later renamed New Westminster) as the capital
of the new mainland colony. In Victoria, administration buildings
for the island colony, to replace Fort Victoria which was sold and
demolished, are built on the site of the present Parliament
Buildings. The "Pig War" on the San Juan Islands (a dispute in
which the only casualty was a Hudson's Bay Company pig shot by

an *American settler) results in a stand-off between the Royal Navy and American troops who land on the island. Joint occupancy is agreed upon until arbitration by Kaiser Wilhelm I in 1872 rules in the United States' favour. Chief Justice Begbie proclaims the Gold Field Act to regulate mining claims and impose the rule of law.*

1860 ✎ THE CARIBOO GOLD RUSH *begins. Fisgard Lighthouse, the first on the coast, is constructed at the entrance to Esquimalt Harbour and followed by a second lighthouse at Race Rocks. Chief Justice Begbie presides over the first case in which a white man is convicted on the testimony of Indians.*

1861 ✎ JAMES DOUGLAS *commands the Royal Engineers to begin construction of the Cariboo Road up the Fraser River to consolidate colonial authority and ensure that trade does not bypass his realm. The first colonial postage stamps are issued.*

1862 ✎ THE CITY OF VICTORIA *is incorporated. Gas street lighting is installed. Barkerville, in Cariboo gold rush country, briefly becomes the largest community north of San Francisco and west of Chicago.*

1863 ✎ THE HUDSON'S BAY COMPANY, *trading by royal charter granted in 1670, is sold to a business syndicate, ending its era of paternalistic colonization of the west.*

1864 ✎ THE CARIBOO WAGON ROAD *is completed. The first Legislative Assembly of British Columbia is convened at New Westminster. James Douglas, knighted by Queen Victoria, retires in Victoria. Two men are required to take his place: Arthur Edward Kennedy as governor of Vancouver Island, and Frederick Seymour as governor of British Columbia.*

1865 ✎ THE ROYAL NAVY BASE *at Esquimalt is permanently established.*

1866 ✎ THE COLONIES *of Vancouver Island and British Columbia are joined. Seymour is appointed governor and New Westminster is named the capital.*

1867 ❧ ONTARIO, QUEBEC, *New Brunswick, and Nova Scotia are the founding provinces of the Dominion of Canada which is formed as a self-governing entity within the British Empire. The United States purchases Alaska from the tsar of Russia.*

1868 ❧ VICTORIA *is declared the capital of British Columbia. The Legislative Assembly of British Columbia sits in Victoria for the first time.*

1869 ❧ THE BRITISH GOVERNMENT, *recognizing the west coast's isolation and strategic importance to the empire, appoints Anthony Musgrave governor of British Columbia with a brief to encourage union with the Dominion of Canada.*

1870 ❧ MATTHEW BAILLIE BEGBIE *is appointed Chief Justice of the United Colony of British Columbia.*

1871 ❧ BRITISH COLUMBIA *enters Confederation as the Dominion of Canada's sixth province (Manitoba joined in 1870). The colony's conditions of entry to Confederation include that the Dominion government in Ottawa assume the provincial debt and build a railway to the Pacific coast within ten years and a graving dock at Esquimalt. Surveyor Sandford Fleming scouts possible routes for a transcontinental railway.*

1873 ❧ A CEREMONY AT ESQUIMALT *marks the anticipated terminus of the transcontinental railway line—but progress is delayed after the "Pacific Scandal" over railway cronyism causes the resignation of the "Father of Confederation," Canada's first prime minister John A. Macdonald.*

1875 ❧ MATTHEW BAILLIE BEGBIE *is knighted by Queen Victoria at Balmoral Castle, Scotland.*

1877 ❧ SIR JAMES DOUGLAS *dies in Victoria. Miners strike at Robert Dunsmuir's Nanaimo coal mines.*

1878 ❧ AFTER DELAYS, *and appeals by British Columbia to the Colonial Office in London in 1874, Prime Minister Alexander Mackenzie announces the terminus of the transcontinental railway will be on Burrard Inlet (present-day Vancouver). Victorians are dismayed—a northern route, crossing to the island, had been expected. The first telephone in Victoria is tested.*

1881–85 ❧ THE CANADIAN PACIFIC RAILWAY, *headed by a group of Montreal's Scottish business elite, is awarded a charter to construct the railway line, completed in 1885. Over 15,000 Chinese enter British Columbia, including 10,000 imported by the CPR and its agents in Hong Kong and San Francisco. Many of the Chinese labourers pass through or later settle in Victoria.*

1886 ❧ THE CITY OF VANCOUVER, *the western terminus of the CPR, is incorporated. Vancouver Island's branch railway, the Esquimalt & Nanaimo, is opened by Prime Minister Sir John A. Macdonald. Atlantic Ocean and CPR telegraph lines connect the west coast with Europe. News from London that previously took weeks or months to arrive, is transmitted instantly (a "Round the World Cable" link, across the Pacific Ocean, follows in 1902).*

1887 ❧ THE FIRST CPR PASSENGER TRAIN *from Montreal arrives at Vancouver. At Esquimalt, HMS* Cormorant *is the first ship to enter the newly completed graving dock.*

1888–90 ❧ VICTORIA'S *first door-to-door postal delivery service begins. Matthew Baillie Begbie opens the new Victoria Law Courts in 1889. Street lights are electrified. The city's tram service is inaugurated.*

1893 ❧ ARCHITECT FRANCIS RATTENBURY *wins the competition to design the new Provincial Parliament Buildings.*

1894 ❧ SIR MATTHEW BAILLIE BEGBIE *dies.*

1896 ❧ GOLD IS DISCOVERED *in the Klondike. Victoria relives the boom of 1858.*

1897 ❧ DIAMOND JUBILEE *of Queen Victoria is celebrated across the British Empire. British Columbia's new Parliament Buildings are illuminated for the event—and officially opened the following year.*

VICTORIA R. I.

1837-1901

The Inner Harbour

THE VIRTUE OF ADVERSITY IS FORTITUDE . . . THE VIRTUE OF
PROSPERITY IS TEMPERANCE . . . GREAT EFFECTS COME OF
INDUSTRY AND PERSEVERANCE—*Victorian epigrams inside the
Parliament Buildings*

PARLIAMENT BUILDINGS

O N a stage set for imperial ceremony, Queen Victoria—cast in
bronze on a granite pediment in front of British Columbia's
Parliament Buildings—gazes across the Inner Harbour of the
city that bears her name. She seems aloof and slightly bemused by the
prospect. A Greco-Roman style cast-iron fountain gushes enthusiastically, but there are no broad boulevards or bellicose government
buildings for her to admire, no battleships in the harbour or Royal
Household Cavalry on parade. Only the slowly cruising red London
buses are double-decked, and the sole sentry to be seen is the Cenotaph's
First World War infantryman, poised, with Lee-Enfield rifle at the
ready. The only legions here are tourists who troop dutifully beneath her

*The statue of Queen Victoria at the Parliament Buildings was
the work of an English sculptor. The gilt figure of Captain
George Vancouver on the copper dome was made by a Viennese
metalsmith. An Italian sculptor, Scottish carver and many other
craftsmen whose names are unrecorded fashioned the Parliament
Buildings' splendid and multifarious decorative effects.* RW

I

plinth, perhaps hearing echoes of an empire on which the sun was never to set. This is the paradox and poignancy of the place, a city so close yet so far away from the imperial age and the queen after whom it was named. The monarch's effigy was installed in colonial cities around the world but nowhere does she, or the empire she ruled, seem so idyllic, so perfectly innocuous, so oddly mirrored as they do here. Surveying her "little bit of old England," the queen seems to have stepped into an eccentric tea party setting like Alice in Wonderland.

The Empress Hotel was named in her honour but its whimsical architecture has its roots in France; the Parliament Buildings are not quite haughty enough to celebrate imperial conquest; the cast-iron fountain was made in New York. The British acquired the Colony of Vancouver Island by accident rather than design and held it through the resolve of one man, commemorated on an obelisk "erected by the people of British Columbia to the memory of Sir James Douglas KCB, Governor and Commander-in-Chief from 1851 to 1864," beside the queen. If size reflected achievement, Douglas's obelisk would have been built on a pharaonic scale. Its inscription, though, and that on the queen's granite pedestal—"Victoria R.I. This stone was laid September 24th 1919 by his Royal Highness the Prince of Wales"—were carved to last a thousand years. No Prince of Wales would erect talismans like those on the lawn of the Parliament Buildings today, any more than a government would choose to be attired with the pretension of the nineteenth century that the buildings, opened in 1898, display. But their presence is still commanding. Their architect too was firmly cast in the imperial mould.

Francis Mawson Rattenbury, who gave architectural substance to Victoria's imperial dream with his design for the Parliament Buildings, was born into a Methodist family in Leeds in 1867. He studied architecture with his two uncles, William and Richard Mawson, whose company was known as Lockwood and Mawson before Rattenbury's apprenticeship. The firm had made its reputation in mid-Victorian England with designs for Bradford Town Hall and Saltaire, a model mill town built for "work, health, education, and moral instruction." Rattenbury won a Soane Medallion in 1890, an award that could have raised his profile from anonymity as a junior member of the firm. But he exchanged his worthy family background for the promise of empire, where distant booming cities brimmed with work for British-trained architects. Lured by Canadian Pacific Railway advertisements promoting the wonders of the Rocky Mountains and the developing west, Rattenbury sailed for Canada in 1892. In Montreal, then the country's largest city, he was struck by fashionable North American architectural styles, particularly the Richardsonian Romanesque facades at Windsor Station which he saw before boarding a train for Vancouver. Within a year, Rattenbury moved to Victoria, having achieved astonishing early success by winning the competition for design of the new provincial Parliament Buildings in 1893. He was twenty-five years old.

Entries to the competition were to be anonymous. While other entrants deployed overblown regal or Latin *noms de plume*, Rattenbury signed his drawings "BC ARCHITECT" to flatter the local judges. Sixty-five entries were received from across North America—although none by heavyweight architects of the day—in styles that ranged from Venetian Gothic to the Roman Empire. Rattenbury's precociously accomplished design caught the spirit of the age and place with its blend of rugged Romanesque and, in polished Renaissance manner, British imperial splendour. Nothing he subsequently designed displayed the confident draughtsmanship of the Parliament Buildings, stirring a rumour that the design had been plagiarized from a Lockwood and Mawson concoction for a maharajah. But while there is a whiff of curry in the squatly domed, arcaded pavilions of the design, the aroma of roast beef is stronger. The buildings reflect mainstream British architecture of the time—Glasgow City Chambers, and the Natural History Museum in South Kensington, for example—that the architect would have known. The plagiarism rumour remains unproven: most of Rattenbury's plans and correspondence were destroyed when his office on Government

Street burned down in 1910. But he was an opportunist, talented enough to conceal his use of other architects' designs. Certainly he was not above embellishing his credentials. He described himself in an advertisement in the Vancouver *Daily World* (coincidentally on the same page announcing the competition for the Parliament Buildings) as having "for ten years erected all classes of buildings in conjunction with the well-known firm of Lockwood and Mawson, Bradford." But his work in England was paltry and the firm's creative force, Henry Francis Lockwood, had died in 1878. By the time Rattenbury joined as an apprentice in 1885, the practice had been renamed Mawson and Mawson. Rattenbury knew that in an isolated corner of the empire it was unlikely anyone would dispute his claim to fame, and after winning the Parliament Buildings competition, he defended the specious Lockwood connection to deflect criticism that he was too inexperienced to be trusted with the job. He then made up for immaturity by overbearing self-confidence. He sidestepped responsibility for mistakes, design changes and cost overruns, blaming administrators, contractors and, on one occasion, the stone (it was the wrong

When Francis Rattenbury saw Victoria for the first time in 1892 from the deck of a steamer approaching the Inner Harbour, he conceived a stone-built provincial capital adorned with picturesque statuary and monumental architecture—an "imperial garden of Eden"—all of his own design. Between 1892 and 1924 he was able to realize his dream. He became the most influential architect in the city and, when the Empress Hotel opened in 1908, the province. But he plummeted to a self-destructive end. Few photographs of Rattenbury survive. This one was taken c. 1897. Many of his notes and plans were lost in a fire in 1910 that destroyed his office on Government Street. A set of his drawings of the Parliament Buildings is displayed in the buildings' foyer—the originals (and other examples of his draughtsmanship) can be inspected in the BC Archives. BCARS B–09502

colour, he said, although he had chosen it from the quarry himself).

Rattenbury's youthful ambition, however, soared above his critics as the Parliament Buildings rose above the wooden houses and kitchen gardens of James Bay. The neo-Romanesque archway frames ceremonial steps and a barrel-vaulted vestibule guarded by palatial iron gates in a portal fit for the most imperious dignitary. Captain George Vancouver and Judge Matthew Baillie Begbie occupy niches respectively left and right of the entrance. Columns are intricately carved with mythical creatures and Greek foliage. Some competition entries placed imperial lions at the entrance, but Rattenbury's building is endowed with more meaning than clichés from Trafalgar Square. Prancing deer and bighorn sheep decorate the provincial coat of arms on a facade that spouts a gallimaufry of gargoyles, griffins, turrets and cupolas, crowned with the architect's great Renaissance dome. A gilded effigy—not of Rattenbury, although he would have enjoyed the conceit (he had actually suggested Britannia), but of George Vancouver—glints on the cupola.

In the loggia by the Legislative Chamber, a superb stained glass window by James Bloomfield celebrates Queen Victoria's Diamond Jubilee (Bloomfield's father Henry was an English immigrant who established the province's first stained glass workshop in New Westminster in 1889). Other windows, most of them made by Powell Brothers, Leeds, in

Nothing Rattenbury subsequently designed displayed the confident draughtsmanship and stirring silhouette of the Parliament Buildings. It was rumoured that the design had been cut from a blueprint drawn for a maharajah's palace in India, prepared by his uncles' firm in England, where he had trained. The rumour was never substantiated. Rattenbury flattered his clients with charm—and infuriated them with petulance when criticized. But he confounded his detractors with a combination of overbearing self-confiidence and an undeniable flair for flamboyant design. RW

Rattenbury's native Yorkshire, and Joseph McCausland, Toronto, and some by Morris & Company, London, illustrate pioneering activities and ambitions. Sheep farming and forestry appear along with the arts, sciences and Greek philosophers' names. There are moralistic Victorian epigrams: "The virtue of adversity is fortitude . . . The virtue of prosperity is temperance . . . Great effects come of industry and perseverance." The latter was noted but apparently misunderstood by the English artist George H. Southwell, commissioned forty years later, in 1932, to paint eight neo-Renaissance murals representing the "historical qualities necessary for the establishment of a civilization." Southwell, an Englishman employed by the government publicity bureau as "provincial artist," persevered with an easy representational style. His tableaux, showing George Vancouver and Juan Francisco de la Bodega y Quadra, Judge Matthew Baillie Begbie, and James Douglas and Indians building Fort Victoria for the Hudson's Bay Company, were painted in the style, but without the artistry, of Italian church frescoes. Southwell's sentimental renderings lack Rattenbury's gusto and confidence.

Throughout his architectural career, Rattenbury threatened to resign when his judgement was questioned, and invariably he got his way. The marbled spectacle of the Legislative Hall, finished in Beaux Arts style complete with Parisian plaster nymphs, was only completed after he threw a tantrum about government penny-pinching. "The whole character of the hall," he announced, "depends entirely on the rich and massive marble columns and we cannot in any adequate way replace these with any cheaper imitation." Magnificent as it turned out to be, the hall was not opened in time for Queen Victoria's Diamond Jubilee in 1897, and the unfinished buildings were disguised with illuminations to celebrate the event (the fairy-lit outline has been a feature of the facade ever since). Legend has it that Rattenbury was not invited to the official opening in 1898 because of his cavalier attitude to his client and contractors. But he chose not to attend. With the impatience and energy that characterized his rise he went to London to drum up support for a steamship venture in the Klondike. His absence was noted after the martial music at the opening ceremony, played by the 5th BC Field Regimental band, echoed away—as were the unsatisfactory acoustics in the Legislative Hall. Professional detractors fluttered angrily round the architect's flame, criticizing his costly ornament and statuary carved by European-trained sculptors Charles Marega, Albert Franz Cizek and George Gibson (immigrants from, respectively, Genoa, Vienna and Edinburgh). Wrought iron gates had been ordered from London. Shiploads of stained glass, mahogany, Italian marble and mosaics had been discharged at the Inner Harbour. But Rattenbury also made use of local building materials: wood floors and finishes, brick for inner walls, roofing slate and granite barged from Nelson Island for the foundations and main floor, and more easily carved Haddington Island andesite to embellish the facades. The building that arose was a tremendous undertaking for a small city of the time and for the battalions of craftsmen who worked on the project. The architect is remembered today, but many anonymous hands created the Parliament Buildings' splendour.

When the accounts were tallied, it was found that the buildings had cost nearly twice the original estimate of $500,000. Rattenbury bounced back and was retained to design the Parliamentary Library, built in 1912–16. If he had learned any lessons from the original buildings, they did not include restraint. His initial proposal for a chateauesque design to match the Loire-style rear roofline on the existing buildings was rejected. Rattenbury, who did not like being sent back to the drawing board, responded with a furious burst of Edwardian baroque. The library rotunda, a marbled space punctuated with seven giant *scagliola* columns flung up around its walls, is completely clad in Carrara marble that reflects the decadence of the late imperial age as much as does the architect's annoyance. The effect is not that you've come to study, but that you have drowned in a Roman bathhouse.

Outside, the building takes on the proportions of a vast mausoleum. Petrified in niches on the rusticated columned facades are statues of provincial explorers and administrators—so many that they were later identified on an explanatory plaque outside. To make sure the building's purpose was understood, Shakespeare, Milton and classical scribes appear on medallions around the walls. Rattenbury's creative flame was extinguished here with a ghostly flicker of inspiration from his early years. The sepulchral sculpted figures from British Columbia's past are thought to have been inspired by Henry Francis Lockwood's Bradford Town Hall, completed in 1873, and garnished with similar statues of English kings.

·⇐ CANADIAN PACIFIC RAILWAY STEAMSHIP TERMINAL ⇒·
468 Belleville Street

Francis Rattenbury saw Victoria for the first time in 1892, from the deck of a steamer approaching the Inner Harbour from Vancouver. He had come to inspect the site for the Parliament Buildings that would transform the three-storey brick town into a stone-built provincial capital dressed with picturesque statuary and monumental buildings—an "imperial garden of Eden," as he visualized it, all of his own design.

After the Parliament Buildings were completed in 1898, Rattenbury won a competition in 1901 to design a new hotel in Vancouver for the CPR. He managed to juggle his responsibilities to other clients while working for the railway almost full-time. As the company's favoured architect he was responsible for all its new buildings from Calgary to the west coast, and he designed everything from palatial interiors for a CPR steamship to chalet-style railway hotels in the Rockies. From this influential perch, his vision for the Inner Harbour began to take shape. In 1903 he sketched in a grand hotel where the Empress stands, a Dominion Post Office and a Beaux Arts public library to the north, and an Anglican cathedral on Church Hill. Only the Empress was built to his design; the post office had already been built to a plan drawn by a government architect in Ottawa, the library was constructed on an inland site by one of his rivals, and cathedral design was not his métier—churches were the only commissions he never sought.

In 1923, toward the end of his career, he was given the chance to almost complete his grand vision of the Inner Harbour when the CPR invited him to design a steamship terminal near the Parliament Buildings. Rattenbury thought it would be "a handsome little building, as good as anything I have ever done." But both Rattenbury and his client exchanged the romantic Victoriana of their youth for the boardroom Neo-classicism of middle age. Solid, dependable and safe, the building was the very image of an imperial establishment that had run out of steam. The colonnaded block that wallowed off Rattenbury's drawing board was designed to impress passengers disembarking from the company's fleet of royally named steamers. The building's incongruous Athenian grandeur—twenty-three Ionic columns, bas-reliefs of the Greek sea god Poseidon, dolphins and CPR cartouche—is firmly moored in the era of imperial expansion when Rattenbury made his name. The terminal seems, like the declining empire, to lack the vigour of earlier years. It was the last major building he designed.

The CPR Steamship Terminal was not the last building to complete the scene. In 1931 a three-level garage and ferry terminal was built at the corner of Government and Wharf streets. Now the Tourist Information Office, the building dates from the time when flying and speed replaced steam power in the public imagination. Its Art Deco pinnacle was designed as a beacon to guide seaplanes to the Inner Harbour at night: it could be seen from sixty miles away, which caused it to be permanently extinguished as a security measure during the Second World War. The floatplanes that now swoop into the harbour are guided by the harbour master. Sometimes he can be seen buzzing about in an inflatable dinghy to chase errant yachts out of the way.

No ships use Rattenbury's steamship terminal today: the provincial government has leased the building to the Royal London Waxworks. But there is a phantom fleet on the seawall parapet in front of the Empress

Hotel. There, a sequence of plaques illustrates Victoria's argosies of empire: the *Princess Marguerite* "with King George VI and Queen Elizabeth," the Hudson's Bay Company steamer *Beaver* "with James Douglas to found Victoria," the *Sea Bird* "with the first four Sisters of St. Ann," the *Thames City* "with Mr. William Hughes, bandmaster of the Royal Engineers, and Mrs. Hughes," the *Panama* "out of San Francisco . . . brought Matthew Baillie Begbie to Victoria as Judge of the Crown Colony of British Columbia," and the sidewheeler *Isabel* "built in Victoria for Captain Edward Stamp, a prime industrialist of BC and a British master mariner." The most illustrious mariner remembered is Captain James Cook, who has been rewarded with a statue that, oddly, faces not the sea but the facade of the Empress Hotel. An inscription on the granite plinth gives an account of his third voyage of discovery: "Capt. James Cook RN 1728–79. After two historic voyages to the South Pacific . . . cruising the waters of the Pacific Northwest on his third and final voyage . . . his two ships *Resolution* and *Discovery* . . . searching for the western exit to the legendary Northwest Passage. In March, 1778, they put into

TOP *The CPR's Clydebuilt steamer* Princess Marguerite, *the "Pride of the Pacific," brought luxury liner style to the West Coast. With her sister ship, the* Princess Kathleen, *she sailed the "Triangle Route" linking Victoria, Seattle and Vancouver. Each ship could carry 1,500 passengers, and each had 290 berths and 136 staterooms for overnight voyages. The ships were fitted with lounges in the glass-domed style of the Empress Hotel. Each had three grand pianos to entertain passengers into the wee hours of the morning.* AUTHOR'S COLLECTION

BOTTOM *The Inner Harbour in 1925, showing the newly completed Canadian Pacific Railway Steamship Terminal. Posters and advertisements—and commercial postcards like the one shown here—publicized the CPR's ships and hotels, enticing tourists to Victoria from around the world.* AUTHOR'S COLLECTION

PRINCESS MARGUERITE

C. P. R. Landing Place, Victoria, B. C. Canada

Nootka Sound for repairs and to trade with the Native people. With him on the voyage were Mr. William Bligh as master of the *Resolution* and midshipman George Vancouver." Cook never entered the Inner Harbour or found the Northwest Passage. He was killed by Polynesians on a beach in Hawaii in 1779. Bligh returned to the Pacific as the captain of HMS *Bounty,* the ship of the infamous mutiny in 1789. Vancouver, promoted to captain of the *Discovery*, returned to explore and chart the coasts of the Pacific Northwest, British Columbia and Alaska between 1792 and 1794. He died in obscurity in England in 1798 but, like Cook and others of his ilk, left his name and those of his lieutenants on every landfall. Spanish navigators too live on in the names of bays, inlets and city streets in Vancouver and Victoria.

·⇐ EMPRESS HOTEL ⇒·
721 Government Street

Every Canadian city and wilderness resort worth its salt boasts a chateauesque railway hotel built in the nineteenth-century baronial manner that the Canadian Pacific Railway made its own. In the 1880s William Cornelius Van Horne, the American general manager of the CPR who was keen to boost revenue on the transcontinental line, conceived a chain of grand hotels from sea to sea. Van Horne was inspired by Cook's Tours, the English company established to cater to the travel whims of the industrial revolution's nouveau riche in the 1860s. "Since we can't export the scenery," Van Horne declared, "we'll have to import the tourists." The railway's mock-medieval architecture, a romantic mélange inspired by Balmoral Castle in Scotland and the Loire chateaux of France, was designed to make the train journey across Canada more

The Empress, named after Queen Victoria, Empress of India,
is one of the legendary imperial hotels—and architect Francis
Rattenbury's most photographed building. RW

comfortable for well-heeled European aristocrats and adventurers. The Banff Springs Hotel, for example, was to be "the finest hotel on the North American continent . . . fit for the richest Highland chieftains."

The Château Frontenac in Quebec, a replica Loire chateau designed by American architect Bruce Price, set the tone for other CPR hotels when it opened in 1893 and established the chateau style as the railway's signature across the country. Price, who had built Windsor Station in Montreal for the railway in 1887–89, reasoned that what was picturesque enough for the aristocracy of sixteenth-century France and Scotland would flatter the CPR's Scottish directors in Montreal and the French Canadians of Quebec. When Francis Rattenbury was invited to design the Empress, the CPR told him to look at the Château Frontenac first.

In 1901, when Rattenbury was retained as the railway's western division architect, Victoria's ruling class hoped it was a sign that the CPR was about to build them a grand hotel like others erected across the country. They were even willing to forgive the railway for locating its terminus in Vancouver, instead of running the line down to Victoria from Seymour Narrows as originally expected. When railway president Sir Thomas Shaughnessy hinted he might build them a hotel, Victoria's businessmen laid out the red carpet. But Shaughnessy played hard to get, despite energetic wooing. Finally, in 1903, the city agreed to give the railway the choicest site in the city, with free water and no taxes for fifteen years. The city would also prepare and landscape the site, a considerable cost since the property was under water at the time. Rattenbury then produced his design promptly, leading to speculation that Shaughnessy had been canny rather than candid in negotiation and had planned to build the hotel all along. The Government Street bridge across James Bay was replaced with a causeway, and the bay to the east (the city dump) was filled to make a foundation for the hotel.

Considering the loss of the railway terminus to rival Vancouver, the hotel was something of a consolation prize for Victoria. But what a prize! What an architect! Rattenbury was the toast of local society after his

Parliament Buildings triumph, and his appointment by the railway was enthusiastically received. The *Colonist*, Victoria's daily paper, claimed the hotel would "make the Western gateway of the great transcontinental system a fitting companion to the historic pile on the heights of Quebec." Van Horne would have been pleased at the newspaper's turn of phrase: the "historic" Château Frontenac was only ten years old. Rattenbury, who could readily turn his pen to most styles, acted in the spirit rather than the letter of the instruction that he tour the Château Frontenac for inspiration. He skillfully adapted the CPR's Franco-Scottish style, adding Elizabethan, Jacobean and Gothic features— "mature chateau style," it has been called (respectfully imitated by a new wing in 1929 and extensive renovations in 1988).

The railway spared no expense in fitting out the hotel to appeal to Van Horne's aristocratic globetrotters. After the Empress opened in 1908, the local beau monde, nostalgic for the palazzos of London clubland and the hunting lodges of the Scottish Highlands, accepted as their own its Neo-classical and baronial salons—which outclassed even Government House as glittering social settings. In 1907 Rudyard Kipling noted, "The hotel was just being finished. The ladies' drawing room . . . carried an arched and superbly enriched plaster ceiling of knops and arabesques and interlacings, which somehow seemed familiar. 'We saw a photo of it in *Country Life*,' the contractor explained . . . 'it seemed just what the room needed, so one of our plasterers, a Frenchman . . . took it and copied it.'" When the Prince of Wales visited Victoria in 1919 there was no question (although he was staying at Government House) where the royal ball would be held. In 1957, after Government House burned down, Lieutenant Governor Frank Mackenzie Ross conducted his vice-regal business from the hotel, already suitably decorated with pastel portraits of the Countess of Aberdeen, Marchioness of Dufferin, Marchioness of Lorne, Lady Tweedsmuir and other titled wives of governors general. In the 1930s, formerly well-off widows lived in rooms upstairs, encouraged to stay on by a depression-era rate of a dollar a day. Along with a

*The Tiffany-style stained glass dome in the Palm Court at the
Empress Hotel, damaged by a snowfall and long boarded up,
was rediscovered and restored during renovations in 1988.* RW

battalion of expiring ex-colonial bureaucrats and brigadiers, they preserved the Empress and Victoria's colonial ambience in the public mind
long after British influence had been diluted elsewhere. Local policemen
wore helmets like London bobbies, and "Land of Hope and Glory" could
be played without affectation or irony in the hotel tearoom.

The potted palms and much else of the original decor lingers, preserving the fin-de-siècle world of blustery brigadiers, beefy baronesses,
bewhiskered business barons and epauletted naval captains. Brass Royal
Mail boxes are as bright as binnacles, and the Tea Lobby is a parade of
classical columns. The Rose Room is vaulted and plastered in Jacobean
style; the dining room looks set for a medieval banquet. Adamesque
scrollwork, oak panelling, sconces shaped like hunting trophies, William
Morris-style wall coverings, massive fireplace mantles, and a grandfather
clock that chimes the notes of Big Ben complete the illusion of antique
grandeur that the railway sought to project.

In 1906 Rattenbury stunned the city, and his client, when he resigned
after completing the Empress design. He flounced off in a temper after
the company's chief architect, Walter S. Painter, summoned him to
Montreal to discuss changes to the interior design. These were suggested
by Kate Reed, wife of the company's hotel superintendent, whose artistic taste had been refined by New York high society. She had advised Van
Horne on his art collection, redecorated the Château Frontenac and prepared the royal train that took the Duke and Duchess of York across the
country in 1901. Rattenbury's irritation was not just that she was a company wife, or that she may have been inspired by English magazines like
Country Life—he was too—but that he worked alone. He insisted on
complete control and rarely chose to share credit with anyone. He had
also begun to freelance for a rival railway, the Grand Trunk Pacific,

Empress Hotel, Victoria,

TOP *"Tea at the Empress" is a highlight of any visit to Victoria and, in keeping with the clinking china and silver-plated cake stands, a dress code is discreetly enforced. Discretion has always been a watchword at the hotel; when Winston Churchill supped at the Empress in the early 1920s, staff apologized for the prohibition then in force and served his whisky in a silver teapot and water in a cream jug.* RW

BOTTOM *The roofscape of the Empress Hotel, a mountain range of chateauesque peaks, was created by additions in 1929 and 1988. This postcard view, by British publisher Valentine & Sons, shows the original 1908 elevation.* AUTHOR'S COLLECTION

which copied the CPR style. Ratz, as he had been nicknamed by then, drew up a plan for the GTP's Prince Rupert terminus that, had it been built, would have outshone even the Empress. But it is for the Parliament Buildings and the Empress that he is remembered. Ironically, the hotel was also the setting of his very public fall, at the end of 1923. Rattenbury was guest of honour at a dinner to celebrate a referendum approving construction of the Crystal Garden, and there he met Alma Pakenham, a young war heroine who had been widowed, remarried, and then divorced. She became his mistress—and eventually his downfall.

·⇐ CRYSTAL GARDEN ⇒·
713 Douglas Street

In 1921, Victoria council approached Francis Rattenbury to design a swimming pool and pleasure garden to be built behind the Empress Hotel. Voters had rejected the plan, but city council hoped that with Rattenbury's name they could revive the project. The chamber of commerce appointed an "amusement centre committee" to drum up popular support. Advertisements promised "the finest salt water swimming pool in Canada . . . dancing floors larger than the Empress ballroom . . . picture galleries and exhibits of all kinds . . . the most beautiful indoor gardens imaginable . . . a building of great beauty which will be a source of pride to the City." Victoria was already home to Canada's first artificial ice rink which had been opened in 1911.

Rattenbury, who had built nothing significant since the Parliamentary Library ten years before, drew up a costly scheme for a sprawling English-style winter garden complete with shopping arcades, a ballroom, banquet hall, three swimming pools, a forty-foot fountain, exhibition rooms and cafes, and four illuminated corner towers. The city couldn't afford it. But in 1923, the CPR stepped in and offered to lease the site and build and operate the winter garden—in return for a twenty-year freeze on the Empress Hotel's taxes, and free water, tax exemption, and profits from the garden for the same period. Rattenbury, having already sketched the plans, was retained as architect. A mid-winter referendum in 1923, timed to make the notion of a tropical pleasure garden irresistible, passed with an overwhelming majority. The chamber of commerce called the measure "a great step toward lasting prosperity." D. C. Coleman, vice-president of the CPR, declared the building would make "Victoria, Vancouver, and British Columbia in general, the playground of the western world."

Faced with such expectations, Rattenbury hired an associate, Percy Leonard James, to help him complete the project. Their relationship was not cordial. Rattenbury, who had effectively retired, disliked having to bow to James's experience designing similar structures in England. James also worked with Rattenbury on the structural design of the CPR Steamship Terminal and would later claim that both buildings were his own creations. Rattenbury dismissed James's claim and bid for a higher share of the Crystal Garden fee by saying he had hired James only as a draughtsman for final details. "The whole conception of the Crystal Garden was designed by me," he claimed in a letter to the *Colonist* in 1925. James was given the benefit of the doubt and was subsequently commissioned to design the swimming pool at the CPR's Chateau Lake

Louise. But Rattenbury can be credited with the exterior trimmings at the Crystal Garden, and also for the vision that helped launch the project: he was arguably a better promoter than an architect. The interior was to be "considerably larger than the Hudson's Bay Store," and the building was to be supported by a concrete raft two and a half feet thick, floated on the James Bay landfill. Seawater for the pool was pumped from the harbour and filtered and heated at the Empress Laundry which stood next door. But neither Rattenbury nor James thought of the long-term effect of salt water in a glass house; the iron and glass roof soon began to rust. In 1954 the pool was filled with fresh water.

In the flurry of enthusiasm when the building opened in June 1925, few noted that the garden's architecture was hardly unique. Numerous provincial cities and seaside resorts in Britain could boast similar structures built years before. The Crystal Garden's name and style can be traced to the iron and glass architecture of the Crystal Palace, built in London for the Great Exhibition of 1851; Rattenbury's roof design is similar to that of the Temperate House at Kew Gardens, London, a botanical glasshouse built in 1860–62. But Rattenbury, showing the intuition and sense of place that had won him contracts for the Parliament Buildings and the Empress Hotel, knew exactly what was required. His conception not only imitated the jaunty seaside pleasure piers and palm houses of his youth in Victorian England, but was also to be the largest winter garden in the British Empire. Tea rooms, soda fountains and a Crystal Garden Beauty Shop were bedecked with bougainvillea and potted palms, wicker chairs, Japanese umbrellas, and birdcages with yellow canaries. After the 1925 Dominion Day parade at Beacon Hill Park, and a ball at Government House hosted by Governor General Baron Byng of Vimy, Lady Byng judged the Oak Bay Rose Show, the Crystal Garden's first but not last horticultural event. Victoria Horticultural Society members so liked the conservatory-style design of the building, they booked it for their annual show. Johnny Weissmuller, later the Hollywood star of *Tarzan of the Apes*, opened the pool and set a 100-yard freestyle world record. Until the 1960s, almost every child in the city who learned to swim did so in the Crystal Garden's pool. During the Second World War, naval cadets were taught to swim there as well—but cautioned to stay clear of the deep end, where the diving board was used for parachute training.

The garden, celebrated for its flower shows, tea dances and college graduation parties, is now much changed from the days when exotic fragrances were trapped inside and the patter of foxtrots and swish of waltzes seeped into the night from the glowing glass roof. In 1964, after the CPR declined to renew its lease, the city took over the Crystal Garden but closed it in 1971. The building sat derelict for a decade until local heritage groups campaigned to have it restored. The swimming pool has disappeared, replaced by a botanical garden boasting "hundreds of tropical plants . . . exotic birds and animals." Outside, Rattenbury's facade has become the "Crystal Garden Shopping Mall, Victoria's Heritage Market Place . . . Novelties and more." The novelty is that the building's history has been completely submerged.

·⇐ UNION CLUB ⇒·
805 Gordon Street

When Victoria's business barons planned a new club building, to be located near the Empress Hotel, they looked to the eminent gentlemen's clubs of London for inspiration—and to Francis Rattenbury for advice. Rattenbury—the popinjay of the Parliament Buildings, as rival architects saw him—was a popular club member, mixing in convivial manner with the bankers, businessmen, lawyers and politicians who were his fellows and potential clients. He creamed off numerous prestigious projects, including an extension in 1902 to the club's first building, next to St. Andrew's Church on Douglas Street. Rattenbury was touring Europe when the new building was tendered, but he was asked to help select submissions when he returned in 1910. The new building, completed in 1912, was designed by Loring P. Rexford of San Francisco in Georgian palazzo style, emulating the aristocratic clubs of St. James. Father Charles John Seghers of St. Ann's seminary wasn't speaking of the Union Club when he commented on "the intolerable pride of the English people," but he might have been. "England thinks she is in every respect the first country in the world, and from her pretended elevation she looks down with pity and disdain upon all other nations. English people keep more or less together in this colony, while all other nationalities . . . mingle and sympathise," Seghers observed. Indeed, at the start of the First World War the club's suggestion book offered the opinion that a notice be posted to the effect that "Gentlemen of German or Austrian birth and parentage, whether naturalised or not . . are requested for their comfort and that of members to abstain from using the Club."

In May 1915, when news of the loss of the *Lusitania* was received, a mob wrecked the old German Club on Government Street, the Kaiserhof Hotel on Blanshard and other German businesses. Eight hundred troops patrolled the streets after the riot act was read by Mayor Alexander Stewart at the corner of Yates and Government streets. Off-duty soldiers started the weekend fracas after the barman at the Kaiserhof refused to fly the Union Jack. A crowd of about 3,000 watched as rioters smashed windows of stores with German-sounding names while the ringleaders held aloft a portrait of King George v. The fire chief refused to turn his hoses on the troublemakers; the police, outnumbered, stood by and watched. The *Vancouver Daily Province* reported "unprecedented scenes took place." Looters acted with "brazen effrontery" and walked "boldly past policemen without hesitation . . . Women were seen holding sacks for their husbands to stuff the loot into, and it is alleged that in some cases people carried home one load and returned for another." The Kaiserhof Hotel "looked as if a cyclone had struck it." In the distemper of the times, the German and Austrian gentlemen of the Union Club were forthwith denied membership.

The architecture of the club certainly looks down from a pretended elevation. The Georgian Revival style is given Florentine elaboration with decorative terracotta tiles, corner quoins, and a looming cornice, all intended to convey Belle Epoque establishment privilege. The first president was the distinguished judge Matthew Baillie Begbie, terror of the Cariboo gold fields, who is displayed in the foyer, in bronze equestrian statuette form. The foppish and crusty names of Begbie's successors—the Honourable Mr. Justice M. Tyrwhitt-Drake, Captain J. Herrick McGregor, Major General F. J. O'Reilly Esquire, and so on—expose a social stratum where "the things that mattered were your school, your college, the trips to Europe, and where you spent the summer." Inside there's still an aura of old money, murmured business deals, and the colonial intrigue of Britain's imperial heyday. The bar is wood-panelled and the reading room carries the *Times* of London.

The Union Club was the first gentlemen's club west of Winnipeg when it was founded in 1879. Its first permanent building, erected in 1885, was noted for its displays of members' hunting trophies which took up "every available square inch of the walls." The mummified menagerie, since dispersed, was so remarkable that the Dominion Government asked to borrow the club's bears and bighorn sheep for an exposition in Vienna in 1910. But the billiard-playing bigwigs who established the club had political rather than sporting motives in mind when they first met above a butcher shop at the southeast corner of Government and Yates streets in 1879. They were determined to block the provincial government's threat to secede from the union with the rest of Canada if the railway to the west coast, promised in the Confederation agreement in 1871, was further delayed. The club's influence was respected by some and resented by others after the offending government was replaced, not quite by coup d'état, but by club members who won seats in the next election. In 1882, the editor of the *Standard* was blackballed after he accused club members of "hoodwinking the public" by playing politics rather than billiards, and one member conceded it was possible that "a few Cabinets were formed within its precincts."

Those precincts were a bastion of male chauvinism. In 1900, local ladies formed their own organization, the Alexandra Club, which met in rooms above Redfern's jewellery and silver shop on Government Street. Women were not permitted to set foot in the Union Club until 1908 when the first Grand Ball was held—"we chaps can't exactly dance with each other," members mused. And of course female kitchen helpers had to be admitted. But it was 1994 before women could become full members. Social events were gushingly reported. When HMS *New Zealand* paid a courtesy call to the city in 1913, the club hastened to organize an inaugural ball which, according to the *Colonist*, was "one of the most brilliant successes of the season." Club affairs were an endless source of gossip in the local press. It was long rumoured that a secret passage led under Douglas Street from the old club building to a nearby brothel. In 1934 the *Vancouver Daily Province* reported, triumphantly but erroneously on the front page, that the impoverished institution had been auctioned for $60,000.

Entries in the club's suggestion book over the years reveal its inimitable character. One member proposed "that very large notices of SILENCE be placed in the silent Reading Room so that members who wish to sleep in the afternoon may not be disturbed by loud and ribald talk." This was countered by the comment that "the silent Reading Room should be SILENT and not filled with grunts and snores from sleeping members." Someone suggested that "the private Dining Room be not permitted to be used for Regimental or other Dinners without a guarantee that the diners . . . conduct themselves in the club like gentlemen." Another entry proposed that any member "found sozzled in the clubhouse" three times be requested to resign, an initiative that was not widely supported. Resident or visiting members could sleep things off in rooms upstairs. During prohibition, a member could keep his own bottle at the bar, marked with his name, or in a nearby locker—a practice maintained to this day.

This upper-class world of perpetual dotage would have been familiar to touring dukes and governors general who regularly arranged luncheon or dinner dates at the Union Club, as well as at Government House and the Empress Hotel. Visiting dignitaries may be few today, but the club can still seem eccentric and amusingly pompous. In 1953, when Josef Stalin died, the club was asked why its flag flew at half-mast. The reply was: "The Union Club's flag flies at half-mast only on the occasion of the death of a member. J. Stalin ESQ. was not a member . . . but the day of his funeral coincided with the death [of one] . . ." A correspondent once assumed that the Union Club could be the only possible local address of the Society for the Preservation of Cigar Store Indians. Another incident is recalled in the club's centenary album: in 1949, a letter arrived for a member who had died. The letter was returned to the sender marked "Dead." The next year a similar letter was received and returned marked "Still Dead." The third year the club secretary returned the letter marked "Deceased." But the sender's faith in the member's longevity, a metaphor for the survival of the institution despite all social evidence to the contrary, was undimmed. For the next thirty years the annual letter arrived, addressed: Charles Ezekiel Ellis—Deceased—Union Club, Victoria BC.

·⇐ CHURCH OF OUR LORD ⇒·
626 Blanshard Street

When the Church of Our Lord was opened in 1875, the waters of the mud flats in James Bay lapped the fringes of Blanshard Street; at high tide, parishioners could arrive at the church by boat. Choppy water on the bay, however, was nothing compared to the sea of religious disturbance that had caused the church to be built.

In 1855, the Reverend Edward Cridge left England and sailed for Fort Victoria on the Hudson's Bay Company supply ship *Marquis of Bute*. Cridge had been appointed by the HBC to look after the fort's church, company school and spiritual well-being. Governor and HBC Chief Factor James Douglas had set aside land on the Fur Trade Reserve for a church, and in 1856 the first Anglican service outside the fort was held on Church Hill with Cridge in the pulpit.

Like everything else in the small community, the church was overwhelmed by the invasion of prospectors during the gold rush of 1858. A bishop, the Reverend George Hills, was sent out by the Church of England in 1859 to administer all the parishes in the rapidly growing colony. Hills relied on the HBC less than his predecessors had—his diocese was funded by an endowment from English aristocrat and banking heiress Baroness Burdett-Coutts. He wrote optimistically that Victoria "must be . . . the most lovely and beautifully situated place in the world . . . In the summer it must be exquisite . . . Sublime mountains, placid sea, noble forest trees, undulating park-like glades." Douglas billetted him unceremoniously in a hastily appointed cabin. Hills, who was nicknamed Beau Brummell for his showy metropolitan manner, had to overcome his irritation at the poor accommodation, and at the state of his diocese, which was overrun by gold seekers, before buckling down to his main task: to ease the church away from its HBC connection.

The HBC, like the British East India Company in Asia, acted as an unofficial agent of imperial expansion: the company saved the British government the trouble and expense of policing and administering the territory its traders explored. Churches took advantage of the company's network of trading posts too, sending missionaries west with HBC trading brigades. The company's London-based governors periodically reminded their traders not to "appear more barbarous than the poor Heathens . . . not instructed in the knowledge of the true God," and followed up this missive with prayer books and preachers. Most fur traders knew that their relationship with Indians, who supplied the company with pelts, was better served with blankets and other trade goods than by bibles. They did not always welcome London-appointed Anglican ministers to their forts.

That is likely the reason the Reverend Herbert Beaver, whose name should at least have guaranteed him a favourable reception, lasted only

The funeral of Sir James Douglas in 1877 at the Church of Our Lord, built in 1874–75 in Picturesque Gothic style after a breakaway from the Anglican

Christ Church Cathedral. The picture shows both churches; the more preten-tious Anglican building is on top of the hill. BCARS A–01266

two and a half years at Fort Vancouver. When the Oxford-educated Beaver was sent to Fort Vancouver in 1836, he encountered a hostile chief factor, John McLoughlin, and his lieutenant, James Douglas. Douglas was the more sympathetic until Beaver made it known how strongly he disapproved of the common-law liaisons between HBC traders and Native women. His dogma was divisive. Beaver "legitimized" Douglas's marriage to his mixed-blood partner Amelia in 1837, but Beaver's wife snubbed her and all other women at the fort. The reverend sailed back to England in 1838, complaining that "the governor is uncivil, the clerks are bores, the women are savages." Douglas remained sensitive to snobbery throughout his life; the higher he rose in authority the more he shielded his wife from the public gaze. Amelia Douglas avoided social appearances by feigning illness, preferring to associate with close friends, mostly HBC families. A grandson remembered, "She wasn't at all frail— in fact very lively; she went out driving three or four afternoons a week; she told such wonderful stories, mostly Indian legends," and was "very kind, especially to poor people and Indians."

The next minister Douglas had to deal with was the Reverend Robert John Staines, who arrived as chaplain to Fort Victoria in 1849. Again, Douglas was not unsympathetic to the church—or, initially to Staines, who on one occasion stood guard with sword in hand while Douglas and Roderick Finlayson destroyed a cache of whisky at the fort. But he did not appreciate Staines siding with settlers who disputed his authority. Furthermore, according to Dr. J. S. Helmcken, the HBC physician, Mrs. Staines was "uppish" and "did not chum at all" with Amelia Douglas. Douglas dismissed Staines, who left in 1854 but perished when his ship, the *Duchess of San Lorenzo*, sank in a gale off Cape Flattery. Staines's replacement was Edward Cridge, and the new reverend soon found his problems were not with the HBC—Cridge, something of an evangelist, found Douglas, a Scottish Presbyterian, tolerant of his nonconformist ways—but with the Anglican church.

Cridge's original church building, completed in 1856, burned down in

1869 and was replaced by an impressive wooden cathedral in 1872—the scene two years later of a stormy schism that in turn led to the construction of the Church of Our Lord. Bishop Hills appointed the Reverend Cridge as Dean, but Cridge opposed Hills's embroidered "Roman" style of service and the introduction of "ritualistic practices." Hills accused Cridge of "brawling in church." Cridge refused to resign his post, barred the bishop from the cathedral, and continued to preach and conduct marriages despite having been defrocked for questioning the Anglican liturgical style. Bishop Hills brought a case against the rebellious and recalcitrant dean. It was heard by a reluctant Judge Begbie, who was about to go on a long-awaited leave. Begbie was dedicated to the rule of law, whether military, church or civil, even in matters of conscience. He ruled in Hills's favour. But en route to Europe, he learned that Cridge had renounced the Church of England and formed his own congregation. Begbie wrote: "I hear by the telegraph and newspapers, with the deepest regret, the very serious step you have taken . . . I hope that you will not consider that anything which has occurred ought to deprive me of the privilege of forwarding the enclosed . . ." Begbie sent Cridge a cheque to cover his legal expenses. There is no record it was ever cashed.

Cridge stomped off down Church Hill followed by numerous supporters and established his own congregation, the Reformed Episcopal Church of Our Lord. Cridge's flock took the pews and prayer books with them when they left. Their new church was designed by English-born engineer and architect John Teague and built by hand by the congregation. Teague, like many early Victoria residents, had come to the town from California during the 1858 gold rush. After adventures in the Cariboo gold fields, he designed buildings for the Royal Navy at Esquimalt and became one of the city's most successful early architects. Teague's association with Cridge and his rebellious congregation did him no harm; shortly after the church was completed, the architect was commissioned to design Victoria City Hall.

Architecturally, the little church seems a perfect expression of its founding members' plain-speaking ways. The California redwood exterior is stoutly built in Picturesque Gothic style, decorative but not, like Bishop Hills's liturgy, overdone. Inside, roof beams and pews are held with wooden pegs in simple but effective pioneering carpentry. The organ, manufactured in Massachusetts around 1815 and salvaged from a shipwreck, was donated to the church by James Douglas, who is commemorated inside, in stained glass, along with other founding members. When the town trooped out for Douglas's funeral service in August 1877 they didn't climb up to Bishop Hills's Anglican Cathedral. Victoria's most illustrious citizen was sent on his way by the Reverend Cridge and taken in a procession through the countryside to be buried in the Presbyterian section of the cemetery at Ross Bay. The differences between Cridge and Bishop Hills were, and still are, symbolized topographically as well as theologically: Emily Carr, whose parents were founding members of Cridge's kirk, remembered old folk speaking of the schism as "the big church kicking the little church down the hill."

·⇐ ST. ANN'S ACADEMY ⇒·
835 Humboldt Street

Bishop Modeste Demers, "the Apostle of British Columbia," arrived on the Pacific coast the hard way—by rivers and lakes with Hudson's Bay Company traders. His instructions from the Bishop of Quebec were to "consider as the first object of your mission to withdraw from barbarity and the disorders which it produces, the Indians scattered in that country. Your second object is, to tender your services to the wicked Christians who have adopted there the vices of Indians, and live in licentiousness and forgetfulness of their duties."

He left Montreal in 1837, wintered at the Red River Settlement and joined an HBC expedition to the Columbia River. Demers and a fellow priest, Father Norbert Blanchet, arrived at Fort Vancouver in 1838. Like most frontier priests, Demers was a skilled craftsman and built a church at his parish in Oregon City in 1845. In 1846 he was summoned to Quebec and briefed on his new mission—to "the Island of Vancouver, the Archipel of the Queen Charlotte, and New Caledonia inclusive of all British and Russian possessions extending to the Arctic Ocean." This was the first Roman Catholic diocese west of Toronto. Demers made a four-year fundraising pilgrimage to France, Belgium, Holland and Italy in 1848–52. When he returned to the west coast he was greeted by James Douglas in Victoria, where their acquaintanceship, formed earlier at Fort Vancouver, developed. Both men spoke French and were often seen walking together or chatting in the evening at each other's homes. Demers was given company credit at Fort Victoria's store, and a company sentry kept watch on his property. His mail was sent out with Douglas's own.

Demers went to Lachine, Montreal to recruit nurses and teachers for his mission in Victoria. He appealed to the Sisters of St. Ann, a charitable group formed in Montreal in 1850. All forty-five sisters volunteered. Four were chosen, three French Canadian and one Irish. In 1858 Demers, the four sisters, three priests and several other recruits entrained at Montreal for New York. They boarded a steamer for Panama, crossed the isthmus by train, sailed for San Francisco, changed ships at Bellingham and arrived at Victoria on the *Seabird* in June 1858, a month after the gold rush had begun. Sister Mary Angèle wrote: "How beautiful it looked to us, with its forest of green trees, grassy slopes and picturesque rocky coast. The steamer rounded a headland, we entered the bay and there Victoria lay before us . . . Our surprise was no less great than the Bishop's. The fort had become a town in his absence. Some 200 neat looking houses had been erected and beyond these stretched a sea of tents." After dinner at the Helmckens' home the sisters were "escorted by His Lordship . . . to a little dwelling on the outskirts of Beacon Hill, that was to be our convent home."

Demers and Douglas set the curricula for the administration and education of the Colony of Vancouver Island. Douglas's formidable British imperial rule was as confident in its purpose and implementation as the religious agenda of the Catholic Church, and the other denominations whose missionaries infiltrated the glens and backwaters of New Caledonia. The schools and hospitals they built were part of a mission to assimilate the Indians into white society by converting them to Christianity, whether they liked it or not. Douglas's pragmatism, however, tempered Demers's sanctimony; the gold rush redirected his focus.

Demers planned to build churches and schools in Indian communities on Vancouver Island. The two-room log cabin convent school in Victoria, however, soon became St. Ann's School for Young Ladies—an indication of the town's growing bourgeois aspirations. James Douglas's three daughters attended the sisters' school; so did the poorest children in the community—the first pupils were said to be orphans. Classes were attended by twelve children in 1858; within a year the school enrolment was over fifty. A new school was opened on View Street in 1860 and twenty-four boarders as well as day students were accepted. St. Louis College, a boys' school, was established. Eight more sisters arrived from Lachine in 1863, and the log cabin was converted to house two sisters and six boy boarders. In 1868 the building was used as a quarantine hospital during a smallpox outbreak.

A new school building was commissioned in 1871, the year Demers died. The four-storey edifice, the centrepiece of the present block, was designed in a Quebec seminary style. Its mansard roof, Baroque stairway and pilastered facade made it look like a palace suddenly risen among the white picket fences and clapboard colonial bungalows that characterized the Catholic compound at the head of James Bay. The building was enlarged three times. The original centre section, designed by Montreal architect Charles Vereydhen, was followed by a pedimented Palladian facade and cupola added in 1886 along with an east wing designed by John Teague. A west wing was built in 1910 by architect Thomas Hooper, who also designed St. Joseph's Hospital for the sisters. The hospital still stands on Humboldt Street facing the school building, which by then was called St. Ann's Academy. Teague's additions concealed St. Ann's Chapel, built in 1858, which was moved from the north side of Humboldt Street and tucked away at the back of Vereydhen's building where its shape can be seen from outside. Inside, the California redwood chapel is preserved, unfortunately not in its original style, but with Hooper's Neo-classical remodelling. It is Victoria's oldest surviving religious building. The grounds, where the Sisters of St. Ann once perambulated in privacy and picked apples from the orchard, were laid out as formal gardens in 1880 and completed in 1914 with a tree-lined avenue framing the original block. It seems pleasant—but St. Ann's picturesque architecture and landscaping symbolize a patronizing agenda. As Demers worked with a carpenter, Brother Charles Michaud, to carve the woodwork and paint icons in the tiny chapel, he never questioned the meaning of his architectural devotion. The building was not meant for local citizens at all. Demers dreamed of a wilderness chapel to civilize the "poor children of the forest," as he described the flock he hoped to gather round him.

·⇐ ST. ANN'S SCHOOLHOUSE ⇒·
Elliot Street Square

The four Sisters of St. Ann—the oldest was thirty-two—and a lay sister helper arrived in Victoria in 1858 from Quebec, to help Bishop Demers fulfill his mission to enlighten "the poor children of the forest," as he imagined the Indians. But when the sisters disembarked, they found that the poor children of the forest had decamped to the Fraser River gold fields. Instead of ministering to the heathen, the sisters taught Hudson's Bay Company employees' children, including Governor James Douglas's three daughters. When they arrived, the sisters were assigned to the pleasant Catholic compound below Beacon Hill Park at the head of James Bay. Demers built a chapel in 1858 and erected other new buildings. The sisters' convent school, however, was a two-room log cabin built by one of the HBC's French Canadians in about 1845. They made the best of early hardship. They were expected to start teaching local children two days after they disembarked, amidst gold rush pandemonium. They had to fix up the cabin themselves, and they taught classes there until a full-size school was built. They slept on mattresses on the floor and stacked them against the wall during the day. They took classes in one room and cooked, ate and slept in the other. In 1859 they squeezed in a piano brought from San Francisco and delighted everyone with their playing and music lessons. In their time off, such as it was, they prayed, planted a garden, sawed wood and fetched water, helped by the bishop's Indian and French Canadian servants.

Classes were basic until Bishop Demers issued the first prospectus in December 1858. His manifesto declared that the Sisters of Charity (as they were also known) would "impart to young ladies the benefit of a good moral and domestic education, accompanied with the knowledge of the various branches of elementary training, together with those which constitute the higher departments of a finished education, such is the object to which the Sisters are devoted by profession, and which they will leave nothing undone to carry through, it is hoped, to the satisfaction of all parents or guardians." Parents were assured that the school would "nourish . . . those principles of virtue and morality which alone can make education profitable." The prospectus was ambitious. "Reading, Writing, Arithmetic . . . Book Keeping, Geography, Grammar, Rhetoric, History, Natural History, English, French, plain and ornamental Needle and Net Work in all their different shapes" were to be made available to all: "Destitute Orphans will be received gratis as Day Schollars; and parents actually not able to pay are requested to call at the Establishment."

The sisters' school was an improvement on the HBC school at Fort Victoria that had been run by the Reverend R. J. and Mrs. Staines. Staines had taught HBC children until he was fired by Douglas in 1854. A former pupil, James Anderson, thought Staines "of rather uncertain temper, and disposed at times to be unduly severe in administering corporal punishment." Sunday at the school, Anderson wrote, was "a day of terror. After morning prayers we had breakfast, such as it was; bread and treacle and tea without milk. Church at eleven in the mess hall . . . summoned by the ringing of the Fort Bell—then dinner, potatoes and meat, sometimes fish—a dreary afternoon learning . . . afternoon service, then tea, a duplicate of breakfast. The only redeeming feature . . . was the evening spent by invitation in the Staines' private apartment, when we would be regaled with one sweet each after prayer; and then, after singing 'Lord, dismiss us,' we were dismissed to bed."

The Sisters of St. Ann were no less disapproving of idle pleasure. Convent girls—even the governor's daughters—were prohibited from attending dances. Douglas withdrew his three daughters from the school, with a courteous letter of explanation, when he and his family were obliged to attend a Royal Navy shipboard ball at Esquimalt. Douglas approved of the school's dictum that "disciplinary government will be mild, yet sufficiently energetic to preserve that good order so essential to the well being of the Institution." His real reason for removing his children was a change in school policy after the arrival of the tough Irish-born Sister Mary Providence in 1859. She became embroiled in controversy when she opened Broad Street School in a rented building next to the Driard Hotel, creating a "select school" for the rich and well connected, and a free one for everyone else. Black children who applied to join the select school, some of whose fathers were serving in Douglas's militia, were turned away. Douglas loathed discrimination. Demers stepped in, but was petitioned by the white parents to support Sister Mary's policies.

There was no mention of this episode in 1882 when the governor general, the Marquis of Lorne, and his wife Princess Louise, daughter of Queen Victoria, visited Victoria and took a tour of St. Ann's Convent. Princess Louise told the Mother Superior: "I shall tell my mother, the Queen, of your great work here. You are caring for humanity from the cradle to the grave . . . I shall tell her of your white-curtained wards, filled with suffering humanity, your bright classrooms, and above all, the self-sacrifice and service your sisterhood contributes to this distant post of empire." The order's achievements went beyond kindergartens and schools for "young ladies," with prize-givings and diplomas decorated with Gothic lettering and a lithograph of the main building's Palladian facade. The sisters ran orphanages and Indian mission schools, organized poor relief and established St. Joseph's Hospital. They worked at more than thirty locations around the province and founded a mission at Dawson City, Yukon, from where they made tours of the Klondike mining camps during the gold rush in 1899. The original pioneer log cabin schoolhouse is now the oldest building in Victoria. It was moved to Elliot Street Square and opened as a school museum next to the Helmcken House when St. Ann's Academy closed in 1973.

Bishop Modeste Demers, "the Apostle of British Columbia," left Montreal on his first posting to the Pacific coast in 1837 with instructions from the Bishop of Quebec ringing in his ears. Demers was told to "consider as the first object of your mission to withdraw from barbarity and the disorders which it produces, the Indians scattered in that country. Your second object is, to tender your services to the wicked Christians who have adopted there the vices of Indians, and live in licentiousness and forgetfulness of their duties"—a reference to Hudson's Bay Company traders who took common-law Indian wives. Ironically, Demers arrived on the Pacific coast by lake and river with one of the company's fur trade brigades and on his second assignment, to build up a mission in Victoria in the 1850s, he was assisted by Governor and HBC Chief Factor James Douglas.

BCARS G–07048

Dr. John Sebastian Helmcken was said to be "the leading physician from San Francisco to the North Pole" when he arrived in Victoria as the Hudson's Bay Company's surgeon in 1850. Like Judge Begbie and Esquimalt's naval officers, Helmcken's education and decency, typical of many British imperial servants, helped smooth the colony's rough edges. BCARS B–02767

·⮌ HELMCKEN HOUSE ⮎·
Elliot Street Square

In March 1850, Dr. John Sebastian Helmcken arrived at Fort Victoria from England on the ship *Norman Morrison* to take up an appointment as physician to the Hudson's Bay Company. Victoria was still a remote wilderness trading post. The colony was so isolated that the doctor was said to be "the leading physician from San Francisco to the North Pole and from Asia to the Red River." Within two months he was enrolled as a magistrate and sent to Fort Rupert. When he returned six months later, he resumed his medical work at the fort and later established a surgery on lower Fort Street, a brisk walk across the James Bay bridge from his home, now preserved as a historic site exactly where it was built in 1852.

Helmcken described his introductory tour of Fort Victoria: "It had been built by Mr. Finlayson . . . was nearly a quadrangle, about one hundred yards long and wide, with bastions at two corners containing cannon. The whole was stockaded with cedar posts about six or eight inches in diameter, and about fifteen feet in length, which had been brought from near 'Cedar Hill' [Mount Douglas]. There were inside about a dozen large block storey-and-a-half buildings, say sixty by forty, roofed with long and wide strips of cedar bark. The buildings were for storage of goods, Indian trading-shop and a large shop for general trade. It contained everything required. The mess room, off from which lived Mr. Douglas and family, was at the corner of Fort and Government Streets. The 'counting house' was near Wharf Street. Mr. Finlayson occupied this post and lived there with his family. A belfry stood in the middle of the yard, and its bell tolled for meals, for deaths, for weddings, for church service, for fires, and sometimes for warnings . . . Outside the Fort, there were no houses, save perhaps a block cabin or two. Forest more or less existed . . . to the north, and the harbour was surrounded with tall pines."

Governor James Douglas granted the doctor a plot of land next door to his own home, one of the first to be built outside the fort. Both houses were set in a grove of Garry oaks and orchard sloping gently north to the tidal mud flats of James Bay. The city's pioneering physician became the governor's son-in-law after marrying his daughter Cecilia in 1852 at a ceremony performed in the mess room at the fort by the Reverend Staines. Douglas's wife, Amelia, had not encouraged the courtship but Douglas "a very self-contained man—rarely giving his confidence to anyone, and to me scarcely ever," had surprised Helmcken by declaring "I am going on this expedition [to Cowichan country to track down the murderer of a compay shepherd]—it is dangerous and what may happen to me is uncertain. I have made my will and so forth . . . it would please me were you to marry before I go, then I would go feeling that if anything happened to me my daughter would be in safe hands and Mrs. Douglas would have someone to look to as well as my children."

Helmcken's house was built by the HBC's French Canadian and Kanaka (Hawaiian) workers, helped by local Indians who split the shingles (and who had also cleared the land). Six-inch-thick logs from local trees, sawn and squared where they had been felled, were floated to James Bay and hauled up the beach to the site of the house by oxen that Helmcken borrowed from his employer. The logs can be seen inside the original single-storey dwelling, which was enlarged in 1856 and again in the 1880s with a two-storey wing. Like St. Ann's Schoolhouse, which stands nearby, the Helmcken House is a reminder of French Canadians' role in early Victoria, not only as Catholic missionaries but also as HBC pioneers. Helmcken recalled the names of some who built his house—"Maurice, Peltier, Dubois—all dead now." Although the HBC's directors in London were mostly Englishmen, most of its men in the field were Scottish, French Canadian or Métis. When James Douglas arrived to build Fort Victoria in 1843, his entourage of three dozen included Scottish lieutenants Charles Ross and Roderick Finlayson, Quebec priest Father Jean Baptiste Bolduc, and French Canadian voyageurs employed to navigate the company's trade routes and build its forts.

Helmcken was born of German ancestry at Whitechapel, London, in 1824. He trained at Guy's Hospital and the Royal College of Surgeons and gained experience as a ship's surgeon on two voyages—to Hudson Bay in 1847 and to India, the Dutch East Indies, Canton and Singapore in 1848–49. But if he entertained thoughts of a future at sea, they were banished while rounding Cape Horn. He wrote "At Cape Horn in the winter season! The weather was beastly—foul wind—fearful gales—hailstorms—a few hours of daylight! Such seas . . . I had seen the huge rollers off the Cape of Good Hope, but these chopping seas were ten times worse and more dangerous." Like other educated pioneers he wrote about his career—with lively, literate accounts of his voyages, life at Fort Victoria and his parallel political positions. Helmcken's medical methods were later deemed "rough and ready, and his diagnosis often arrived at by trial and error; but if medical success be judged by the esteem, confidence and love of patients, then Dr. Helmcken was outstanding in his profession." He was a founding member of the Legislative Assembly (the first west of the Great Lakes when it convened in 1856 in the Batchelors' Hall at the fort) and was elected Speaker of the House. In 1867, he used his standing in the community and at the naval base at Esquimalt to persuade the Colonial Office to approve Victoria as the colonial capital in 1868, and was one of the British Columbia delegates who travelled to Ottawa in 1870 to negotiate the colony's entry into Canadian Confederation. He could have been the first premier—certainly a senator in Ottawa—had he accepted Prime Minister Sir John A. Macdonald's entreaties. But he declined, preferring the security and income of his medical practice—that had enabled him to send his two sons to boarding school in Scotland—to an unpredictable future as a political appointee.

The provincial government bought the house from the family estate and opened it to the public in 1941. It has undergone gradual restoration and is filled, if not entirely with Helmcken's possessions, at least with those of HBC colleagues. The doctor's armchair is in the dining room; the dining table and chairs came from the estate of Dr. William Fraser Tolmie, who worked for the company at forts Vancouver and Nisqually before arriving in Victoria in 1858; the Steinway piano (said to have been the first in Victoria) was owned by John Wark, also an HBC man— known as John Work after his name was misrecorded when he joined the HBC. In 1822, Wark had been one of the first HBC traders to penetrate the Rocky Mountains and he led an expedition to Oregon and northern California in 1832–33. He was posted to Victoria from Fort Vancouver in 1849 and became one of the HBC's prominent landowners and a member of the Legislative Assembly. Helmcken wrote that "Work joined the Hudson's Bay Company, A.D. 1814, and entered on the company's books as John Work. John's Irish friends were indignant that the time-honoured name of Wark should have been Anglicized . . . however . . . He had been entered on the company's book as Work and this was unalterable."

The most evocative items in the house are a chest of drawers made from two sea chests, which was the doctor's only furniture at his first surgery at the fort, and his battered medicine chest, still with the original Victorian travel labels on the lid—faded, but quite legible: Pacific Transfer Company, 110 Sutter Street, San Francisco, and Pacific Coast Steamship Company, Victoria. The chest is packed with glass bottles of Victorian cures which he brought from England, the only source of palliatives for his shipboard companions and patients at the fort—and those at outlying farms like Craigflower. The farms "were distant and trails only existed and these none of the best and very circuitous," he wrote, adding "I had a good deal of riding sometimes at night to do, and in fact led a very active existence." The most poignant item is a child's rocking horse: two of the Helmcken children died young. His wife died of pneumonia in 1865 at age thirty-one and he brought up their three surviving offspring. He retired in 1910 and lived until 1920. His grave is at the Quadra Street burial ground.

Elliot Street, which the house faced, vanished when the Royal British Columbia Museum was built. But beneath the Garry oak grove on Helmcken's land there is a sense of the original pastoral setting, and the balmy evenings Douglas and Helmcken spent strolling in the gloaming. The doctor recalled "The district of Victoria was . . . like a large park— patches of forest and open glades . . . Gardens and flowers were cultivated about the houses and in fact the country became like and as civilized as any respectable village in England . . . The Governor had a gardener, an old Englishman named Thomas . . . the Company's men from Kent were decent gardeners too . . . daisies were imported from Scotland by Douglas in seed—and the shamrock by Mr. Work—the thistle was an accidental coming." Shamrocks, thistles and daisies still grow in the area but Douglas's home, which stood directly west of the Helmcken property, was demolished in 1906. Its site, behind the museum entrance, is marked by an iron fence and cherry tree—a cutting from one that Douglas planted in 1854. The fence is another relic, salvaged from Hollybank, the manor built by R. P. Rithet, one of the businessmen who superseded the original HBC landowners as the city's élite.

·⇐ THUNDERBIRD PARK ⇒·
Belleville and Douglas streets

In 1858 the Secretary of State for the Colonies, Sir Edward Bulwer Lytton, wrote from London to Governor James Douglas: "I have to enjoin you to consider the best and most humane means of dealing with the Native Indians. The feelings of this country would be strongly opposed to the adoption of any arbitrary or oppressive measures towards them." Lytton left Douglas to decide how to avoid "affrays between

Indians and immigrants," and committed the government to subsidize the Indians after treaties had commandeered their land. He went on: "It is the earnest desire of Her Majesty's Government that your early attentions should be given to the best means of diffusing the blessings of the Christian Religion and of civilisation among the natives."

Douglas had intended to give the Indians clear title to village sites, fishing and hunting grounds so that they could fend for themselves. Between 1850 and 1854 he negotiated fourteen treaties that wrested title from the Indians around Nanaimo and Victoria, all to the Indians' considerable disadvantage. After British Columbia entered Confederation in 1871, the Dominion Government allowed them only 20 acres to settlers' 160. Between 1876 and 1908, Royal Commissions allocated reserves and adjusted boundaries to benefit logging, mining and fishing companies rather than Natives. The *Colonist* quoted one chief in 1880: "The Whiteman has taken all our land and all the salmon, and we have nothing . . . in the middle of a magnificent land that was once our own all we ask is land enough to live like whitemen . . . we are not beggars."

White men took not only Indian land but also cultural possessions. In the nineteenth century, totem poles, masks and other collectable ceremonial objects were removed by missionaries and museum and private collectors in exchange for blankets, copper, money or other goods. Thunderbird Park, near the entrance to the Royal British Columbia Museum, is a legacy of this trade. The park's collection of totem poles, deprived of their original significance and settings, gaze north across the Canadian Pacific Lawn Bowling Club toward the coastal villages where, if they were original, they would first have been erected. But Thunderbird Park's poles are replicas. The park was set up in 1940 as an outdoor display of northern village totem poles, which were later moved indoors to be preserved and protected behind plate glass. The museum's "totem pole restoration programme" commissioned substitutes from Kwakiutl Chief Mungo Martin, who was employed to revive the art of totem pole carving in the 1950s. His example helped establish a cottage industry and fine art community that produces new masks and totems for sale in shops and galleries, as well as for traditional ceremonial use. Martin was rewarded with a visit to England in 1967 when a Canadian Centennial pole he carved was presented to Queen Elizabeth II at Windsor Castle.

The debate over how to treat Native artifacts, especially those already moved from their settings, is as slippery an issue for museums in North America as the question of whether the Elgin Marbles in the British Museum should be returned to Athens. In Native culture, poles were allowed to decay, weathered by wind and rain, disintegrating piece by piece to the land where they were originally erected. They were not intended to become preserved curiosities. Museum curators argue that the pieces should be saved for posterity. But what posterity will make of Thunderbird Park is unclear. It seems a harmless tourist attraction but, from a historical perspective, it is misleading.

Totem poles were carved and placed to announce wealth and authority, assets that the Indians have for more than a century been denied, and to deify natural creatures that the Indians depended on. Ceremonies passed on hereditary privileges and publicly confirmed social status. Thunderbird Park's imagery and material is correct: the aromatic, straight-grained Western red cedar provided the raw material for Native architecture and canoe building—and carving that made the supernatural visible. Thunderbirds carved and mounted atop totem poles are guardian spirits; other creatures record clan myths and identities; each animal, bird, fish or human image has a symbolic role and identity. It is ironic that European immigrants, while zealously preserving the physical evidence of the culture, thoroughly disrupted the parallel spiritual world that the artifacts represented.

The spiritual power of the totem poles gave Native society no protection against the relentless march of traders, missionaries and settlers. Whole communities were rendered dysfunctional by colonial intrusion in all its forms. Meanwhile, Indian artifacts ignored by collectors found a ready market among tourists and residents in search of souvenirs and macabre mementos to give meaning to their own lives. Victorian and Edwardian travellers noted with amazement the oddities that came into their ken. When Dr. Helmcken paddled over to the Songhees village on his first evening at Fort Victoria, he observed "five or six hundred Indians. By far the greater number had a blanket only for clothing, but 'King Freezy' had on a tall hat and a long coat and considered himself somebody, as indeed he was, and friendly to the whites. He had a most remarkably flattened head—indeed all the Indians had flattened heads—fearful foreheads, retreating backward." Flattened skulls, dug from burial grounds, were later sold as souvenirs.

All that was symbolic—totem pole creatures, masks, hypnotic dances by firelight—was undermined by white contact. The fur trade in the early nineteenth century had brought wealth to the northern coastal tribes, and their carvers used iron tools to create even more adventurous and sophisticated works. But between the 1880s and the 1950s, the traditional art of carving was almost lost. Today, reproduction Indian artifacts have never been more sought after since the scramble by American and European collectors for the real thing around the turn of the century. Some Natives approve of the new work and museum sponsorship; others are offended by it. In 1995 two Shuswap Indians pointedly chose Thunderbird Park as the location for a public hunger strike. They sought

A totem pole image at Thunderbird Park. The park was created in 1940 to display a collection of poles taken from northern coastal Indian villages. Native spiritual beliefs were more sophisticated than Christians like Bishop Demers, who planned to preach to the "poor children of the forest," realized. In their original setting the poles made the supernatural visible: thunderbirds carved and mounted atop totem poles are guardian spirits; other creatures record clan myths and identities; each animal, bird, fish or human image has a symbolic role and identity. RW

the return of ancestral bones found at an archaeological dig during high-way construction and sent to the museum. The hunger strikers also main-tained that the band and tribal council system, imposed by the federal government in the nineteenth century, was an "illegitimate structure of control." Mungo Martin's replicas of stable tribal society, and his rela-tionship with his museum benefactors, are clouded with more sombre meaning than the quaint display of his poles intended.

·⇐ ROYAL BRITISH COLUMBIA MUSEUM ⇒·
675 Belleville Street

The British Columbia Museum of Natural History and Anthropology was opened in 1887 in a room in the Colonial Administration Buildings, after thirty of "the most prominent persons, scholars or otherwise" in Victoria petitioned the provincial government. They wanted BC to com-pete with collectors and museum curators from the United States and Europe who were scouring the coastal communities of British Columbia for Native art and artifacts. Chief Justice Matthew Baillie Begbie, a pri-vate collector in his spare time, was among the group who declared: "It is a source of general regret that objects connected with the ethnography of the country are being yearly taken away in great numbers to the enrichment of other museums and private collections . . . their loss is fre-quently irreparable, and when once removed from the locality of their production their scientific value and utility to the country are greatly lessened." The petitioners' loyalty to Victoria was not entirely sincere: some of them were actively engaged in the artifact trade. For example,

Curator John Fannin's numerous attributes did not include an appreciation of Native culture; he was more responsive to the call of the wild. Taxidermy was his passion. When the museum opened, its main exhibit was a collection of his well-stuffed and glass-eyed hunting trophies. BCARS G–03172

Israel W. Powell, federal Indian superintendent for coastal British Columbia, collected for the Canadian government and the American Museum of Natural History. In 1881 he had pocketed nearly 800 items for his clients while on an official cruise aboard the gunboat HMS *Rocket*. Dr. William Fraser Tolmie, who became a noted anthropologist and compiled the first Haida language dictionary, sent his collection as a gift to Inverness Museum in his native Scotland.

All the nineteenth-century European empires—British, French, Dutch and German—were engaged in an obsessive cult of collecting the art and artifacts of the cultures that colonization was destroying. No European or North American city's status was assured until it had a great museum overflowing with "ethnic" curiosities; no imperial regime could resist displaying the booty of conquest. In 1877 the British barged Cleopatra's Needle, a 180-ton ancient Egyptian obelisk, from the Nile and triumphantly re-erected it on the Victoria Embankment, London. Museums in London, Paris and Berlin dispatched expeditions across the globe in search of aboriginal objets d'art—the more grotesque the better to measure against European cultural superiority.

Collectors behaved as if they were on a holiday shopping spree, and they did not always pay fairly for their souvenirs. Between 1881 and 1883 a German-funded expedition to British Columbia amassed over 2,000 items and shipped them to the Neues Museum, Berlin. Even the director of the Imperial Museum of Natural History in Vienna had turned up on the coast in 1873. Museums in the US vied with each other to see which could gather the largest collections. In 1903 George A. Dorsey, curator of the Field Museum in Chicago, wrote of the rival American Museum of Natural History in New York and its formidable Prussian-born ethnologist Franz Boas: "at the present time they have at least twenty seven [totem] poles in New York and we have twenty three in Chicago. I do not like to have the difference in number remain against us."

When the Provincial Museum was founded, it appointed a curator who turned out to be completely indifferent to Native culture. John Fannin, an

Ontario-born adventurer, naturalist and surveyor, arrived in British Columbia in 1862 after a six-month trek from Winnipeg. He prospected for gold but never struck it rich, except perhaps in the spiritual sense. He became absorbed by the flora and fauna of the natural world, an interest that reflected the nineteenth-century quest for knowledge about colonized territories, but failed to see how these were connected to Native art. As curator of the museum, he founded and organized field trips for the British Columbia Natural History Society and collected and catalogued rocks, sea shells, plants, insects and animals.

In 1891, *Victoria Illustrated* claimed: "Visitors to Victoria are pleasantly surprised by one of the prettiest little museums on the American continent; it is thoroughly unique and did our visitors but know its history they would be amazed." The government was "very fortunate in the acquisition of Mr. John Fannin, who had for thirty years previous collected and made a study of the habits of animals and birds . . . Mr. Fannin makes bi-yearly excursions to the favourite game haunts in search of new specimens, and he and his friends have contributed a vast number of the animals and birds adorning the museum . . . Mr. Fannin has personally done or superintended the taxidermy of every animal and bird and his labors have met with such great success that his name is known among naturalists and sportsmen all over North America."

Fannin consistently refused offers of cultural items for the museum's collection. A "Collection of Relics and Antiquities" amassed by adventurer Captain Newton Henry Chittenden during an 1884 trip to the Queen Charlotte Islands was eventually given to the province in 1891, but when the museum opened in 1887 its main exhibit was a collection not of Native artifacts but of its curator's hunting trophies. When the museum was transferred to the new Parliament Buildings in 1898—a move that their architect Francis Rattenbury "deemed highly intemperate"— Fannin's opening display featured the same stuffed animals that Victoria's residents had come to know well. Only after foreign museums had taken

A forest of Haida totem poles lines the shore at Skidegate Village, on the Queen Charlotte Islands, in 1878. There are more poles in this one photograph than there are in the Royal British Columbia Museum. The museum

brims with enough Victorian bric-a-brac to stock every antique shop in the province, but most of the totem poles from the Queen Charlottes are in Chicago, New York, London and Berlin. BCARS B–03660

their pick of aboriginal cultural items did local interest develop in the preservation, rather than the export and eradication, of Native culture.

Perhaps it is to his credit that Fannin took no part in what turned out to be a distasteful trade. During his tenure, from 1886 to 1903, he stood by while tons of material, the loot of the coast, was shipped to Europe and America from Victoria. The 1893 Chicago World's Fair featured a complete Haida log house, totem poles and a troupe of Indians who performed in front of a Kwakiutl house on the shore of Lake Michigan. In 1900 an outraged *Colonist* reported the "LOSS TO BRITISH COLUMBIA —Through the Depredations of United States and Other Foreign Collectors of the Province's Most Valuable Indian Relics." In another report, "How the Province is Plundered," the paper quoted a Victoria visitor to New York who found a "veritable forest of totem poles" at the American Museum of Natural History in Central Park.

Many Indians soon learned to hide heirlooms away, but some Natives and mixed-bloods were quick to adapt to the cash economy, exploiting the cultural collapse of their own people. There were Hudson's Bay Company traders and missionaries who also took part as intermediaries or as collectors themselves. Officially the HBC was more concerned with trading furs than collecting artifacts but the churches, in their mission to convert the Indians from pagan to Christian ways, coerced them into disposing of their relics. Epidemics of European diseases, especially smallpox, and the banning of the potlatch ceremony in 1885, left more masks than wearers and more ceremonial objects than people to use them. When the supply of artifacts began to run out, collectors dug up Indian graves. Victoria's Beacon Hill Park, once a Native burial site, was plundered early on; only the cairns on top of the hill remain.

Local specialists like Charles Frederic Newcombe made a handsome living as agents for the likes of George A. Dorsey of the Field Museum. In 1901 Dorsey commissioned Newcombe to make "a clean sweep" of the Queen Charlotte Islands for remaining Haida artifacts and bones. In 1902, while on the Queen Charlottes looking for a pole for the British

Museum, Newcombe excavated a burial site for Dorsey while one of his party kept the local chief occupied. Dorsey wanted to show "every phase of [Haida] life and industry . . . to do it better than it has been done by any other museum." By the turn of the century, competition for relics had become less a matter of scholarly recording of a "dying culture" and more a matter of an avaricious quest for prestige within the academic and curatorial community. In 1911, the provincial archivist, gazing at Fannin's legacy of stuffed creatures—deer, bear, lynx, wolves, birds, bighorn sheep—observed that "If the formation of . . . a collection is not undertaken at once, and vigorously prosecuted, it will be soon, very soon indeed, once and for all too late for the Province to acquire an exhibit worthy of the great ethnological field which it covers."

In a belated effort to build a credible collection, Newcombe, by then well connected on the coast, was persuaded to venture north. Between 1911 and 1914 he worked to increase the Victoria museum's meagre collection, and today there is a hall with poles he gathered. But the most prominent feature inside the museum is a Kwakiutl house of a type that now survives only in old photographs: the house is a replica, in its setting as artificial as the cedar aroma piped in. Newcombe's poles are impressive but all the best material had been shipped to American and European museums years before. Clever design and theatrical presentation at the museum today conceals the paltry size of Victoria's collection of Native work. As for Fannin, his esoteric, rarely displayed legacy still looms large. When the Royal British Columbia Museum was moved to its purpose-built complex in 1968, the tallest block was a storage tower named after him. It was erected to house the thousands of botanical and fossil specimens he sought, and the ducks and bighorn sheep he shot. ✍

James Bay

GINGERBREAD CONTRIVANCES . . . SOMETHING BETWEEN A
DUTCH TOY AND CHINESE PAGODA—*the* Colonist'*s verdict on
the Colonial Administration Buildings, 1860*

COLONIAL ADMINISTRATION BUILDINGS

THE superb site of British Columbia's Parliament Buildings, at James Bay, was selected not by architect Francis Rattenbury but by Governor James Douglas when he commissioned a group of colonial administration buildings to replace Fort Victoria after it was overwhelmed by the gold rush of 1858. Douglas showed no sentiment when prestige was to hand, and he sold land around the Hudson's Bay Company fort (for which the company was later reimbursed) to pay for the new buildings. The fort's stockade was removed in 1860 and the buildings demolished. "Alas, poor old bastion!" the *Colonist* moaned. "Thy removal should be enough to break the heart of every Hudson's Bay man in the country. Such an ornament to the city and yet doomed to destruction." James Bay was a shallow tidal inlet that flowed east from the Inner Harbour to wash up on mud flats bordering Blanshard Street. When construction of the Colonial Administration Buildings began in

*The bargeboard detail at 151 Oswego Street, James Bay,
is an example of mechanical jigsaw carving—a process
that allowed Victorian builders to mimic intricate "hand-
carved" decorative effects.* RW

1859, a bridge was built to carry Government Street across the inlet from the old town to the new government quarter. The James Bay bridge was later dismantled when a causeway was constructed, and the flats were filled in as the site for the Empress Hotel. As a coastal feature the bay vanished but left its name on the peninsula southwest of the hotel and the Parliament Buildings. The peninsula was wooded and dotted with farms and vegetable gardens that produced food for residents of the fort and town. When Douglas set aside land for the Colonial Administration Buildings, he built a home nearby. Many of the local gentry duly followed. James Bay became a fashionable residential district, and remained so until the turn of the century. By 1900, most of the peninsula's western shoreline had be-come heavily industrialized, and the middle classes began to move to the fashionable suburbs of Rockland and Oak Bay.

The architecture of James Bay, from the Parliament Buildings to the most humble labourer's cottage, is uniquely layered with urban evolution, decay and restoration. Despite the proximity of the government buildings, the area was not developed as a formal town plan. The well-to-do who followed Douglas to the area to escape from the wharves and saloons that gold fever had brought to the old town, built Italianate homes on large wooded properties. On some streets James Bay's old homes stand in clusters that strongly evoke the horse-drawn, gas-lit era in which they were built. Elsewhere, they pop up at unexpected corners in a way that gives the area an aura of serendipity and charm. Beacon Hill Park, which Douglas set aside as park land, gave the community a thick, wooded edge. One early homeowner, Emily Carr's mother, "cried at the lonesomeness of going to live in the forest," although the home her husband built in 1863 was only one mile out of town. The Carr house, originally built on a large estate, is one of the few of its period to survive—in the kitchen there is a copy of an 1878 *Bird's Eye View of Victoria*, in which James Bay is still shown as a semi-rural setting. Colonial properties of the Douglas era were subdivided and sold as building lots in the 1880s and 1890s, the period from which most of the neighbourhood's old homes date. Here are little villas built for government bureaucrats, insurance agents, ships' engineers, and railway superintendents; for the proprietor of Rutland and Company Gentleman's Outfitters and the landlord of the Palace Saloon; for butchers, bookkeepers, post office clerks, mining engineers, real estate agents, schoolteachers and contractors.

This bourgeois world had its share of offbeat residents. With the proceeds from the sale of a Vancouver Island gold claim, Ayrshire-born William Wallace Gibson built the first Canadian flying machine, in a coach house at 146 Clarence Street. He made his first flight in 1910 from the slopes of Mount Tolmie. Emily Carr opened a boarding house in 1913 at 646 Simcoe Street. Guests at the "House of All Sorts" shared lodgings with the artist's menagerie, which included rabbits, hens and a pack of sheepdogs. "Honest John" Robson, New Westminster newspaper publisher, politician and premier of British Columbia from 1889–1892, built a Victoria residence at 506 Government Street—with a twin next door for his married daughter. Robson, a radical democrat and editor of the *British Columbian*, the mainland's first paper, was a ceaseless critic of Douglas's autocratic government and its lackeys. When Judge Matthew Baillie Begbie once jailed him in New Westminster for contempt of court, Robson sent out a barrage of furious editorials from his cell. The Robson family's Victorian Italianate twins are now government offices. Numerous homes, after being used as rooming houses, have awakened as bed and breakfast inns. Many others remain, or have been restored as family homes. All preserve a Victorian village patchwork of gingerbread gables, columned porches and stained glass front doors on the narrow streets and well-tended gardens, below Beacon Hill Park and hidden behind the Parliament Buildings and Belleville Street's apartment buildings and hotels.

The Colonial Administration Buildings set the scene, and whimsical architectural tone, for the area's future development. The buildings were to house a colonial secretary's office, the legislative chamber, supreme court, governor's residence, a land office and registry, the colonial treasury's fireproof vault, and a barracks for a military guard. Construction was halted in 1860 when tax revenue from the gold rush ran out and the colony began to run up a debt—the Colonial Office insisted that the colony, which had invested in roads and public buildings, should pay its way. The population declined by 1,000 people, and real estate prices plunged as half-finished buildings were abandoned. The most visible half-built project was the new government compound. Only one structure was opened and had to be shared by the Legislative Assembly and the courthouse until the remaining buildings were completed in 1864, the year James Douglas retired.

Many architectural styles are evident at James Bay: Italianate, Queen Anne, Craftsman cottage and Colonial bungalow. But few homebuilders attempted to replicate the Administration Buildings, designed by the government's Berlin-born surveyor-architect, Hermann Otto Tiedemann, who had arrived in Victoria in 1858. The buildings, spaced so that if fire engulfed one it would not spread to the others, were Tiedemann's first effort—and the town's first public buildings—and the press hastened to identify their architectural sources. The *Colonist* ventured that they were "gingerbread contrivances . . . something between a Dutch Toy and Chinese Pagoda." The *Gazette* thought they were "the latest fashion for Chinese pagoda, Swiss-cottage, and Italian-villa fancy birdcages." The "birdcages" epithet caught on. Tiedemann went on to supervise other government projects in Victoria, including Fisgard Lighthouse and the Victoria Law Courts, but never quite lived down the joke that was made of his first big contract.

The nickname was echoed on Government Street, which was called Birdcage Walk where it ran past the buildings. (The name may also have referred to Birdcage Walk at St. James's Park, London.) While many citizens were amused by the image of politicians strutting, preening and pecking inside, few were impressed by the buildings. The half-timbered

Birdcages sported bricks part-painted to look like stone, imitation marble mantlepieces, Georgian doorways and pine grained to look like oak. The buildings' bungaloid grandeur became even more embarrassing in 1868, when the capital of the united colonies of Vancouver Island and the Mainland moved to Victoria from New Westminster.

The Administration Buildings' "Picturesque Eclectic" style began to seem a symbol of a fragile alliance rather than a permanent one. Loyalty to the Crown and the British Empire was already being questioned, especially by the numerous Americans in Victoria. In 1869 "forty prominent businessmen"—dismissed by the *Colonist* as "foreigners"—signed a petition calling for annexation by the United States and sent it to the White House. There was no reply from Washington but the petition provoked debate in Victoria, a city where during the gold rush most businesses closed not only for Queen Victoria's birthday but also for the Fourth of July. In 1858 Douglas refused permission for Americans to fire a salute on Independence Day and American members of the police force resigned rather than swear allegiance to the queen. To judge by its bars, Victoria was already merrily American: there was a Sacramento Restaurant on Waddington Alley, an American Hotel on Yates Street, and a California Saloon on Johnson Street—which displayed both the Union Jack and Stars and Stripes on British and American public holidays. The *Colonist* called the petition "rank sedition and treason." A Queen's Birthday editorial declared: "It is on occasions such as these we are brought to contemplate the magnitude and grandeur of the British Empire, and to realize the beauty as well as the correctness of the expression that on its extensive territory the sun never sets . . . No other country can make so great a boast."

Tiedemann's buildings rattled with rhetoric as pro-American and pro-British and Canadian members harangued each other across the floor of the legislative chamber. Articles in the *Times* of London ventured that if British Columbians wished to join the United States then the British government should not stand in their way, and the *Colonist* responded:

"Loyalty to the Crown must be contingent upon loyalty to the colonies. If the Crown should prove disloyal to the colonists, they cannot be expected to continue loyal to it . . . the immediate destiny of this colony is either that of an important province of a great and successful British North American empire, or a state of the powerful Republic. There is no happy medium here." But some loyal British-born members of the legislature pointed to the absurdity of Victoria's geographical and economic isolation from Ottawa, never mind London. Dr. Helmcken questioned the efficacy of maintaining an alliance "with a people 3,000 miles away, without any settlement of the intervening country, with no communication, except through the United States . . . Canada is for all practical purposes further removed from us today than England . . . I feel certain that Her Majesty's government has no wish . . . to be involved in quarrels with the United States . . . I say that the United States will probably ultimately absorb both this Colony and the Dominion of Canada . . . No union between this Colony and Canada can permanently exist, unless it be to the material and pecuniary advantage of this Colony." Others like Joseph Trutch, Chief Commissionor of Lands and Works, supported confederation "because it will secure the continuance of this colony under the British flag and strengthen British interests in this continent." He might have added that British rule meant that he and other civil servants would keep their influential posts.

The Douglas house on James Bay, a blend of Georgian Colonial and provincial Quebec styles, was built for James Douglas by his French Canadian Hudson's Bay Company carpenters. A cairn behind the entrance to the Royal BC Museum marks its site. In 1902 an "Auction Sale . . . Joshua Davis, Auctioneer—Unique, Historical Furniture—Old Colonial Residence of the late Sir James Douglas, K.C.B.—Terms Cash" dispersed the contents. The governor's residence was torn down in 1906.
BCARS A–04621

In 1870, confidence in British interest in the colony was revived by the appearance around Albert Head of the Royal Navy's Flying Squadron, a fleet of warships which had been showing the flag at ports in South Africa, South America, Australia, New Zealand and Japan. A deal that promised the new province a transcontinental railway, a naval dry dock at Esquimalt, and a write-down of the colony's debt, was thrashed out in the legislature, and British Columbia joined Confederation the next year. The deal did not allow for replacement of the Birdcages, although newspaper commentators spasmodically sniped at them from behind their typewriters. Amor de Cosmos, editor of the *Colonist*, wrote: "Mean and insignificant public buildings are outward and visible signs of a sordid, narrow-minded, and uncultivated state or province . . . visitors are sure to judge the whole people by the buildings they erect." Eventually, when officials unveiled Rattenbury's design for Parliament Buildings to replace Tiedemann's tumbledown ensemble, Victoria's status seemed manifest. The Birdcages were finally demolished when government departments moved into Rattenbury's building. Their brickwork was used as a foundation for its driveways.

TOP *The new Parliament Buildings rose like a mirage of progress and prosperity above the old Colonial Administration Buildings in 1898. Captain George Vancouver and Judge Matthew Baillie Begbie occupy niches respectively left and right of the entrance. Captain Vancouver (the English navigator who explored the west coast in the 1790s) also glints on the cupola.* RW BOTTOM *Tiedemann's follies, the Colonial Administration Buildings, begun in 1859 and thought "mean and insignificant" by the local press, looked as if they had been inspired by willow pattern china. Their bungalow style was typical of colonial architecture in remote corners of the empire. Shown here c. 1860, they were torn down after Rattenbury's more elaborate building opened in 1898.* BCARS A–02574

·⇐ PENDRAY HOUSE ⇒·
309 Belleville Street

When Edwardian shipboard passengers sailed into Victoria's Inner Harbour, the first sight they were rewarded with was not Rattenbury's Parliament Buildings or the Empress Hotel, but the typography, tin sheds and smokestacks of William J. Pendray's British Columbia Soap Works. Rudyard Kipling must have been looking the other way in 1907 when he wrote that the view was "worth a very long journey." But those who stayed on deck were reassured when the Empress Hotel and the Parliament Buildings hove into view—along with the mansion of the man whose industry had given them that unexpected first impression.

Pendray's picturesque home was the talk of the town when completed in 1897. The brightly dressed new arrival made neighbouring Italianate villas look distinctly dowdy. The Pendray house is a flurry of gables and turrets, interior ceiling frescoes and stained glass. It was a true "painted lady"—a term for the residential architecture style of nineteenth-century San Francisco. The style was toned down by the time it was applied in James Bay: Victoria's residents flirted with fashionable American architectural styles as the city grew, but they eventually overpainted the new ideas with British colonial respectability and expressed themselves in the Cotswold cottage and Tudor Revival styles of Rockland and Oak Bay.

The *Colonist* wrote that Pendray's fresco artists Muller and Sturn—no less restrained in self-promotion than the house is in Queen Anne style decoration—"worked in the largest castles and residences in Germany and Switzerland," and that the fresco style applied "was originally acquired in the ruins of ancient Pompeii." Victorian industrialists were flattered by this sort of cultural association. Few, however, chose to live as close to their work as Pendray did. Even as his home was being built the city's plutocrats were moving to Rockland, where the coal baron Robert Dunsmuir had built Craigdarroch Castle. Pendray's palace stood a stone's throw from its owner's factories, painting an image of Victorian capitalism's two worlds in unusual proximity: private privilege amidst industrial squalor. Pendray's British Columbia Soap Works despoiled Laurel Point, the gateway to the Inner Harbour, but its owner could leave the steaming vats and greasy tanks, return to the gaudy turrets and wood-panelled rooms and reflect, as he trimmed his tidy topiary, on his contribution to local well-being. Pendray's skill with secateurs ensured that his garden, which was featured on postcards, became as well known as his best-selling White Swan brand soap.

Pendray had worked in the California gold fields, made a fortune in the Cariboo gold rush, and returned to England—only to lose everything in South African mineral speculation. He settled in Victoria in 1875 and started the soap works on the premise that, as he put it, "if people are ever to become contented, happy, and prosperous, they must first be made clean." By 1881 he was making 9,000 pounds of soap every day. Pendray also established the British American Paint Works on the basis that contented and clean citizens would wish to keep their James Bay bungalows freshly painted. Pendray's life ended in 1913, when a pipe fell on him in his factory. The soap works was sold by his son and eventually closed, but the paint plant survived until 1965. There are no plaques to mark Pendray's businesses at Laurel Point today. But his radiant residence, built at the gates of the factories almost as an advertisement for both products, has survived a change of use and name, as has the topiary Pendray tended so well.

James Bay was partly redeveloped with apartment blocks and hotels in the 1960s, but the traditional architecture still seems much as it was in the 1890s, when Francis Rattenbury rented rooms on Menzies Street while preparing plans for the Parliament Buildings. Rattenbury's main rival in Victoria, fellow Englishman Thomas Hooper, also lived in the area and established his reputation building villas for the neighbourhood's well-off residents. His most notable designs were the Pendray House and Pinehurst—built in 1889 at 617 Battery Street for retired lumber baron and banker William James Macaulay. Almost as elaborate as the Pendray

House, Pinehurst—restored but hidden in a townhouse development—boasts Gothic bargeboard gables and a corner turret. There was a wood-panelled billiard room and eighteen fireplaces throughout the home—some decorated with Minton tiles featuring scenes from the novels of Sir Walter Scott (the writer's Victorian baronial home in Scotland inspired countless imitations wherever his books were read). Pinehurst once commanded views of the Olympic Mountains which Macaulay could contemplate from his turretted belvedere; the estate once extended to the shore beyond Dallas Road. Hooper designed a Queen Anne style home for himself in 1902 at the corner of Belleville and Menzies streets just west of the Parliament Buildings. Hooper's house, christened Hatherleigh after his birthplace in Devon, is less ostentatious than those he designed for others. Only the front survives in original form, with curving verandah, Tuscan-columned porch, pediment, bay window, balcony and period stained glass. The house was moved to 243 Kingston Street in 1912 because, according to an apocryphal story, Hooper built it on the wrong lot.

·⇐ OGDEN POINT ⇒·

Toward Ogden Point on the peninsula's western edge, James Bay dissolves into workers' housing and an industrial waterfront that developed in the 1880s with shipyards, machinery works and an ocean terminal for Canadian Pacific Railway's Empress liners. Victoria could have become Canada's west coast commercial and industrial metropolis, but for the quirk of history that made Vancouver the terminus of the CPR. Even in the 1920s the Inner Harbour was choked with ships, sawmills and the Pendray soap works. One of the largest dry docks in the British Empire was built at Esquimalt in 1921–27. Thousands of men and women were employed at the now derelict Yarrows shipyard at Esquimalt and the vanished Victoria Machinery Depot at Ogden Point. The wharves at Ogden Point were enlarged during the First World War and dominated by a massive concrete grain elevator. But the shipyards and the grain elevator have gone. At Ogden Point, Victoria's dreams of industrial grandeur washed away.

All that remains are the terraced granite blocks of the Ogden Point breakwater, built by the Sir John Jackson Company, a British contractor, in 1911–19. Crushed stone was excavated from Albert Head, and massive twenty-ton granite blocks were quarried at Hardy Island and barged to Victoria. The Hardy Island quarry at Jervis Inlet was one of the largest operations of the time. Its granite face was one hundred feet long and sixty feet high. One hundred quarrymen and engineers, accommodated in almost Siberian conditions, blasted out the 1,500,000 cubic feet of granite used for the contract. Few ocean-going ships now seek the breakwater's protection; it is Victoria's nearest equivalent to an English-style pleasure pier, attracting visitors to its mile-long mole and lighthouse, and providing recreation for anglers.

In 1901, when the Duke and Duchess of York disembarked at Rithet's Wharves during a royal visit to the city, Victoria was a port of call for the finest liners afloat. Robert Paterson Rithet had developed Ogden Point as an ocean terminal in the 1890s after the master of the CPR's new liner *Empress of India* discovered his ship was too big to negotiate the Inner Harbour. Rithet, a Scottish farmer's son, was one of the breed of immigrant entrepreneurs who succeeded the Hudson's Bay Company landed gentry at the top of the city's social scale. His rise in status was not hindered by his marriage to the daughter of Alexander Munro, an HBC chief factor at Fort Victoria. Lured by gold fever, Rithet had arrived in the city in 1862 and worked as a stevedore and bookkeeper. After partnerships with other British merchants, and experience in San Francisco working as agent of Gilbert Sproat, a Victoria wholesaler, he formed his own company.

Rithet's marine interests included the Canadian Pacific Navigation Company (which was sold to the CPR in 1901), insurance and import agencies, a wholesale business on Wharf Street, investments in Albion

Ironworks, sawmills, canneries, the sealing trade, and a trans-Pacific tele-graph. He imported sugar from Hawaii and China, and served as the Hawaiian consul in Victoria until the American putsch that deposed the Hawaiian royal family in 1893. *Victoria Illustrated* boomed in 1891 that "the harbor and shipping facilities cannot be surpassed. By the expendi-ture of hundreds of thousands of dollars, private enterprise has con-structed at the entrance to the harbor proper, docks capable of accom-modating and sheltering in the roughest gale that blows, the largest steamships and sailing vessels of the Pacific . . . Mr. R. P. Rithet deser-ves the gratitude of Victorians." The *Colonist* clamoured "Rithet for Mayor" in 1884 and described him as "a public spirited, useful and ener-getic citizen . . . who, having made his money in this city, has invested it here . . . the presence of a man like R. P. Rithet at the helm is indispens-able. We hope he will consent to stand." He did, and he was elected.

TOP *The Canadian Pacific Railway Company's* Empress of Japan *at Rithet's Wharves, c. 1897. Robert Paterson Rithet, the very model of a mercantile maharajah, built the docks at Ogden Point for ocean-going ships, particularly the CPR's* Empress of India, Empress of Japan *and* Empress of China. *From 1891, "The White Empresses of the Pacific, Fastest to the Orient" sailed the Pacific stretch of the All Red Route (around the globe with every port of call on British territory). Canadian Pacific, still one of the country's largest corporations, seems diminished since dropping its stirring slogan "Canadian Pacific Spans the World."* BCARS G–00917

BOTTOM *The James Bay Bridge (present-day Government Street), c. 1869. The bridge was built to connect the Colonial Administration Buildings—and Governor Douglas's house—with the town. It was demolished when the bay was filled to build the Empress Hotel.* BCARS D–03568

The Carr House and garden's picket fences and circular driveway
look exactly as they were when Emily Carr, British Columbia's
most famous artist, was born in an upstairs bedroom in 1871. The
house is a picture-perfect Victorian Italianate villa. Like many
other early buildings in Victoria, it was built of California red-
wood (the local forest industry was unprepared to cope with the
sudden demands of the 1858 gold rush boom). RW

Rithet lived on Dallas Road from where he could watch the activity on his wharves. The area close to the docks was handy for his workers too and a handful of labourers' cottages remain on St. Lawrence Street. But this end of James Bay was never fashionably residential. Rithet later moved to Hollybank, a villa on Humboldt Street, now demolished. The Dallas Hotel, Victoria's first seaside hotel, built in 1891 on Dallas Road for CPR passengers, lent the neighbourhood a leisurely air. But it lost out when the Empress opened in 1908. Despite having been upgraded by Rattenbury, the Dallas was later demolished. The only other substantial property at Ogden Point belonged to William John Macdonald, HBC Collector of Customs during the 1858 gold rush, a militia captain and gold commissioner who settled near Ogden Point in a mansion built in 1876. Macdonald, a merchant and property investor after his career with the HBC, became the city's third mayor in 1866. His stone villa was called Armadale after Macdonald's clan home on the Isle of Skye. Macdonald Park is all that survives of the estate. The point was named after another nineteenth-century HBC trader, Peter Skene Ogden.

·⇐ NEWCOMBE HOUSE ⇒·
138 Dallas Road

Dr. Charles Frederic Newcombe, a native of Newcastle, was the epitome of a Victorian scholarly adventurer. He had studied medicine in Scotland and Germany and practised in England before emigrating to America where his collector's instinct, originally for natural history, prompted an interest in ethnography that became his life's work. He gained international renown as an authority on Native culture and artifacts, venturing up the west coast as far as the Queen Charlotte Islands in a quest, as he saw it, to record and preserve the "vanishing race." Had Newcombe been in Victoria earlier, he wouldn't have had to travel far to witness the decline of British Columbia's Native population. Smallpox had a catastrophic effect on aboriginal groups in the 1860s. Local newspapers reported that Indians were dying by the score; only fifteen of one hundred Natives camped at Ogden Point survived the outbreak of 1862 (Dr. Helmcken vaccinated five hundred Songhees Indians that year).

Newcombe and his wife and three children moved to Victoria in 1889. He joined the local natural history society and met John Fannin, the curator of the Provincial Museum. With an income from British stocks and bonds, he led the comfortable life of a semi-retired gentleman until his wife died after bearing their sixth child in 1891. Newcombe took a year off in Britain and on the Continent renewing old acquaintances and making new ones in the scientific community. When he returned, he found the scramble for coastal Native artifacts had intensified dramatically. He began work as a freelance collector and self-styled ethnological authority. Thereafter, he rarely missed a trinket. He worked for anyone who would help him enhance his status as an expert. In 1897 he accepted a commission from J. H. Turner, premier of British Columbia, to find a Haida totem pole to present to the Royal Botanical Society, Kew Gardens, on Queen Victoria's Diamond Jubilee that year. He worked for George A. Dorsey, curator of the Field Museum in Chicago—who was determined to acquire the most extensive collection of Native artifacts in North America—and for Franz Boas, Dorsey's New York rival who, while dismissing Newcombe as an amateur, thought he was a useful contact. Newcombe accepted Boas's opinion that pieces should be preserved in "a large accessible museum," and not "in a remote place like Victoria where, at best, few scientists will have the chance to see them."

In 1906 Newcombe's contract with the Field Museum ended. He sold off some of his private collection to the Brooklyn Institute of Arts and Sciences, but most of his material was sold to the Canadian Geological Survey in Ottawa for $6,500 which conveniently paid for Newcombe's new home, a Renaissance-style villa with distinctive columned verandahs in the British East Indian manner, which he built at Ogden Point in 1907. By 1911 the American museums' appetite for Indian artifacts had been sated. Newcombe was only then prepared to help Victoria's Museum of Natural History and Ethnology increase its lamentable collection by sailing north in search of poles. He also filled a few back orders for other museums: a Haida pole was sent to Melbourne; two more went to Brooklyn; another was shipped to the Royal Scottish Museum, Edinburgh. Victoria gained a handful. By the time the Royal Ontario Museum asked him for a pole there were almost none left, but he found one on his last trip north in 1923.

Newcombe's talent for totem pole hunting was not entirely matched by an appreciation for art. He once advised the Provincial Museum to refuse an offer of paintings from Emily Carr because he thought her Indian village scenes were too vividly coloured to meet curatorial standards of accuracy—although he did buy some of her paintings for himself. His public opinion, however, scuppered her hopes for a commission to decorate Rattenbury's library at the Parliament Buildings. After Newcombe died in 1924, his son William was employed as a curator in the Provincial Museum from 1928–32. He was more receptive than his father had been to Carr's work, but he rarely mentioned the contents of the family's colonial home where he lived with his books and research. When he died, a large collection of Indian arts and crafts, rare books, glass plate photographs—and dozens of Carr's paintings—was discovered in the Dallas Road house. It was finally obtained by the museum that C. F. Newcombe, who had been passed over as curator in 1904, had chosen to ignore.

·⇐ CARR HOUSE ⇒·

207 Government Street

Emily Carr, British Columbia's most famous artist, was born during a snowstorm in an upstairs bedroom on Government Street in December 1871, the year British Columbia joined Confederation. The house was built for her father, a moneyed merchant named Richard Carr, originally from Devon, by architect John Wright. Richard Carr worked in Ontario, New Orleans and California, where he made his fortune in the gold rush of 1849 (California was the source of much early investment in Victoria). In 1863 he opened a store on Wharf Street, importing wine, cigars and other provisions. That same year he hired Wright, the city's most established architect, to design his new home on a large wooded estate in James Bay, then the city's up-and-coming middle-class neighbourhood.

Wright was born near Glasgow and had arrived in Victoria from San Francisco in 1859 on the tide of gold fever. As the first professional architect in Victoria he was soon employed by the colonial government and he designed Fisgard Lighthouse, among other structures. Wright was familiar with the fashionable styles of the day and composed them to picturesque effect. The Carr House, a formal composition detailed with bracketted overhanging eaves, round arched and bay windows, a hooded verandah, and a circular entrance carriageway, is a perfect example of a Victorian Italianate villa. Like many other early structures in Victoria, it was built of California redwood. (At the time, Victoria's trading patterns made it as much an outpost of California as it was of the British Empire.)

Along with the Helmcken House, Point Ellice House and Craigflower Farmhouse, the Carr House is a "BC Heritage Attraction" where visitors are invited to "Share the adventure of Victoria's past at British Columbia's oldest historic sites." This means being escorted around by guides in period costume—a coy embroidery that is neither quite theatrical nor authentic enough to bring the past to life. At the Carr House there is a room-by-room tour tape-recorded by Emily herself. But whatever voices of the past are present, they are silent when the costumed guides are around. There's a disorienting charm about the familiarity with which they speak of their heroine "Emily," as if she were about to walk down the stairs for tea. Emily Carr's writings about her upbringing are the basis for tours of the home, but echoes of Carr are not resonant in the redecorated downstairs rooms, despite the well-meant whispers of the guides. And in the anodyne accounts of life here, there is little sign of the complex, disturbed artist that is revealed in her paintings and letters. Carr became a cantankerous character, more at home in the wilderness painting decaying totem poles than she ever was in the tidy family dining room, taking part in pious teatime conversation. Yet her memories of childhood—of Sunday dinners and afternoon tea—can also be seen in the homely refurnishing of the house.

Carr remembered her father as "a stern autocrat" who fenced off the pasture to keep the cows away from the garden which he wanted to "look exactly like England." He planted "Englishy flowers" in the garden to erase "all the wild Canadian-ness," turning semi-rural life in Victoria into a pastoral idyll. Local gardeners, loyal to the gardening legacy of the empire, continue the tradition today. Carr wrote more affectionately of "Bong," the family's Chinese houseboy, and "Wash Mary," their Indian help, than of her father. The garden, though, was an enchantment that nourished the young artist's imagination and feeling for nature. Her father, she recalled in softer tone, "loved trees, but cleared away the scrub to make meadows and a beautiful garden . . . there were hawthorn hedges, primrose banks . . . an orchard and a great tin-lined apple room, wonderful strawberry beds, and raspberry and currant bushes, all from imported English stock . . . we had chickens, cows and a pig, a grand vegetable garden—almost everything we ate grew on our land." But her father's demure English plantings were not far from the wilderness and the gloomy, sodden forests and derelict coastal scenes which were the inspiration for Carr's life as a painter. She sensed the world beyond the gate, once flanked by two Lombardy poplars, planted by her father to frame the Italianate dwelling.

Carr had an eye for the bizarre aspects of colonial life, not least her own; in later years she was often seen walking with her favourite pet, a Javanese monkey which she dressed in costume. She wrote how her father fenced off the eastern edge of his property to obscure the notorious Colonist Hotel on Douglas Street after a dispute with the owners, William and Henrietta Lush, whose clientele lived up to the proprietors' name. She recalled Captain and Mrs. Lewis, who lived on Belleville Street and are said to have imported the first piano to British Columbia from England round Cape Horn. It was landed at Esquimalt and carried by Indian porters through the bush trail to Victoria. Carr noted that when "the tired Indians put the piano down in a field outside the house to rest for a minute," Mrs. Lewis and her sisters "rushed out with the key, unlocked and played the piano out there in the field." The astonished Indians peered "up into the sky and into the woods to see where the noise came from," and ran away.

Few of the antique furnishings in the Carr House today belonged to the Carr family. They are "in keeping" with the period that the restoration, begun in 1976, seeks to revive. Layers of paint, wallpaper and varnish have been peeled away to show the original surfaces, and the original nineteenth-century colour scheme has been replicated inside and out. Some rooms have been refinished as they were in Carr's time, but other panels have been left unrestored to show the work in progress. The main rooms have been "furnished as the family would have known them in 1865." The dining room table is set with Spode "Blue Italian" china delicately printed with Neo-classical ruins—tasteful imagery for middle-class homes when it was first manufactured in 1816. Whether or not Carr slurped her soup from plates like these, they do contrast with her rebellious nature. Nothing could be further removed from the pretty garden and doll's house Italianate architecture that characterize both the Spode service and her old home than the brooding, mystical world of her mature paintings. Carr's mother died in 1886; her father in 1888. She was an unsettled sixteen-year-old by the time her guardian allowed her to study art in San Francisco in 1890. Although she returned to the house in 1893 and taught art to local children in her father's barn, she seems never to have been at home here, and finally went to study in London in 1899. She might well abhor the precious reverence that would greet her if she were to return to her childhood home. In the "literary garden," signs with quotes from her books do their best to bring her back.

·⇐ BEACON HILL PARK ⇒·

James Bay may appear as just another gentrified Victorian neighbourhood with cozy nooks and charming turn-of-the-century architecture. Behind the Parliament Buildings, where Government Street sheds its urban tempo as it extends through the area's leafy lanes, this seems to be so. But James Bay has weathered edges that the little lanes cannot entirely conceal. When it reaches Holland Point the neighbourhood butts abruptly into the seashore, part of which was called the "Bay of Falling off Cliffs" by the Salish Indians. On a clear day the panoramic vista of the Strait of Juan de Fuca shimmers with the floating snowcaps of the Olympic Mountains in Washington state. Container ships from Vancouver head for open sea, flags fluttering as if to remind Victoria of her decline as a port city since the heyday of the nineteenth century.

Beacon Hill Park was named after beacons that were first lit by the Hudson's Bay Company in 1846 as a warning to ships to avoid a reef offshore and to guide them safely into harbour. A granite marker on the bluffs at Lewis Street recalls the wreck of the collier *San Pedro* in 1891—not the first on Brotchie Ledge. Captain William Brotchie was born in 1799 in Caithness, Scotland and became an experienced skipper as master of the HBC brig *Cadboro*. In 1849 Brotchie, a member of the Pioneer Cricket Club which played at Beacon Hill Park, was stumped on the reef that bears his name, thus gaining first-hand knowledge of local hazards, which led to his appointment as Victoria Harbour Master in 1858. Brotchie Ledge has a doleful ring that echoes the many maritime calamities that washed up on Victoria's shores. Sewell Prescott Moody, an American lumber baron whose Moodyville sawmill on the Burrard Inlet was the genesis of North Vancouver, went down with the steamer *Pacific* in 1906 off Cape Flattery in 1875. A fragment of the ship was later washed up on the beach below Beacon Hill bearing a scrawled message from the doomed vessel: "S. P. Moody, all is lost."

The park, which the HBC had used for recreation and as a site for the beacons, was spared from development by a far-sighted James Douglas in 1850. After 1858 it was administered by the colonial government and a board of trustees until Parliament handed it to the city in 1882. City council's first act was to introduce a bylaw that prevented locals from gambling, cleaning carpets, grazing their cattle or discharging firearms in the park. This ordinance did not apply to Finlayson Point Battery, manned by local militia, where coastal defence guns had been mounted in 1878 during a diplomatic flurry when there was fear of a Russian attack, or to the Royal Artillery which used the park for gunnery practice. Military manoeuvres on its grassy plateau, the city's most expansive piece of open ground, were as keenly watched as the local cricket club's games. On royal visits and other ceremonial occasions the park was decked with flags and podiums, dressed with ranks of regimental tunics, and dinned with gun salutes and the pipes and drums of imperial celebration. The unveiling of the Robert Burns monument in 1900 drew Lieutenant Governor Sir Henri-Gustave Joly de Lotbinière and Mayor Charles Hayward to an elaborate ceremony attended by a kilted guard of

A cairn on the windy summit of Beacon Hill notes the origin of the name—from two beacons that were first lit by the Hudson's Bay Company in 1846 to warn ships of the treacherous Brotchie Ledge offshore. In 1850 the site was set aside by Governor James Douglas as a public park. RW

BEACON HILL PARK

WHEN VICTORIA WAS SETTLED IN 1843 THIS AREA
WAS A NATURAL PARK. IT WAS RESERVED IN 1858
FOR A PARK BY SIR JAMES DOUGLAS, GOVERNOR OF THE
COLONY OF VANCOUVER ISLAND AND GIVEN IN TRUST
TO VICTORIA BY THE PROVINCE OF BRITISH COLUMBIA
IN 1882. IT WAS SO NAMED FROM TWO BEACONS
PLACED ON THE HILL IN 1846 TO MARK THE POSITION
OF BROTCHIE LEDGE. AREA 154 ACRES

Mushroom Seat, Beacon Hill Park, Victoria,

honour. Commissioned by the local William Wallace and St. Andrew's and Caledonian societies, the memorial is reputed to have been the first erected in Canada to the Scottish poet.

Beacon Hill Park is one of the few sites where the Garry oak, a tree peculiar to southern Vancouver Island, still grows. Garry oak meadows were commonplace when the park was created but are now rare. A Garry oak preservation society campaigns to protect them. The tree was named by David Douglas, a Scottish botanical explorer who was trained at Glasgow Botanic Gardens and sponsored by the Royal Horticultural Society, London. Douglas named the oak after Nicholas Garry, a deputy-governor of the HBC. In 1825–27, he explored northern California and the Columbia River while based at Fort Vancouver. (It was for him, not James Douglas, that the Douglas fir is named.) Douglas was feted for his "zeal and spirit," having collected nearly 500 plant specimens and 100 varieties of seeds. After going back to London for a time, he reappeared to explore New Caledonia—or New Scotland, as British

TOP *An Edwardian postcard view showing one of Beacon Hill Park's ornamental lakes and the "Mushroom Seat," a typically Victorian folly. The park's oddities also included a "Rustic Stone Medieval Bridge"—built in 1889.* AUTHOR'S COLLECTION
BOTTOM *Victoria may have been the only place in the British Empire where a cricket match ended in a duel. In 1858, the* Gazette *reported that two Americans, John Collins and William Morris, "had a misunderstanding at the cricket ground on Beacon Hill . . ." and they chose the gentlemen's way with pistols to settle their quarrel. "The combatants met later in the afternoon at the fort and proceeded as far as Vancouver Street . . . Collins said that was far enough and they would fight it out there. Those who were with them endeavoured to dissuade them, but the principals were determined . . . Three shots were exchanged. At the third, Collins fell, mortally wounded . . . Morris fled the country."* RW

Columbia was then called. In 1833 he lost everything, including a year's worth of notes, in a canoe mishap west of Fort George. He later sailed for the Sandwich Islands and became the first European to scale the two highest peaks there.

In 1884, when the city proposed building agricultural exhibition buildings in the park, former HBC factor Alexander Caulfield Anderson took the city council to court. Judge Matthew Baillie Begbie pronounced in Anderson's favour: "Whoever can, like myself, remember the ostensible and accepted dimensions of Beacon Hill Park, twenty-five years ago, and observes the comparatively scanty dimensions to which it is now reduced . . . must feel some anxiety that at least the poor remainder shall be preserved intact . . . The neglect of a young city to provide open space for the supply of light and air to its maturer growth is one of the great sources of anxiety, on sanitary grounds to many towns in England. The improvidence of the earlier citizens is severely visited on and dearly redeemed by their children and successors." City council then arranged a competition to lay out the site as a formal civic park. The result is a classic nineteenth-century urban park that owes much to British civic design and cultural thought of the time.

Civic parks were unknown before the nineteenth century. In England, there were village commons where people played games or grazed their cattle, and there were royal parks and hunting grounds that were occasionally opened to the public—but with restrictive admission rules. When Regent's Park in London was opened in 1838 there were no public footpaths, only aristocratic carriageways that effectively deterred the poor from entering. The notion of public parks for all social classes was a result of the industrial revolution. Social reformers campaigned for green space to be planted and natural features protected in densely populated and polluted industrial towns. Parks were seen by well-meaning Victorian thinkers as places where "the intellectual character of the lower classes" might be raised; it was thought that persuading the proletariat to appreciate nature along with their betters would lead to social harmony.

Today this idea may sound naive. It was certainly condescending. But public parks, with their fountains, statuary, flowerbeds and tree-lined avenues—like public libraries, also aspects of Victorian civic improvement—were the saving graces of many dour nineteenth-century British mill and shipbuilding towns.

Sir Joseph Paxton, the English landscape architect and engineer, laid out the first public park at Birkenhead near Liverpool in 1843. In 1857, Frederick Law Olmsted, the American landscape designer of Central Park, New York, wrote of Birkenhead Park: "in democratic America, there was nothing to be thought of as comparable with this People's Garden . . . and all this magnificent pleasure-ground is entirely, unreservedly, and for ever the people's own. The poorest British peasant is as free to enjoy it in all its parts as the British Queen." Beacon Hill Park was laid out by John Blair, a Scottish landscape architect whose competition-winning design of 1888 was influenced by Paxton and Olmsted's styles. Blair, who had previously worked in Chicago, displayed a typically Victorian desire to re-create nature with a tidy formula for the park's northern and western sides facing the city and James Bay. His plan, with rural vistas, winding leafy carriageways, ornamental fountains and artificial lakes, nods to Paxton and Olmsted—and, in its pastoral sweep, to the eighteenth-century landscape gardens of English stately homes. A "Rustic Stone Medieval Bridge"—constructed in 1889—and an octagonal bandstand added to the park's novelty for citizens of the time. But Blair's design also left some rough edges. He preserved Beacon Hill's southward open slopes, panoramic ocean views and wooded landscapes as a semi-wild setting. Emily Carr, who took daily walks in the park, noted the frisson inspired by its windy spaces and grassy braes. "When you climbed to the top of Beacon Hill and looked around," she wrote, "you knew that the school geography was right after all and that the world was really round." ❧

Fort Victoria

IT HAS BEEN THE UNIFORM POLICY OF THE HUDSON'S BAY
COMPANY NEVER TO SUFFER THE BLOOD OF A WHITE MAN TO BE
SHED BY AN INDIAN WITH IMPUNITY—*Hudson's Bay Company
Governor Sir John Henry Pelly to Earl Grey, Secretary of State for
War and the Colonies, 1852*

FORT VICTORIA

ORT VICTORIA was founded in 1843 by James Douglas, chief factor of the Hudson's Bay Company, on a site now bounded by Broughton, Wharf, Bastion and Government streets. The fort became the HBC's main trading post on the west coast, but it was not the earliest. The fur trading company built Fort Vancouver at the mouth of the Columbia River in 1824 and Fort Langley on the Fraser River in 1827. Fort Vancouver's operation was moved to Victoria when Oregon Territory was ceded by Britain to the United States and the frontier drawn along the 49th parallel by treaty in 1846. While visiting Fort Vancouver in 1841–42, Sir George Simpson, the governor of the HBC in Canada, reconnoitred Fort Victoria's site from the deck of the company

*Fort Victoria on the Inner Harbour, before the gold rush of
1858 transformed the settlement. The Hudson's Bay Company
ship* Otter *is anchored offshore. Nothing remains of the fort,
except for an iron mooring ring on the rocks below Wharf Street
where the* Otter *and the* Beaver *tied up.* BCARS A-04103

ship *Beaver*. Simpson observed that "the Southern end of Vancouver Island . . . appears to be the best situation for such an establishment . . . a harbour . . . safe and accessible [an] abundance of timber for home consumption and exportation . . . a range of plains nearly six miles square containing a great extent of valuable tillage and pasture land."

In March 1843 James Douglas, with lieutenants Charles Ross and Roderick Finlayson, Father Jean Baptiste Bolduc, and three dozen French Canadian company employees, landed to construct the fort. Finlayson noted in his journal that there was "dense forest along the water of the harbour," but that the site for the fort was "an open glade with oak trees of a large size." The company's armed vessels *Beaver* and *Cadboro* stood offshore to guard the work crew from Songhees Indians, but after Douglas explained his plans the Natives helped build the fort. They were paid one point blanket for every forty pickets they cut for the stockade, under the direction of the company's French Canadian carpenters. A quadrangle 300 by 500 feet was cleared and an 18-foot high palisade erected to protect the buildings inside—the chief factor's residence and officers' mess, chapel and schoolhouse, Batchelors' Hall, office and storehouses, blacksmith's and carpenter's workshops. An octagonal bastion, like a scene from *Treasure Island*, was equipped with cutlasses and four nine-pounder cannons for defence. Initially Fort Victoria was as much a military strongpoint as it was a trading post.

Douglas returned to Fort Vancouver, leaving Ross and Finlayson to complete construction of the fort. The melancholic Ross, who viewed his life with the HBC as one of "dreary solitude," was in charge. He was glad to have escaped the incessant rains of Fort McLoughlin for the sunnier climate at Fort Victoria. But after supervising the construction and defence of the fort he gasped, "I never before was in such a turmoil." Ross died in 1844 and was succeeded by Finlayson. Born at Loch Alsh in the Scottish West Highlands, Finlayson had emigrated to New York in 1837, and was hired by the HBC in Montreal after a relative put in a good word for him. In 1839 he was sent to Fort Vancouver and acted as relief manager at Fort Simpson before being posted to Victoria. Finlayson's leadership was the true foundation of Fort Victoria: after Ross died he was in charge until Douglas returned to take over in 1849. A salmon store, coal depot, farm buildings and a mechanic's house were built outside the fort. Horses and cattle were brought from Fort Nisqually on Puget Sound. Two dairy farms supplied the fort with milk and beef. In 1848 a company sawmill was opened at the head of Esquimalt Harbour. Lumber was exported to sugar plantations in Hawaii and gold fields in California. The community evolved more in the manner of a bucolic medieval settlement than a conventional fur trading post. In 1848 George William Courtenay, captain of HMS *Constance,* noted "300 acres under tillage, and a dairy farm of 80 cows . . . under the superintendence of a civil but hard Scot [Finlayson] who has about 30 people of all descriptions under him." John Moresby, a lieutenant on HMS *Thetis* based at Esquimalt in 1852, described the surroundings as "Trees, trees everywhere, many of them 200 feet high, laced with undergrowth, hoary with lichen . . . and the majestic silence and loneliness of the place." Captain John Gordon of HMS *America* said that he would "not give one of the bleakest knolls of all the bleak hills of Scotland for twenty islands like this arrayed in barbaric splendour."

The brooding wilderness heightened the sense of isolation, bringing a claustrophobic aura to recreation at the fort. Dr. Helmcken wrote: "Batchelors' Hall was a portion of a large storey-and-a-half block building, having a common-room in the centre, and two rooms on each side with a door opening into each . . . Every room had sporting weapons in it—muskets, and rifles of great variety—swords, a saddle and bridle, tobacco and pipes, lots of dust, and the usual utensils." Saturday nights in the hall, described by Helmcken in 1850, were like scenes from a Shakespearian tavern. "In the evenings there was singing . . . much to the annoyance of the parson and his wife, but not to the girl boarders in the Staines School. Batchelors' Hall was the rendezvous of all visitors—if they were socially acceptable, so sometimes there was a goodly number, including Captain Grant and the captains and mates of Her Majesty's ships when in harbour. Of course, sometimes they were a little boisterous, but never much, because the parson was on one side and Mr. Douglas only 50 feet away." James Anderson, a pupil at the fort's school, recalled compensation for boarders' draughty, rat-infested quarters: "One of our greatest joys was feasting our eyes on the sumptuous suppers enjoyed by the batchelors ... who had quarters immediately under our dormitory. By dint of raising up a board in the flooring ... we were enabled to view the mild orgies of the batchelors: oysters, sherry, port, and brandy in abundance ... How they ever missed seeing the row of hungry little faces above beats me."

Douglas, who had moved back to Victoria in 1849, allowed his men to let off steam. But he ruled the colony like a feudal potentate until he retired in 1864. His haughty bearing and strict conduct gave him the nickname "Old Squaretoes." Douglas insisted on dressing for dinner. Helmcken recorded his first meal at the fort: "The mess room was more than thirty feet long, by say twenty wide, a large open fire at one end ... A clock on the wall, a long table in the middle, covered with spotless linen, the knives and forks clean, decanters bright, containing wine and so forth ... everything European ... there must have been more than twenty people in the room, when Mr. Douglas made his appearance—a handsome specimen of nature's noblemen—tall, stout, broad-shouldered, muscular, with grave bronzed face, but kindly withal." The only absentee was the Reverend Staines, the company chaplain and schoolteacher, whose relationship with Douglas had been cool from the day he had arrived in 1849.

After well-practised greetings, Douglas "took the head of the table, Mr. Finlayson the foot. Capt. Dodd, Capt. Wishart, Capt. Grant, and myself were guests ... Grace having been said by Mr. Douglas, on comes the soup, then the salmon, then the meats—venison on this occasion and ducks—then pies and so forth ... Having done justice to the dinner and taken a glass 'to the Queen,' many of the junior members left. We remained; the steward, a Kanaka, brought on tobacco and long clay pipes ... Mr. Douglas took his pipe ... everyone appeared to smoke calmly and deliberately." The doctor had been "informed that no frivolous conversation was ever allowed at table ... Mr. Douglas as a rule came primed with some intellectual or scientific subject, and thus he educated his clerks. All had to go to church every Sunday, the mess room serving every purpose—baptisms, marriages, funerals, councils, dances, theatricals, or other amusements." Helmcken was pleasantly surprised to find his colleagues "well read and well educated" and their loquacious boarding school rivalry amused him. During the dinner "there was conversation ... newspapers of the latest dates—that is to say nearly six months old—had come out and Mr. Douglas commenced about some Scotch battles fought long ago ... Douglas and Dodd seemed to know how many men were engaged in each ... all at once they tumbled into the battle of Waterloo, the one claiming that the Scotch did best, the other that the English did most execution, whilst a third claimed that both Scotch, English, and Irish would have been beaten had it not been for Blucher and his host coming up just in the nick of time to save the lot. 'Old Tod' [a retired HBC factor] was chaffed for having fired a salute four years after the victory, i.e., as soon as he heard of it. He was indignant and said it was less than three. His post had been somewhere near the North Pole."

The names of HBC staff and other early residents, engraved on commemorative bricks on Government Street, reveal the social make-up of the settlement: Scots James Douglas, Charles Ross, Roderick Finlayson and John Wark; French Canadians Joseph Charbonneau and Pierre Versailles Baptiste Bottineau; and assorted Europeans, Sandwich (Hawaiian) Islanders, and captains and commodores of the Royal Navy based at Esquimalt. The fort was the hub of the isolated society. The company store was the only source of imported goods, sent once a year on an HBC sailing ship from England. It stocked everything from boots and blankets to pots, pans and pilot biscuits. HBC farmers and the handful of early independent settlers would visit to buy supplies and to seek companionship—coffee was always ready on Batchelors' Hall's cast-iron stove. Indians who set up camp in the lee of the fort to trade were generally peaceful—especially after Royal Marines from the *Constance* put on a show of force. There was also a Hawaiian watchman from the company's outpost on the Sandwich Islands, employed to lock and unlock the gates and to announce church services and meals from the belfry. The daily dinner bell also alerted the fort's dogs, which howled for attention in the compound. But between lights out and reveille, the watchman's sporadic "All's well," called out on his nocturnal promenade, was the only sound to be heard above the creaking of the anchored *Beaver* and *Otter*, the dogs' spasmodic barking, and the wind and the tidal wash on the harbour.

Everyone knew their place within the fort's stable, disciplined social structure. The HBC and Royal Navy's British officers were at the top along with French priests and English chaplains; French Canadian craftsmen were in the middle ranks; Métis and Kanakas were lower down; and the Indians were at the bottom. The pyramid was eroded when the settlement became a colony in 1849. "Drunkenness is now the crying and prevalent sin of this colony," Douglas wrote in 1853, "and will, I fear, continue to be so, until a better and more responsible class of people are sent to the country, or a great improvement takes place in the moral tone of the present population." Royal Navy Lieutenant C. W. Wilson thought that "many English people, most of a rather questionable standing at home, have come out here & pretend to look down upon the old settlers," and he gave a reason why. In 1858 he wrote: "We all went to a ball given by the officers of the *Plumper*, where we were met by all the young ladies of Vancouver Island, they only number about 30 and are not very great beauties, however I enjoyed myself very much, not having had a dance for such a time. Most of the young ladies are half breeds and have quite as many of the propensities of the savage as of the civilised being."

The HBC factors' marital habits certainly caused eyebrows to be raised.

John Tod retired with a young Indian wife, his fourth, having abandoned the earlier ones at various trading posts. Douglas was married to a half-Cree, half-Irish woman. John Wark's wife was half Indian, half French Canadian. Charles Ross's wife Isabella was also a Native mixed-blood woman. More and more of these trading post relationships were legitimized by the church at the earliest opportunity as pious Victorian values began to permeate colonial life. Douglas's wife's Indian blood caused snobbish gossip among second-generation settlers.

An exaggerated Britishness came to characterize the colony— almost as if Douglas had taken HBC Secretary Archibald Barclay's "Land Policy of the Colony of Vancouver Island" to the letter. In 1849 Barclay wrote that "the object of every sound system of colonization should be, not to re-organize Society on a new basis . . . but to transfer to the new country whatever is most valuable and most approved in the institutions of the old, so that society may, as far as possible, consist of the same classes, united together by the same ties and having the same relative duties to perform in one country as the other." Douglas moved out of the fort to his house on James Bay where he began to lay out a croquet lawn. Helmcken thought the settlement was "as civilised as any respectable village in England." In 1852 Lieutenant John Moresby and the crew of HMS *Thetis* played the first cricket match on Vancouver Island at Beacon Hill Park, roundly beating a local team. The cricketing sailors also chopped a road through the forest from Esquimalt to Victoria.

Douglas, faced with a new role and responsibilities after Vancouver Island became a British colony, ordered *Burke's Peerage, Baronetage, and Knightage* for his library when he was appointed governor in 1851. He took quickly to the flowery diplomatic language of the time, writing to Lord Grey: "I have the honour to acknowledge the receipt of your Lordship's communication . . . transmitting a commission under the Great Seal of the United Kingdom, appointing me to be Governor and Commander in Chief in and over the Island of Vancouver, and its dependencies . . . I beg your Lordship convey to Her most Gracious Majesty my humble thanks for those distinguished marks of confidence which it shall be my endeavour to prove are not misplaced." Helmcken observed: "Before long rude simplicity gave way before the . . . desire to . . . put on airs and graces . . . what we were in England and Scotland was burnisht and made the most of." By 1854 there were approximately 230 white residents at Fort Victoria and 150 to the west where the land (from the Songhees Indian village to beyond Esquimalt Harbour) was divided between four HBC farms: Viewfield, Constance Cove, Colwood and Craigflower. An 1858 map of local property prepared by surveyor J. D. Pemberton also showed that apart from Beacon Hill Park, Victoria townsite and James Bay, virtually all land northeast of the Inner Harbour, reaching to the HBC's Uplands Farm at Cadboro Bay, was owned by company officers. The HBC pioneers had exchanged the blankets and buckskins of the fort for the tweeds of the landed gentry.

A trapper and a Hudson's Bay Company trader in an imaginary fur trade scene at Fort Victoria. The image—one of a collection of stained glass panels showing local activities—was made in Edinburgh and installed at Christ Church Cathedral where the glass can be seen today. RW

·⇐ JAMES DOUGLAS ⇒·

James Douglas was born in 1803, son of a Glasgow merchant and his Creole sugar plantation mistress at Demerara, British Guiana. One of Douglas's daughters thought he was born in Lanarkshire where he was sent to boarding school when his father married a Glasgow sweetheart in 1809. Little is known of his family background, and Douglas himself was reticent on the subject throughout his career. His real mother died in 1839 and his father in 1865. When he left school he found a substitute for the family stability he never enjoyed. In 1819 he joined the fur trading North West Company in Montreal as a clerk. When it was amalgamated with

FUR TRADE

the rival Hudson's Bay Company in 1821, Douglas stayed on and rose through the new company's ranks. He married Amelia Connolly, the part-Cree, part-Jewish daughter of an Irish HBC factor at Fort St. James, New Caledonia. In 1830 he was posted to Fort Vancouver, where he became assistant to the company's chief factor John McLoughlin, also a former Nor'wester.

In 1842 Douglas was instructed by HBC Governor Sir George Simpson to sail to Vancouver Island and establish a new trading post as Fort Vancouver was vulnerable to American territorial expansion. Simpson made thumbnail assessments of his employees' personalities and abilities in a notebook, an *aide memoire* that became as legendary as his travels by canoe and his surprise visits to the company's scattered fur trading posts. With Iroquois voyageurs paddling and a kilted piper playing, the "Little Emperor" would arrive at the remote posts to be greeted by astonished staff—astonished not just by the skirl of the bagpipes that heralded his unexpected approach, but by Simpson's attire: he made a point of disembarking wearing a top hat and cape like a London gent. Measuring up Douglas in 1832, Simpson wrote: "A Scotch West Indian . . . a stout powerful active man of good conduct and respectable abilities: tolerably well educated, expresses himself clearly on paper, understands our Counting House business and is an excellent Trader . . . well qualified for any Service requiring bodily exertion, firmness of mind and the exercise of sound judgement, but furiously violent when roused . . . has every reason to look forward to early promotion." Simpson sent Douglas to

Sir James Douglas, the "Father of British Columbia," was Victoria's autocratic but honourable Hudson's Bay Company factor and colonial governor. In 1852 Lieutenant John Moresby of HMS Thetis *wrote: "It was easy to see that here indeed was a man, middle- aged, tall . . . alert and kindly . . . the type that has broken out of our island home in all centuries to colonise and civilise—the born pioneer."* BCARS A—01232

Alaska to negotiate with the competing Russian American Company in 1840 and, the following year, to Monterey to discuss trade with Mexican authorities. In Mexican California, Douglas noted that the Spanish governor's status was not matched by power, which was held by a junta elected by property owners. He remembered this when he became colonial governor of Vancouver Island in 1851, establishing his own authority and resisting elections.

Douglas's firm judgement and courage survived all tests. He never backed away from confrontation. At Fort St. James in 1828 he strode into an Indian village and arrested and promptly dispatched the murderer of two HBC employees. The Natives stormed the fort where, according to a Kiplingesque account by John Moresby, Douglas was "surrounded by a horde of maddened Indians, was at his last struggle, when . . . an Indian girl, the daughter of a chief, tore her way to his side, held back the savages, and pleaded his cause with such passion that the red man granted his life to her entreaties. She lived to share his honours, and to become Lady Amelia Douglas, wife of the Governor and Commander-in-chief of British Columbia." It is a measure of Douglas's appeal that his exploits were so colourfully embroidered. The "Indian Girl" was not Amelia Douglas nor was she the daughter of a chief.

Queen Victoria, the formidable Empress and "Great White Queen," as Natives were instructed to call her, ruled through loyal ambassadors like Douglas, who reinforced the rumour of her wealth and conquering influence when they travelled around her colonies. In November 1852 a company shepherd was shot dead by Nanaimo and Cowichan Indians on the outskirts of Victoria. Douglas, acting out HBC Governor Sir John Pelly's dictum that "it has been the uniform policy of the Hudson's Bay Company never to suffer the blood of a white man to be shed by an Indian with impunity," investigated the case in January 1853, and organized an expedition to the Cowichan Valley to apprehend the two murderers. The Cowichans, particularly, had a hostile reputation and Douglas, aboard the *Beaver* with his French Canadian bodyguard, was accompanied by Royal Marines in naval cutters from HMS *Thetis*. The flotilla anchored off the mouth of the Cowichan River, where it encountered a force of 200 Natives in war canoes. Douglas and the Cowichan chiefs agreed to talk, and the armed party landed and raised the Union Jack. John Moresby, gunnery lieutenant on the *Thetis*, recorded Douglas's words as he stood outside his tent where he received the chiefs' delegation: "Hearken, O Chiefs! I am sent by King George [at the time the former monarch was still recognised by the Indians] who is your friend, and who desires right only between your tribes and his men. If his men kill an Indian, they are punished. If your men do likewise, they must also suffer. Give up the murderer, and let there be peace between the peoples, or I will burn your lodges and trample out your tribes." The Indians agreed to help catch the fugitive—a face-saving way out for both parties. The culprit was caught near Nanaimo and hanged after the first jury trial in the colony, held on board the *Beaver*.

Throughout his career Douglas exceeded Simpson's assessment. He developed Fort Victoria as the western headquarters of the HBC's trading empire and became the first governor of the united colonies of Vancouver Island and British Columbia in 1858. Almost single-handedly he safeguarded British sovereignty in New Caledonia during the turbulent 1858 Fraser River gold rush. His address to a rough-and-tumble group of American miners at Yale is a classic of high-minded imperial braggadocio: "Gentlemen, I understand that you assembled . . . not only to welcome the Representative of Our Most Gracious Lady, the Queen, but also to learn from me the views of the Queen's Government about this country. It is not the custom with Governors of British provinces to address the public, but as this is a particular occasion, and the circumstances are peculiar . . . Our gracious Queen commands me to . . . allow you to dig for gold in her dominion, and to offer you the protection of British laws, as long as you obey those laws, and pay the Queen's dues like honest men."

Douglas was a belligerent statesman, suggesting once that Indians, whom the Americans had "treated . . . in such a manner as to arouse their worst passions," could be used as guerrilla fighters against the United States. He claimed he could raise 50,000 Indian riflemen at Victoria to settle the San Juan Islands Pig War. During the American Civil War, he proposed the British should retake the Oregon Territory and invade Alaska. (In both cases he was restrained by cooler heads in London.) In 1846 Colonial Secretary Earl Grey and Sir John Pelly discussed colonization of Vancouver Island. In 1848 it was agreed that if a colony was not established within five years, the HBC's 7 shillings annual lease would be lost. The colony was established in 1849. Douglas, the obvious choice for governor, was passed over because of political opposition to the HBC in London where the company was accused in Parliament of "frightful despotism" in keeping the Natives in a "state of degradation." The Colonial Office appointed Richard Blanshard instead.

Blanshard, who had previously served in the West Indies, expected to lead the life of a country gent with an estate and a mansion. But when he arrived on HMS *Driver*, Douglas made it plain who was in charge. The hapless Blanshard suffered a humiliating tenure. He found himself ruling a colony with few colonists. He had brought a servant, but had no staff. He had no troops. And he had no governor's mansion—he was quartered aboard the *Driver* until Douglas reluctantly had a house built for him. He was given none of the perks to which he was accustomed; he didn't even qualify for discounts at the HBC store. Blanshard found few duties to perform. With the assistance of the Royal Navy, he attempted to mediate a Native–white dispute at the HBC post at Fort Rupert on northeast Vancouver Island in 1850, but ended up bombarding two Native villages from a navy ship. The following year he set up an executive council in Victoria, the forerunner of the provincial legislature, in response to complaints about Douglas's dictatorial ways and the HBC monopoly. But he was disillusioned and plagued by malaria he had caught in the tropics, and he soon resigned. When he sailed back to England he had to pay his own way home. Douglas was appointed his successor.

Communication from Europe to Victoria in the 1850s took three to five months by sail via Cape Horn and forty or fifty days by steam via Panama. Even so, Douglas felt the modern industrial and democratic world closing around his feudal pedestal. The HBC's trading palisades were disintegrating as bartering was replaced by a capitalist wage and cash economy. The more he saw this happening, the more stubbornly he clung to his power and benign autocratic authority as he struggled to maintain order when the gold rush washed over the fort's walls in 1858. Few of the gold rush incomers thanked him for this. Amor de Cosmos, writing in the first issue of the *Colonist* in 1858, said Douglas "wanted to serve his country with honour and at the same time preserve the grasping interests of the Hudson's Bay Company inviolate. In trying to serve two masters he was unsuccessful as a statesman . . . his policy approximate to masterly inactivity." Alfred Penderill Waddington, an English merchant and property owner, did not treat Douglas kindly when he wrote *The Fraser Mines Vindicated*, the first book published in the colony. Waddington's fifty-page tract—the result, as he put it, of "a few days scribbling at spare hours"—criticized "the stifling influences" of the HBC. Douglas, Waddington wrote, had been "habituated almost from childhood" to the company's "mean, petty, despotic dealings." A temporary slump after the first months of gold fever provoked further complaint. Waddington wrote: "hundreds came down [the Fraser River] quicker than they went up, and filled the place with consternation . . . The storekeepers of Victoria felt annihilated . . . goods ordered [from San Francisco] during the rush piled up on wharves . . . traders sold out . . . at ruinous prices." Douglas was on the receiving end of miners' and merchants' frustration, although high water on the Fraser River rather than the HBC had prevented fresh discoveries of gold.

As colonial governor, Douglas faced a clear conflict of interest. As HBC chief factor, he had one foot lingering in the fort as the other stepped into Government House. The company's wish to preserve its trading monopoly and the colonial office's desire for settlement were incompatible aims. The new colonial secretary, Lord Lytton, wrote to Douglas: "You fully understand that, unless you are prepared to assure me that all connection between yourself and the Company is terminated, or in the course of speedy termination, you will be relieved by the appointment of a successor . . . It is quite impossible that you should continue to serve at once the Crown and the Company, when their respective rights and interests may possibly diverge, and when at all events public opinion will not allow of such a connection." Douglas was aware of the greater cause and resigned from the company in November 1858, when he was appointed Governor of British Columbia—and appointed Alexander Grant Dallas, an HBC colleague and his son-in-law, his successor. He wrote to the Colonial Office: "all claims and interests [of the HBC] will be rendered subordinate to the great object of peopling and opening up the new country, and consolidating it as an integral part of the British Empire."

Douglas was knighted in 1863 and, after British Columbia's first Legislative Council was held at New Westminster in 1864, he retired. He attended farewell banquets in Victoria and New Westminster before taking his family on a European grand tour. When he set sail in March 1864, the *Colonist* recorded: "the city was decked in all directions with flags and banners, and the shipping in the harbour gaily ornamented with streamers and signals . . . the *Enterprise* lay awaiting her distinguished passenger . . . His Excellency, preceded by the band playing 'For He's a Jolly Good Fellow' . . . was greeted by hearty cheers from the assembled multitude . . . he stepped on board the steamer. The gallant little craft then moved slowly off, backing out into the stream, amid the most vociferous cheering, the band playing 'Auld Lang Syne' and the battery on the opposite wharf sending forth a thundering salute." Douglas returned to his croquet lawn and library with its forty-five-volume set of English classics that he had carried for years. HBC men were not noted for airs and graces, but Douglas acquired a love of ceremony. Sir George Simpson would have been amused to learn that when Douglas visited the

HBC's Craigflower Farm he expected to be greeted by a cannon salute. He also, with justification, ended correspondence with the flourish "His Excellency, James Douglas, Governor of Vancouver Island and its Dependencies, Commander-in-Chief and Vice-Admiral of the same." He died in Victoria in 1877 and is buried in Ross Bay cemetery.

·⇐ BASTION SQUARE ⇒·

Bastion Square takes its name from the stockade and watchtowers that protected Fort Victoria. Nothing now remains of the fort, which was demolished in the property boom during the 1858 gold rush, except for an iron mooring ring on the rocks below Wharf Street. The buildings that replaced the bastion have also disappeared, as has topographic evidence of the fort's parade ground (erased in the 1860s when Bastion Street was extended to the waterfront). Bastion Square's architecture dates from the 1880s when the Victoria Law Courts replaced the gold rush-era police barracks and jail, a severe castellated Georgian style block built in 1859. Its facade was the last sight for prisoners who were executed at public hangings and buried in the barracks yard.

The new building, designed by Hermann Otto Tiedemann, was the grandest of more than thirty new courthouses built around the province in the late nineteenth century. But it was not quite grand enough. The brick facades were thought to lack the *gravitas* appropriate to the building's purpose, and they were later stuccoed and banded at the base to look like stone. In 1899 Francis Rattenbury added new courtrooms and filled in the arched Langley Street entrance. A new portal—that skewed Tiedemann's symmetrical design—was built on Bastion Street. The interior was modernized with the notable installation of an elaborate open-cage elevator, said to have been ordered for the convenience of a portly senior judge. The antique lift is the oldest still operating in the province.

Bastion Square's heritage buildings have kept much of their late-nineteenth-century character, if not their occupants. Rattenbury reputedly designed the law chambers, built at the southwest corner of Bastion and Langley streets in 1899. The building now houses shops and offices. The Board of Trade Building, designed by Andrew Maxwell Muir and described by the *Colonist* as "Free Italian Renaissance" style when it opened in 1892, has a different design on every floor—but no merchants gaze out over the harbour watching for their ships from the belvedere (since removed) on the seaward corner. The Burns Building, built by John Teague in 1886 at the corner of Chancery Lane as a hotel for an Irish saloonkeeper, was a law office, a warehouse and, when the area slipped into decay in the 1940s, a brothel.

When the police barracks, jail and neighbouring buildings were demolished to accommodate Tiedemann's structure, the most inconvenient loss for jurors was the Boomerang Inn, to which they would repair—on judges' recommendations—to consider their verdicts. Nothing remains of this bar, or of the boardwalks, horse hitching rails, dirt streets or public hanging ground. Tiedemann's building replaced these with four-storey metropolitan pretension. The law courts' self-contained community of lawyers, press reporters and stenographers also vanished without trace after the courts were closed in 1962 and refitted as the city's maritime museum. Apart from Bastion Square's facades—and a pub at the southeast corner of Bastion and Langley streets that stands on the site of a saloon frequented by judges and jailors—the only evidence of history here is a plaque outside the former law courts summarizing Judge Matthew Baillie Begbie's career.

> *German-trained architect Hermann Otto Tiedemann was said to have based the design of the Victoria Law Courts, built in 1887–89, on an Italianate courthouse in Munich—a rumour of middle European grandeur that lends the portals of justice a Ruritanian air.* RW

·⇐ MATTHEW BAILLIE BEGBIE ⇒·

The building that dominates Bastion Square was opened in 1889 as the Victoria Law Courts. Hermann Otto Tiedemann, the architect, was said to have based the design on an Italianate courthouse in Munich, or Berlin, where he was born—a rumour of *mittel Europa* that lends the portals of justice a Ruritanian air. But when completed, the Victoria Law Courts edifice had an august presence. It was the first major public building constructed by the provincial government after British Columbia joined the Dominion. In 1889 its pinnacled, fortress-like girth sat solidly above the tumbledown architecture of the early town much in the way that its most celebrated panjandrum, Chief Justice Matthew Baillie Begbie, held court and dispensed justice inside.

Begbie was born to a Scottish army captain and his wife at Cape Town in 1819. He was educated in Guernsey, and at Trinity College, Cambridge. He then trained in London at Lincoln's Inns Fields, became a barrister and practised law from chambers in Chancery Lane for fourteen years. In 1858 he accepted a colonial appointment as Stipendiary Magistrate of the mainland colony of British Columbia. Begbie's character and experience at the bar had been noted by Solicitor General Sir Hugh Cairns. Writing to Home Secretary Spencer Walpole, Cairns said of Begbie: "I think him personally, physically, and mentally well qualified for the ... peculiar office that is to be filled: and I know of no other person of whom the same could be said."

Begbie, duly outfitted with his robes of office from Ede & Sons,

Chief Justice Matthew Baillie Begbie made his reputation for rough justice in the gold fields of the Fraser River and Cariboo country. His direct approach—"Aye, we'll give ye a fair trial— and then we'll hang ye," to coin a Scottish expression—brought him the morbid moniker "the hanging judge." This picture was taken c. 1870. BCARS A–06955

Chancery Lane, boarded a Cunard liner at Liverpool, sailed to New York, changed ships for Panama, crossed the Isthmus by narrow-gauge train, and sailed for Esquimalt via San Francisco. Begbie travelled light. His luggage, which included a prefabricated iron house—Governor Richard Blanshard's difficulties were well known at the Colonial Office —was sent around Cape Horn with a regiment of the Royal Engineers who had been posted to the colony at the same time. Begbie arrived in Victoria in November 1858 and stayed in a Victoria hotel. In March 1859 he set off from New Westminster, then the provincial capital, on the first of many biannual judicial circuits to hear cases in mining camps and settlements in the interior.

In the popular and memorable image of Begbie, he rides into isolated, lawless gold rush shantytowns accompanied by his Indian servant and a constable to hold rudimentary but effective court, formally robed and bewigged for the occasion. He displayed exceptional strength of character—some would say stubbornness—as he made his reputation for rough justice in the gold fields of the Fraser River and Cariboo country. His direct approach—"Aye, we'll give ye a fair trial—and then we'll hang ye," to coin a Scottish expression—brought him the morbid moniker "the hanging judge." At his first murder trial in 1859 at New Westminster, a jury of American miners convicted one of their compatriots of manslaughter. The accused, who had shot a man in a barroom brawl, expected to get off with a plea of self-defence—as he probably would have done in the us. Begbie told the prisoner, "Your crime is diabolical murder, you deserve to be hanged." Turning on the jury, he delivered a typical Begbie broadside. "Gentlemen . . . it would give me great pleasure to see you hanged, each and every one of you, for declaring a murderer guilty only of manslaughter." When another prisoner came before him and ventured that jail would be inconvenient, Begbie replied, "That is why I send you there."

His delivery from the bench, and notes in his bench books, where he recorded every case, were peppered with literary asides and dry wit. His style was patrician and puckish depending on the severity of the case. Passing judgement on a collision after two ships left the harbour, he said: "it was in evidence that these vessels never race—that is forbidden by the Pilot Rules—yet it was ingenuously confessed that they never meet without seeing which of them can go the fastest." He so irritated one council, by interrupting the questioning of a witness, that the member threw down his wig and gown and exclaimed, "I shall never appear before you while you are trying a case alone." Begbie replied, "I shall survive the loss, Mr. Richards."

Begbie gained a working knowledge of Native languages, helped initially by his fluency in French, and whenever possible took an aboriginal interpreter with him on his judicial circuits. Indians often were wrongly accused because of linguistic misunderstandings, and Begbie was well aware that Natives held title to land that many European immigrants saw as free for the taking. Few cases involving Native–white disputes were clear-cut, and Begbie sometimes acted with compassion. He was sensitive to the difficulties of applying colonial laws that ignored tribal social structures and spiritual beliefs. In 1873 he advised his magistrates to allow Indian chiefs to exercise "their customary jurisdiction over drunken and disorderly members of their own tribes" and to dispense "the salutary discipline usual in the tribe." When the Dominion Government banned Native potlatch ceremonies in 1884–85, Begbie ruled that the act was imprecise and forced Ottawa back to the drawing board.

Begbie was as willing to sentence a guilty aboriginal or Chinese person to death as he was a white one. In 1864 he sent five Indians to the gallows for the "Waddington Massacre" after twenty-one white roadbuilders were murdered in a series of attacks. His report on the trial was tinged with regret. He described the ringleader as "the finest savage I have met with yet." He acknowledged that the road crew and their leader, Alfred Waddington, had provoked the Natives, withheld food from them and failed to respect their lands. He admitted that the murderers had been tricked into surrendering. But, he concluded, "the blood of twenty-one whites calls for retribution. These fellows are cruel, murdering pirates—taking life . . . in the same spirit in which you or I would go out after partridges or rabbit-shooting."

Begbie did not hesitate to overturn emotional or prejudiced jury verdicts if the evidence did not support them—and he could weather scurrilous attacks in the press. In 1866, after he ruled on a mining claim dispute, the *Cariboo Sentinel* and the *Colonist* reported that more than five hundred disgruntled miners protested and passed a resolution calling Begbie "dictatorial and arbitrary." One of his fiercest critics, John Robson, publisher of the *British Columbian* in New Westminster, called him "the tyrant judge." Amor de Cosmos, editor of the *Colonist*, wrote that Begbie was the "bugbear of the Colony," and added that "the sooner the inhabitants call on the Home Government to fill his place with a more suitable man, the better." In his own defence, Begbie wrote to the Earl of Carnarvon claiming that "the criminal statistics of the colony appear highly favourable when placed beside those of any other gold-producing country. Crimes of violence are extemely rare; highway robberies almost unknown . . . stabbing and pistolling, so common in the adjacent territories, are almost unheard of on the British side of the line; although the population is composed of the same ingredients." His status at the colonial office rose, and in 1871 he accepted a promotion to Chief Justice of the Supreme Court of British Columbia. In 1875, while on leave in Britain, he was summoned to Balmoral Castle and knighted by Queen Victoria.

Throughout his colonial career, Begbie tried to interpret British law based on common sense coloured by local customs and conditions, not bookishly impose it as if he were still practising in London. A century after he made his rulings, they were being cited as legal precedents. His education in Greek, Latin, arts and sciences was shared by many able British administrators and army officers posted to the far corners of the Empire, but few matched his physical stamina and intellectual interests. In London, he had been a well-known bon vivant who frequently toured the Continent. He was an amateur cartographer whose work was once presented to the Royal Geographic Society, the first president of Victoria's exclusive Union Club and a founding member of the Victoria Philharmonic Society. When he returned from his European trip in 1875 he regaled the society's members with an account of his visit to the newly opened Paris Opera House.

Begbie died in 1894 and is buried at Ross Bay Cemetery. A plaque outside Victoria's former courthouse sums up his career: "36 years of fearless, impartial service . . . a lasting contribution to the administration of justice in the Pacific region of Canada." At Ross Bay, the tombstone erected in his honour, a tall granite cross on a conspicuous three-tiered pedestal, was designed to match his public status, but it ignored his request for "no other monument than a wooden cross."

·⇐ SONGHEES INDIAN RESERVE ⇒·

Before the arrival of the Europeans, aboriginal groups lived in settlements on the shores of the inlets and bays around Victoria and in inland valleys. Their semi-nomadic habits, based on salmon runs, seasonal trading and food-gathering, were irrevocably changed when the Hudson's Bay Company expedition landed to build Fort Victoria. Songhees and other Salish Indians ventured to the fort out of curiosity and stayed to work and trade. The HBC traded biscuits, beads, blankets, tobacco, gunpowder and iron tools in return for pelts and fish. But it took time for mutual confidence to be established. Roderick Finlayson wrote: "The natives for sometime after our arrival kept aloof and would not come near . . . some came round gradually and, finding them inclined to steal anything they could get, a watch was kept night and day, while we lived in tents before the houses could be built. The natives . . . soon got rid of their shyness and began to remove from the village of Cadboro Bay and erect homes for themselves along the bank of the harbour . . . some of the men were employed clearing the land . . . to raise vegetables and cereals for the use of the place. In these operations we gradually got some young natives to assist, paying them in goods, and found them very useful as drivers in ploughing the land."

As a trading company, the HBC had no designs on Indian land—the Natives were left alone to supply the company with the animal pelts from which it profited. But as the west was settled, the Indians became a troublesome presence to the immigrants. They did not share the white man's concept of property ownership or the desire to treat natural resources as capital. Their relationship with the natural world was based on a spiritual rather than commercial culture. The company's traders generally treated the Indians with muscular paternalism and occasional respect but they were prepared to use force when diplomacy failed.

Finlayson's *sang froid* was tested after some of the company's dairy cattle grazing on Church Hill were butchered by Songhees Indians who had been incited by the antagonistic Cowichans. Finlayson warned the chief and demanded payment. The chief "went away in a rage, assembled some Cow- ichan Indians to his village," Finlayson wrote, "and the next move I found on their part was a shower of bullets fired at the fort . . . I had then to gather our forces and man the bastion, and I did not allow any of our men outside the fort until I could settle the matter." Finlayson suggested a truce, but warned the Indians that he "was fully prepared to carry on the battle but did not like to kill them without explaining to them that they were wrong and giving them another chance of making restitution." He then blasted the chief's lodge with grapeshot from the bastion's nine-pounder gun. The lodge "flew in the air in splinters like a bombshell. After this was such a howling that I thought a number had been killed . . . but they were much frightened, not knowing we had such destructive arms. The chief, with some of his men, shortly after this came to the gate and asked to see me. I went and assumed a warlike attitude and mentioned that unless the cattle killed were paid for I would demolish all their huts and drive them from the place . . . the next day payment in full of furs was made." He told the chief that "we came here to trade peaceable with them, and did not want war unless we were forced."

The fort attracted trading bands from the Queen Charlotte Islands and the HBC's former headquarters at Fort Vancouver. In the 1850s several thousand aboriginals arrived every summer in Victoria to trade or to find work. They camped around the fort and across the water from the HBC compound. Many were armed, especially the Haidas from the Queen Charlotte Islands who, according to Douglas, were "the most warlike, ignorant and barbarous people on the coast," but who were also canny traders who had been dealing with whites for over fifty years. In 1853, five hundred Haida Indians paddled south to Nanaimo and Victoria to trade and seek work. Douglas sent them packing but they returned annually for many years, and worked and traded until smallpox epidemics in the 1860s and missionaries in the 1870s devastated their culture. Indians frequently outnumbered the fort's Europeans who, at such times, felt they were under siege. But the sight of Royal Navy vessels in the harbour gave the fort's denizens some reassurance—and reminded the Natives of the possibility of reprisal if they misbehaved. After a group of Haidas fired shots at a schooner in the harbour in 1860, the appearance of HMS *Plumper* from Esquimalt and a detachment of marines were required before the Natives could be disarmed. In 1848, at Finlayson's urgent request, Captain George Courtenay of HMS *Constance* sent a squad of Royal Marines and the ship's band to march aggressively in front of the fort after Indians fired shots. Courtenay's men paraded and drilled all day. Finlayson noted, "This display of arms from the *Constance* had a good effect on the natives, as they were evidently afraid to pick any quarrels with us for some time afterward." But one chief cheekily told Finlayson that Indians were not stupid enough to fight the British on open ground.

James Anderson, remembering schooldays at the fort, told how "dogs would swim over from the Indian village opposite the Fort and get after Mr. Finlayson's fowls; so of course we naturally hailed the chance of exercising our cruelty by chasing and stoning the dogs, sometimes being lucky enough to corner one and kill him . . . The dogs were handsome white animals resembling a Pomeranian but larger, with long wooly hair which was regularly shorn and woven into blankets and articles of clothing, so the dogs were of economic value to the natives, and we were doubly blameable." George Henry Richards, captain of the *Plumper*, observed in a report to Rear Admiral Baynes: "It appears to me that in the present relations existing between our people and the Indians, it cannot be a matter of surprise if many wrongs are committed on both sides, and my opinion is that the Natives in most instances are the oppressed and injured parties." But relations among aboriginal groups were no less troubled than between Natives and whites. Finlayson intervened in 1845 to forcefully persuade a group of Songhees Indians to return some HBC trade goods that they had pirated from an American Indian trading party's canoes off Clover Point. He later remarked, "Thus these wild savages were taught to respect British justice."

In 1851 after Natives attacked white settlers, Douglas wrote to Earl Grey: "I would take the liberty of remarking to your Lordship, how very important it is to the peace and security of the settlement that instant

TOP *The Royal Navy's "Flying Squadron" anchored in Esquimalt Harbour, 1870. The presence of the navy was crucial to the protection of the early settlement in Victoria. On more than one occasion, the navy's ships sailed into the Inner Harbour at the HBC's request to show the Songhees and Cowichan Indians who was in charge.* BCARS A–04916

BOTTOM *The* Beaver, *the first steamship on the northwest coast, anchored off Songhees Point, c. 1874 (the building on the point is the colonial hospital). Built on the Thames for the Hudson's Bay Company in 1835, the* Beaver *arrived from England in 1836 after a seven-month voyage via Madeira, Trinidad, the Falkland Islands and Honolulu.* BCARS A–00011

attention should be paid to the complaints of the Indians, and their wrongs receive speedy redress, as nothing will tend more to inspire confidence in the governing power, and teach them that justice may be obtained by less dangerous and more certain method than their own hasty and precipitate acts of private revenge." He considered every person "without distinction residing on our premises as free British subjects, who may, at any time, under the Company's protection, assert the exercise of their absolute and legal rights." Douglas recognized the imperial imperative that clear title be held, if not by conquest then by negotiation, so that both Indians and white settlers knew where they stood and could avoid conflict. He did his best to eliminate Native title by signing fourteen treaties with Indian bands on southern Vancouver Island. In the first land surrender negotiated, he bought the Songhees Esquimalt land title "forever." It cost him 27 pounds and 10 shillings. (The federal government still pays Indians $5 "treaty money" every year, and it is accepted without insult; the token hand-out is proof that the treaties exist.) Douglas, who promised to promote "the honour and advantage of the Crown, as well as the interests of Her Majesty's subjects in this Colony," subsequently entertained Native chiefs at elaborate treaty ceremonies in the name of Queen Victoria, celebrating agreements that effectively banished the Indians to reservations.

In 1860, as gold seekers pressed north after the Fraser River gold rush, Chief Justice Matthew Baillie Begbie wrote: "Indian title is by no means extinguished. Separate provision must be made for it, and soon: though how this is to be done will require some consideration."

A Songhees Indian woman, photographed by Hannah Maynard, wearing Hudson's Bay Company point blankets, the company's ubiquitous trade item. The English-made woollen blankets were dyed with primary coloured stripes and marked with a sewn-in scale of "points" representing fur trade value for pelts and other forms of barter. BCARS F-09011

Douglas's treaties were virtually the only ones signed in BC. Lord
Dufferin, the governor general, criticized Douglas's heirs in 1876, saying:
"British Columbia neglected to recognize what is known as Indian title.
In Canada this has always been done: no government, whether provincial
or central, has failed to acknowledge that the original title to the land
existed in the Indian tribes and communities that hunted and wandered
over them." However, Land Commissioner and Lieutenant Governor
Joseph Trutch took the view that the Indians were "lawless and violent
uncivilised savages" who were undeserving of the privilege of property
ownership and with whom negotiations were not required. Trutch
refused to recognize Native land title and scoffed at the idea of treaties
during his term of public office in Victoria. Ninety years after his death,
the effects of his attitude are still being felt, as unresolved Indian land
claims in BC continue to simmer. Their subtext of cultural differences,
tribal traditions and the rule of law, is as contentious as ever. In 1991
members of an Indian group claiming 22,000 square miles of northern
BC were dismissed by the provincial chief justice as descendants of primitive people. Now these "descendants of primitive people" commission
Vancouver accountants to estimate their economic loss from the non-
Native fishing, mining and lumber industries that have exploited tribal
lands since the nineteenth century.

In Victoria, the Native population seems to have been banished from
its former territories. The Songhees were forced to move across the harbour after white settlers convinced Finlayson that the Indians were living
too close to the fort for safety and comfort—although they continued to
trade with the fort and work in the town. Songhees women sold clams
on the streets. The men raced with Royal Navy oarsmen during regat-
tas on Selkirk Water. During the 1858 gold rush they worked as packers
on horse teams taking supplies to the gold fields. But in Victoria, the
effects of 1858 were less favourable to aboriginals. Indian maids and
washerwomen lost their jobs to Chinese immigrants. Prospectors did not
share the HBC's self-interested paternalism toward them.

The Reverend Matthew Macfie (who was sponsored by the colony to tour the British Isles to encourage prospective emigrants six years later) witnessed scenes "to shock even the bluntest sensibilities" on what is now a swank residential site across the harbour from the old town. Macfie wrote of scenes that could have sprung from the pages of Dante: "fires of Native tents pitched upon the beach casting a lurid glare upon the water; the loud and discordant whoopings of the natives, several of whom were usually infuriated with bad liquor ... crowds of the more debased miners strewed in vicious concert with squaws on the public highway." On the Esquimalt Road, he observed "Indian slaves, squatting in considerable numbers in the bush, for what purpose it is not difficult to imagine ... encouraged by the crews of Her Majesty's ships ... a disgrace to the service they represent and a scandal to the country. Hundreds of dissipated white men, moreover, live in open concubinage with these wretched creatures. So unblushingly is this trade carried on, that I have seen the husband and wife of a native family canvassing from one miner's shanty to another, with a view to making assignations."

As the town paved its frontier streets, citizens repeatedly complained about the "proximity of this wigwam settlement, with its possibilities of depravity and vice being injurious to the appearance, morals, and business of the city, and to the character and best interests of the Indians themselves." The problem was lobbed back and forth between Victoria and Ottawa until 1910 when the remaining forty-three band members accepted compensation of $10,000 each and moved to a new reserve at Esquimalt. Premier Richard McBride, who engineered the removal of the Indians, then promoted industrial development on the site. Today, the only reminder of the once-thriving local Native community is the "Songhees" development—a garish group of faux-chateau apartment blocks—and a totem pole, the world's tallest but not of local design, erected for the Commonwealth Games in 1994. ❧

On the Waterfront

BIG BEND GOLD MINES! BRITISH COLUMBIA . . . THE SAFEST,
THE SHORTEST AND THE CHEAPEST ROUTE TO THESE EXTRA-
ORDINARY MINES IS BY WAY OF VICTORIA, VANCOUVER ISLAND!
—*Victoria Chamber of Commerce poster, 1858*

MARITIME MUSEUM
28 Bastion Square

T HE Maritime Museum was established as a naval museum on
Signal Hill, Esquimalt in 1953 and relocated to the former
Victoria Law Courts at Bastion Square in 1965. The museum
charts Victoria's salty past with an engaging clutter of items, all beached
high and dry in the age of sail and steam. Nothing here seems to date
much after the Second World War. The gleaming ship models in glass
cases and the silent, polished machinery seem so ready for sea, that entering the museum is like stumbling aboard the *Mary Celeste*. One cleaning
lady quit her job after hearing footsteps and laughter in the night; the
building is said to be haunted by a convict imprisoned by Judge Matthew
Baillie Begbie. Many ghosts from the maritime past surface here, but the
most notable is the Hudson's Bay Company paddle steamer *Beaver*. She
was the first steamship on the coast—ordered after a company brig went

Sail training schooners Robertson II *and* Pacific Swift
*evoke the salty world of barquetines and square-riggers in
the Inner Harbour's heyday in the nineteenth century.* RW

down at the mouth of the Columbia River in 1829, with all hands and cargo for London. HBC Governor George Simpson wrote: "the melancholy fate of the *William & Ann* deranges all our plans for business on the coast for this year." Simpson recommended the company purchase a steamship, which would be less vulnerable to coastal tides and currents. "A steam vessel," he wrote, "would afford us incalculable advantages over the Americans, as we could look into every creek and cove while they were confined to harbour by head winds and calms, we could ascend any stream of any consequence on the coast . . . in short, a Steam Vessel would, in our opinion, bring the contest [between the HBC and American fur traders] to a close very soon, by making us masters of the trade."

Her skipper, a Boston man named William Henry McNeill, charted Victoria Harbour and the coast of southern Vancouver Island in 1837. At times McNeill could behave like Captain Bligh. The *Beaver* consumed forty cords of wood a day, an amount that took six men two days to cut. A mutinous crew was flogged in 1838 for refusing to carry it aboard. James Anderson, a schoolboy at the time, saw another side of McNeill's nature: "The bright particular spots in our existence were the occasions of the arrival of the *Mary Dare* from Honolulu, when Captain McNeill with his never-to-be-forgotten thoughtfullness and good nature presented the boys with oranges, sugar cane, firecrackers etc."

Dr. J. S. Helmcken saw the ship at anchor in the Inner Harbour when he arrived in Victoria in 1850. He thought her "so spruce, as well outside as in, with cannon on deck, muskets and cutlasses arranged in their proper places, beautiful cabins and good furniture, with a trading place for Indians, who . . . were only allowed a few at a time on board, when on trade. She had a large crew—active, robust, weatherbeaten, jolly good tempered men—fat from not being overworked—some grey, some grizzled, some young." He also noted the true purpose of the *Beaver*: "She had the appearance of a small man-of-war, had four brass cannon, muskets and cutlasses in racks around the mainmast, and hand grenades in safe places."

When she arrived from England in 1836, the *Beaver* became HBC Chief Factor James Douglas's one-ship navy, and he ruled the fjord-like coast of New Caledonia from its bridge. Simpson, who sailed with Douglas on the ship on his tour in 1841–42, understood gunboat diplomacy and advised Douglas accordingly: "the mysterious steamer, against which neither calms nor contrary winds were any security, possessed, in our estimation, this advantage over stationary forts . . . besides being convenient for the purposes of trade, she was the terror, whether present or absent, of every tribe on the coast." The steam-powered *Beaver* impressed the Indians more than sailing ships. One band built a thirty-foot replica canoe complete with deck and painted portholes, hoping that they could replicate the power of the *Beaver* as well.

The Maritime Museum's exhibits range from the renowned clipper ship *Thermopylae*, the only full-rigged sailing ship registered in Victoria, to Canadian Pacific liners and warships of the Royal Navy; from Captain Cook's eighteenth-century voyages of exploration to the travels of Captain Voss, who set off from Oak Bay in 1901 on a lone voyage around the world. There is Captain Joseph Spratt, who established the Albion Iron Works in 1863 at Chatham and Store streets. Steam engines and ship's boilers were assembled or repaired at the foundry—the biggest north of San Francisco—which also made cast-iron shopfronts, some of which still stand on Wharf Street. Spratt established the Victoria Machinery Depot in 1880, whose shipyards at Ogden Point could compete with the Scottish builders that dominated local shipping and marine engineering. A polished brass engine plate from the CPR coastal steamer *Princess Joan* stamped "The Fairfield Shipbuilding & Engineering Co. Ltd. Govan, Glasgow" is a reminder of this connection. Yarrows shipyard at Esquimalt, established in 1913, is another; the parent company was based on the Clyde.

Ships' stern nameplates and oil paintings of James Cook and George Vancouver haunt the museum's stairway. There is the chilling tale of the *Valencia*, an American steamer en route from California to Victoria in

January 1906. Miles off course in fog and with the leadsman's voice charting her doom—"sixty fathoms . . . thirty five . . ."—the *Valencia* grounded on an undersea pinnacle sixty feet from cliffs west of Port Renfrew. Heavy seas battered the ship as night fell. Lifeboats packed with terrified passengers were lowered, only to be swept against the cliffs by heaving breakers. One survivor wrote: "What a sight! The searchlight showed every detail of the terrible tragedy—the men and women struggling in the water, their faces ghastly in the glare . . . the bodies of children swept toward the terrible rocks, in a wild chaos of boiling surf." Those who remained on board, clinging to the rigging or pinned to the scuppers, perished when the ship broke up and went down two nights after hitting the rocks. Rescue ships that had steamed out from Victoria stood offshore, unable to assist. One hundred seventeen people were lost. Thirty-seven survived, washed ashore or picked up from a lone lifeboat. For years afterward seamen claimed to have seen a ghost ship resembling the *Valencia* drifting by in the mist, her masts and rigging festooned with corpses. All that remains of the vessel is a battered nameplate from a lifeboat that washed up twenty years later and miles away on the Alberni Canal.

The museum's collection tells stories of lighthouses, their builders, and their keepers, like George Davis, British Columbia's first lightkeeper, a Welshman sent out in 1860 to man Fisgard Lighthouse, and there is Colonel William P. Anderson, Chief Engineer and Superintendent of Lighthouses, Department of Marine and Fisheries, in the 1890s. Anderson, an engineer with "a passion for beauty as well as function,"

The City of Kingston *and a souvenir montage of its crew by Hannah Maynard, c. 1891. The Puget Sound and Alaska Steamship Company's ship, which steamed between Tacoma, Seattle and Victoria in the 1890s, was one of several American vessels that competed with the local Canadian Pacific Navigation Company's ships for coastal traffic.* BCARS F–05113

designed Estevan Point lighthouse, a colossal concrete pillar braced with flying buttresses, which was built in 1909 on the northwest coast of Vancouver Island. It was his finest achievement. His "great blunder" was Triangle Island. Forty-two miles off the north tip of Vancouver Island and 680 feet above sea level, Triangle Island light's nine-foot diameter lens shone for fifty miles out to sea—or would have done but for the foggy location. Anderson had ignored the "no more than 150 feet below the cloud base rule." The station, built in 1900, was dismantled in 1918 and the lens is preserved at Ogden Point Coast Guard station. (The light outside the museum was originally installed on Trial Island, Oak Bay in 1906.)

Estevan Point leapt onto the front pages in 1942 when it was bombarded, it was reported at the time, by a Japanese submarine that had surfaced offshore. The gunfire missed the target but caused panic on the coast. Troops were alerted and the naval batteries at Esquimalt trained their guns to the horizon. Lighthousemen were issued with rifles in case of invasion. But the Japanese submarine vanished, leaving only shell fragments now displayed in a glass case in the museum. The incident was the only time enemy shells landed on Canadian soil during the Second World War. There is some evidence that it was staged for propaganda purposes, that the shelling was "friendly fire" intended to drum up support for the war effort. For instance, the attack eased a controversial conscription act through Parliament in Ottawa. An eyewitness report from Robert Lally, a lightkeeper, identified a cruiser, not a submarine, and was censored by the War Measures Act. Lally found a shell fragment with English markings under freshly painted Japanese letters—and the relevant day's page in the lighthouse log went missing. After the raid the

The German-built barque Pamir *in a rolling sea off Cape Flattery. Fog banks, tides and tempests earned the desolate coastline on the west of Vancouver Island the grim moniker "Graveyard of the Pacific."* AUTHOR'S COLLECTION

threat of future attacks, and possible landings by Japanese sabotage units, was taken so seriously that an armoured train was built in Winnipeg. Fortified with a 75-mm field gun, anti-aircraft guns, and 120 soldiers, No. 1 Armoured Train puffed its way up and down the Prince Rupert line until 1944.

The museum's collection of ship models includes the I-26, the Japanese submarine of Estevan Point fame. There are models of Canadian Pacific liners, including the second *Empress of Japan*, built in 1929 as the flagship of the company's Clydebuilt trans-Pacific fleet (the liner's name was changed to the *Empress of Scotland* during the Second World War). Here too are CPR coastal steamers like the *Princess Marguerite* and *Princess Alice* displayed in magnificently carved wood and glass cabinets. Models like these were often made as builders' test tank hulls and later fitted out for display in ship-owners' boardrooms. "The World's Greatest Travel System," as the CPR was known, pioneered the "All Red Route" where no around-the-world traveller, or message sent by Royal Mail, needed to stray from British imperial ports of call—or from the company's ships, trains and hotels (CPR liners also steamed across the Atlantic Ocean, from Montreal to Liverpool and Glasgow). Posters in the museum evoke the Empress liners' era: scenic embarkation at Vancouver; shipboard salons glittering with silverplate and china, mahogany and stained glass; svelte voyageurs lingering on promenade decks and fragrant landfalls at Honolulu; the bustle of rickshaws on the docks at Yokohama.

·⇐ WHARF STREET ⇒·

Wharf Street was a bustling commercial waterfront at the turn of the century. Its wharves and jetties were forested with the masts and spars of sailing ships and foggy with the smoke of steamers. Its boardwalks and cobbled streets were crisscrossed by stevedores, sea captains and shipping agents. Saloons were awash with inebriated sailors—an era when the biggest warehouse on the waterfront, built in 1905 at 1019 Wharf Street, belonged to Pither and Leiser, "importers of wines and liquors." In the 1890s Victoria was an industrial city, not a tourist attraction.

During the 1858 gold rush Fort Victoria was demolished and the land was sold for development. Warehouses, stores and offices sprang up along with hotels and bars in a hectic expansion that, with intermissions of economic slump and political uncertainty, culminated in a second bout of gold fever during the Klondike gold rush of 1897–98. The Hudson's Bay Company warehouse built on the water's edge (its stone retaining walls and mooring rings can still be seen at the foot of Fort Street), and HBC factor W. J. Macdonald's warehouse at 1205–13 Wharf Street, were the old regime's last fling after the company made windfall profits when the fort was sold. A commercial aristocracy, personified by the likes of wholesaler Robert Paterson Rithet, replaced the HBC's pioneering landowners as the city's ruling class. The Rithet Building, completed in 1885 at 1107–21 Wharf Street, stands on what was the west palisade of Fort Victoria. Rithet's empire included the Canadian Pacific Navigation Company, Albion Iron Works, the California and Hawaii Sugar Refining Company, and deep-water port facilities at Ogden Point.

Local industry and Wharf Street's wholesalers supplied mines, logging camps and salmon canneries throughout the province. In 1891 the Board of Trade had over 150 members. A business directory published by the *Colonist* the same year listed a commercial cornucopia: the Victoria Roller Flour and Rice Mills, the British Columbia and Victoria Soap Works, and the Star, Union and Clyde shipyards were among the largest firms—along with six breweries, two soda water makers, coffee and spice mills, a piano factory, carriage, boot and shoe manufacturers, brush works, stair building works, sash and door factories and saw and planing mills. There were shirt and clothing manufacturers, pottery and terracotta works, marble, granite and brick yards, bakeries, lithographing and printing establishments, a harness maker and tannery, tin can, box, and match manufacturers.

The Inner Harbour was a maze of ships—from CPNC coastal steamers to a fifty-schooner sealing fleet which docked in the harbour for annual refits. The most beautiful vessels to sail in were the clipper ships *Titania*, which the HBC ran between Victoria and London, and the *Thermopylae*, the only full-rigged sailing ship registered in Victoria. Launched at Aberdeen in 1868 as a China tea clipper, the *Thermopylae* was famed for record-breaking voyages from Shanghai to London. She was bought by Mount Royal Rice Milling & Manufacturing, Montreal, to land rice at the company's Victoria mill (now Capital Iron) on Store Street . The crew of the *Thermopylae* entertained boys and local barmen with Conradian tales of typhoons in the South China Sea and how, after passage from Bangkok in 1892, the ship limped into the Inner Harbour with her sails in shreds and her crew reduced to eating the cargo for the last ten days of the voyage. She was a ship to squeeze a romantic gesture from the most weatherbeaten seaman. The captain of HMS *Charybdis* at Esquimalt was moved to semaphore, as the *Thermopylae* overhauled him on her maiden voyage from Victoria, "Good bye. You are too much for us. You are the finest model of a ship I ever saw." Her memory is kept alive in an evocative song: "My ship came from China with a cargo of tea, all laden with gifts for you and me," that can still be heard sung by children in Victoria's school playgrounds.

After James Douglas reported to the Colonial Office in 1855 that he could supply enough spars and masts to fit out the entire Royal Navy, thousands of spars for British shipyards were cut from virgin forests on Vancouver Island and the Burrard Inlet. Lumber was also shipped to Australia, San Francisco and China. Captain Edward Stamp, a British mariner who arrived on the coast in 1857, opened a general store in Victoria and a sawmill at Alberni which he managed for British backers. The famous steamship *Great Eastern* was fitted with masts from Stamp's coastal mills. He managed Hastings Mill (present day Vancouver), named after one of his customers, Rear Admiral George F. Hastings, Commander in Chief, Esquimalt. Stamp invested in property, building a three-storey block on Government Street across from the Bank of British Columbia, and opened a salmon cannery at New Westminster to process some of the abundant Pacific salmon that were caught, salted, pickled and canned for export.

Victoria was the main port for exporting salmon. Sailing ships landed European imports and loaded salmon for the return voyage. The Delta Cannery on the Fraser River could pack 25,000 cases (over one million cans) a month, most of which was shipped to London and Liverpool from Victoria by Welch, Rithet & Co. Thousands of Native and Chinese workers were employed filleting and canning fish, until the trade began to be mechanized around 1900 with steam-powered machines. One mechanical processor, displayed in the Royal BC Museum, was advertised as the "Iron Chink" because it replaced a dozen Chinese workers. Civic services in Victoria at this time included water mains, a sewerage system planned by a New York engineer, paved streets, electric street lighting, and the third electric tramway to be opened in Canada. Beacon Hill Park had been laid out in 1888, with carriageways and romantic landscape design to match the best in Europe. In 1891 city hall received its finishing touches when a huge clock arrived from London and was installed in an Italianate bell tower.

There were no grand public clocks to tell the time on a Sunday morning in April 1858, when the ship *Commodore* sailed in from San Francisco. Over four hundred gold seekers tumbled off onto the peaceful sabbath streets of the settlement and besieged Fort Victoria for supplies. Among the arrivals was Alfred Waddington who opened a branch of his San Francisco grocery store Dulip & Waddington. Waddington recorded the impact of the gold rush on the settlement where "no noise, no bustle, no gamblers, no speculators" disturbed the "few quiet gentlemanly behaved inhabitants, chiefly Scotchmen, secluded as it were from the whole world." Victoria "was assailed by an indescribable array of Polish Jews, Italian fishermen, French cooks, jobbers, speculators of every kind, land agents, auctioneers, hangers on . . . bummers, bankrupts, and brokers of every description . . . swindlers, thieves, drunkards, and jail birds let loose by the Governor of California for the benefit of mankind."

Douglas had anticipated the gold rush but even he was taken aback by its sudden, dramatic effect. In 1856 he had informed the Colonial Office in London: "A discovery of much importance made known to me by Mr. Angus Macdonald, clerk in charge of Fort Colville, one of the Hudson's Bay Company's trading posts on the Upper Columbia river district . . . That gold has been found in considerable quantities within British territory on the Upper Columbia, and that he is of the opinion that valuable deposits of gold will be found in many other parts of the country." In 1857 the HBC factor at Fort Kamloops, Donald McLean, bought 800 ounces of gold from Indians on the Thompson River and sent it to Fort Victoria for analysis. Douglas played down rumours of gold on the Fraser and Thompson rivers, but when some was coined by the purser of the HBC steamer *Otter* at the US Mint at San Francisco, word got out. Within weeks the first party of prospectors arrived on the *Commodore* and headed for the Fraser River.

The Victoria Chamber of Commerce quickly printed advertising flyers that were scattered around the docks and saloons of San Francisco: "BIG BEND GOLD MINES! BRITISH COLUMBIA. The Safest, the Shortest, and the Cheapest Route to these Extraordinary Placer Mines is by way of VICTORIA, VANCOUVER ISLAND! Passengers going this way have not to cross the dangerous Columbia River Bar, and the distance is over ONE THIRD SHORTER by way of Victoria, than by way of Portland." A fleet of vessels, from geriatric riverboats to newly launched seagoing steamers, sailed into Victoria. Douglas, anxious to control the invasion, subsidized HBC and California Steam Navigation Company steamers to carry miners from San Francisco to Victoria where passengers could connect with river steamers to Yale, where a government wagon road was to be built by the Royal Engineers.

Douglas, in a dispatch to London that played down the miners' capacity for alcohol and mischief, wrote: "our little town, though crowded to excess with this sudden influx of people, and though there was a temporary scarcity of food, and dearth of accommodation, the police few in numbers, and many temptations to excess in the way of drink . . . order prevailed and there was not a single committal for rioting, drunkenness, or other offences, during their stay here." But Victoria's sober church-goers thought the California miners "the worst of the population of San Francisco—the very dregs, in fact, of society." "When, oh when shall we have a bath?" ran a headline in the *Gazette* in 1858, referring to the conditions in the tentville the miners had set up. Although most of those the *Commodore* disgorged moved on, subsequent arrivals turned the town into "a dust bowl in summer, a mud hole in winter . . . the populace was constantly falling through holes in the rickety wooden sidewalks." Douglas quickly drafted a plan to pay for civic improvements by a levy on the town's innumerable public houses.

The Sisters of St. Ann were astonished to land in the middle of this quagmire. So too were the British Columbia Emigration Society's "bride ship" passengers—"respectable, industrious women [sent] to the colony, not only as domestic servants, but as a step towards supplying wives for the miners and settlers, thus establishing a solid basis of colonial existence." In 1862 the *Colonist* reported the arrival of "the good steamer *Tynemouth*, with 60 select bundles of crinolines [among its 270 passengers from England] . . . a large number of our male citizens visited Esquimalt and endeavoured to board the vessel, but were generally ordered off, and returned from their fruitless effort with heavy hearts." Most ocean-going vessels anchored at Esquimalt and disembarking passengers had to haul their baggage on wagons along the muddy, rutted Esquimalt Road to Fort Victoria. The lucky ladies from the *Tynemouth* were transferred to the Colonial Administration's marine barracks on the gunboat HMS *Forward*. One observer noted: "two by two the girls were marched up the quay to the Parliament Buildings where each was handed a bucket of soapy water . . . To have to tidy themselves under the ogling scrutiny of hundreds of males was a terrifying experience." The

The Wharf Street waterfront with a clipper ship (possibly the Titania *or the* Thermopylae*) berthed near the site of Fort Victoria, c. 1890. The Customs*

House, built in 1873–75 and now the oldest federal building west of Ontario, can be seen above the stern of the sidewheeler Olympian. BCARS A–03848

Colonist thought they "would give a good account of themselves in what ever station in life they may be called to fill—even if they marry lucky batchelor miners from the Cariboo," and the clergy in England who had sponsored them hoped that by providing wives for miners, they could eliminate prostitution among Native girls.

One clergyman, Matthew Macfie, who sailed into Victoria in 1859, was amazed at the mixed population: "Among the many remarkable matrimonial alliances to be met with, I have known Europeans married to pure squaws, Indian half-breeds and Mulatto females respectively. One case has come under my observation of a negro married to a white woman, and another of a man descended from a Hindoo mother married to a wife of Indian extraction." Even James Douglas, "a gentleman of large property, reported to be of Mulatto origin, is married to a half-breed Indian." Macfie sketched a graphic picture of the boom: "individuals of every trade and profession in San Francisco . . . threw up their employments, in many cases sold their property at an immense sacrifice . . . The rich came to speculate, and the poor in the hope of quickly becoming rich . . . The limited supply of provisions in Victoria was speedily exhausted . . . Twice the bakers were short of bread, which had to be replaced with ship biscuit and soda crackers. Innumerable tents covered the ground in and around Victoria far as the eye could reach. The sound of hammer and axe was heard in every direction. Shops, stores, and 'shanties' to the number of 225, arose in six weeks. Speculation in town lots attained a pitch of unparalleled extravagance. The land office was besieged, often before four o'clock in the morning, by the multitude eager to buy town property . . . no one being allowed to purchase more than six lots . . . sales were obliged to be suspended in order to allow the surveyor time to measure the appointed divisions of land beforehand."

Several blacks from San Francisco moved to Victoria after writing to Douglas. Thirty-five arrived on the *Commodore*. Some headed for the gold fields but most settled in the town, where they were joined by a further 250 black immigrants during the American Civil War. Forty-three volunteered for the local militia and were organized in 1860 as the "Africa Rifles." Douglas allowed them to hold an annual ceremony to commemorate the freeing of slaves in the British West Indies. Not all citizens approved. A black visitor in 1864 wrote: "In some places of public accommodation, such as barbershops, barrooms, restaurants and hotels, coloured persons are denied the usual privileges. But such places are invariably run by Americans or foreigners. In many of the finest establishments, where the proprietors are Englishmen, there is no distinction; they are free of the prejudices which the Americans have introduced. There are, however, many Englishmen who are as full of prejudice . . . moreover, receive you with an aristocratic, patronizing air."

In 1861 there was a fracas at a charity theatre performance when Americans objected to blacks seated in the auditorium. There were letters to the *Gazette* objecting to blacks sitting with whites in Reverend Cridge's church—and ripostes that the blacks had come to Victoria "to escape the tyranny and oppression of Republican Democratic churchgoing California"—or, as Helmcken put it, "the land of the free, and the home of the slave." Some farmed or worked in the boatyards. Wellington Moses owned the Pioneer Shaving Saloon and Bath House and ran a superior boarding house that was recommended by visiting upper crust ladies. Philadelphia native Mifflin Gibbs came north with a load of mining supplies and, with fellow black Peter Lester, founded Lester & Gibbs "Dealers in Groceries, Provisions, Boots, Shoes etc." Gibbs—and Chinese merchants—competed with the HBC, which many newcomers thought was "generally owned by old fogies, who are destitute of Yankee enterprise." Gibbs built a house on James Bay, was the most admired citizen in Victoria's black community, and won a seat on city council before returning south, as had most others by 1870. Gibbs then studied law, served as a judge and became US consul in Madagascar.

Of the 450 prospectors on the *Commodore*, only 60 were British. Most of the others were American—"Californians" as they were called. Douglas, unable to communicate quickly with the Colonial Office in

London—it took months for messages to be exchanged—acted on his own initiative to preserve British influence and the HBC's trading monopoly in the mainland interior, where the gold fields were and where few British administrators were stationed. He issued a "Proclamation, By His Excellency James Douglas, Governor and Commander-in-Chief of the Colony of Vancouver's Island and Dependencies, and Vice Admiral of the same . . . at Government House, Victoria, this eighth day of May in the year of our Lord One thousand eight hundred and fifty eight, and in the twenty first year of Her Majesty's reign . . . God Save the Queen." Delivered with more verbiage than real power, it was astonishingly effective.

Douglas declared Victoria a free port, where miners could obtain provisions duty free and 25 to 50 percent cheaper than in California or Oregon. He declared the gold fields the property of the Crown. Mining licences had to be purchased in Victoria. Land had to be staked and registered with a sketch and written application (in duplicate) to one of Douglas's frontier land commissioners, along with a $2 fee and a declaration under oath that it was a true claim and would be occupied within thirty days. Unlicensed miners ran a gauntlet of Royal Marines from the warship HMS *Satellite*, which Douglas sent to patrol the Fraser River estuary and seize unlicensed goods and vessels. From the gunboat Douglas personally defused the "Fraser Canyon War," after skirmishes between local aboriginals and the first miners to find gold nuggets on the river's banks and sandbars.

The *Times* of London quoted Fort Langley's chief factor berating "Yankee" miners for their "coarseness, bad manners, and vulgarity." (The men had stolen supplies from the HBC fort.) "If these people don't know the practice of decency, they must be taught it [or] go back to their own country where they can indulge in their propensities." But the ragtag cross-section of society that came north was generally law-abiding. Arguments were more often about politics than gold, so intensely did American miners resent British colonial authority. But miners developed their own code of conduct—a gold seeker's ten commandments—that allowed them to work their claims in peace. Judge Begbie, on judicial circuits around the gold field camps, found little evidence of the cheating, thievery and murder that might have been expected. Douglas advised an assembled group of miners in Victoria: "Be careful of your revolvers—and be not too ready to use them in your own cause. The law of the land will do its work without fear or favour. Therefore, appeal to it in all cases; let it do justice between man and man; let it defend your rights and avenge your wrongs . . . The miner who acts in submission to the laws, and pays the Queen's dues like an honest man shall be protected in person and property." He promised that as soon as "good and trusty men could be found," the government's "gold escort" would transport gold dust from the mines to the treasury in Victoria where, on production of an official receipt, prospectors could claim their property. Thus did British bureaucracy, naval power—and James Douglas—pacify the frontier.

·⇐ AMOR DE COSMOS ⇒·

Amor de Cosmos founded Victoria's first independent newspaper, the *British Colonist*, on Wharf Street in 1858, with a banner headline sign as broad as the building's facade and as big as its publisher's personality. A self-styled "Lover of the Universe," de Cosmos had been christened William Alexander Smith in Nova Scotia in 1825, but changed his name. "It is an unusual name," he told curious colleagues, "and its meaning tells what I love most: order, beauty, the world, the universe." To his admirers he was "a brilliant editor and clever politician, a hot-tempered batchelor and eccentric." Critics thought he had "all the eccentricities of a comet without any of its brilliance." Dr. Helmcken thought de Cosmos a "a radical and demagogue—a sort of socialist," but also noted his power as a public speaker, whether debating in the legislature or electioneering on stage at the Victoria Theatre.

De Cosmos's mentor was Joseph Howe, the Nova Scotian publisher and political reformer, who campaigned for democratic government as de Cosmos would do in British Columbia. In 1851 at Halifax he boarded a steamer for New York, and travelled overland to the California gold fields. He claimed to have fought off Indian attacks in the Sierra Nevada, and in Sacramento he worked as a photographer recording mining claims. He invested in mines, was a vigilante in mining camps, became a freemason—and was also said to have been converted by Mormons at Salt Lake City. Nothing in this tangle of half-truth explains why he changed his name in the California gold county of El Dorado in 1854, other than speculation that he had stolen sacred Mormon texts.

De Cosmos sailed into Victoria on the *Brother Jonathan*, disembarking like a bearded prophet. His prayer mat was a newspaper, founded after a meeting with investors in a drugstore on Yates Street. His only competition was the *Gazette*, a speculative but conservative paper that had been started by two Americans. He obtained a Parisian flatbed printing press that had been imported by Bishop Demers, and the services of Demers's typographer and printer, Count Paul de Garro, who typeset de Cosmos's editorials and printed the four-page weekly paper from a Wharf Street office. De Garro, a French political refugee, had published the colony's first paper, the short-lived *Le Courrier de la Nouvelle Calédonie*, in 1858. Supported by Bishop Demers, it was intended to bring culture and enlightenment to the sizable French community in Victoria. De Garro also printed the first book published in the colony, Alfred Waddington's account of Victoria and the gold rush in 1858.

More readers were taken by Waddington's breezy prose than De Garro's liberal, intellectual French-language journal. *Le Courrier* folded and the count found himself working as a waiter; then, in a case of one eccentric recognizing another, he was hired by de Cosmos. The only other staffer on the *Colonist* was its sole reporter, David William Higgins, a Nova Scotian who had also arrived in 1858 from California. Fate dealt De Garro an unlucky hand: he was killed in a shipboard explosion in

Victoria Harbour in 1861. Higgins could only tolerate de Cosmos for so long; he set up a rival paper, the *Victoria Daily Chronicle*, in 1862. He was then elected to city council and to the provincial legislature, where as Speaker of the Legislative Assembly and Deputy Premier he criticized his former editor. After de Garro's demise de Cosmos hired a one-legged printer, Pegleg Larkin, who churned out his comments under the byline "Monitor."

In an editorial in the first issue of the paper, de Cosmos declared: "We intend, with the help of a generous public, to make the *British Colonist* an independent paper, the organ of no clique or party—a true index of public opinion." De Cosmos, who had seen the free (and profitable) press at work in the rough-and-tumble of the United States, was not content to play the role of uncritical publisher and small town booster. His manifesto was an unprecedented attack on Governor Douglas and the ruling Hudson's Bay Company establishment. He judged "the present constitution . . . radically defective, and unsuited to the advanced condition of the colony. We shall counsel the introduction of responsible government—we shall advocate a constitution modelled after the British, and similar to that of Canada." He criticized Douglas's autocratic rule and nepotism in appointing his brother-in-law, David Cameron, who had no legal experience, as the colony's judge. De Cosmos described the colony as "filled with toadyism, consanguinity, and incompetency, compounded with white-washed Englishmen, and renegade Yankees." He wrote that the Douglas administration "was never marked by those broad and comprehensive views of government which were necessary to the times and to the formation of a great colony. It appeared and belonged to a past age."

By 1859 Douglas had been so provoked that he attempted to drive the *Colonist* out of business by invoking an arcane English law that required newspaper publishers to post a bond of £800. But public opinion was on de Cosmos's side and supporters, who shared his concern about the colony's future, raised the bond. Most of all, many colonists thought that a deflation of Douglas's ego was overdue. By 1860 the *Colonist* had become a daily. By 1864 circulation was up from 200 to 4,000 copies, figures that did not amuse Helmcken, who thought the *Colonist* "pleased the dissatisfied and made them more so." In 1860 the government's sergeant at arms appeared at de Cosmos's Wharf Street office and arrested the editor for libelling the assembly's Speaker, Dr. Helmcken. De Cosmos was led to the Birdcages to appear before the elected burghers and backwoodsmen whom he described in the next edition, after they let him off with an apology, as "vain, puffed up, tyrannical, corrupt, short-witted, conceited mummies and numbskulls." Outbursts like this suggest that there may have been some truth in de Cosmos's later, somewhat disingenuous, claim that he "started the *Colonist* for amusement during the winter months," and that his kindred spirits in Victoria were not local worthies but touring theatrical groups whose performances he enjoined his readers to attend. Helmcken remarked that newspapers could not print de Cosmos's speeches in full "because they did not have a sufficient number of capital I s!"

Within a few years he had tired of the paper, and he made three attempts at being elected to the Legislative Assembly. In two elections in 1860—which he thought were rigged to exclude him—he was accused of changing his name to escape criminal charges in California. At a rally at the Victoria Theatre, Helmcken wrote, "De Cosmos appeared on this stage—performed all sorts of semi-theatrical attitudes—boasted of travelling through California with a revolver in each boot . . . was vainglorious and egotistic to the utmost degree. The theatre was crowded—De Cosmos was drunk! This settled the matter, he lost the election." He was elected on a third attempt in 1863.

Those who may have thought that his strident vocabulary and combative nature had been exorcised in his *Colonist* columns were proved

During the 1858 gold rush Victoria was a boisterous frontier town with dozens of hastily erected buildings whose ornate cornices hinted at grandeur to come. RW

wrong. Speaking in the Legislature in 1870, the maverick de Cosmos said, "I would not object to a little revolution now and again in British Columbia, after Confederation, if we were treated unfairly; for I am one of those who believe that political hatreds attest the vitality of a State." He crossed swords with Lieutenant Governor Joseph Trutch, who reluctantly swore him in as British Columbia's second premier after John McCreight, a Trutch-appointed toady, lost a no-confidence vote in 1872. Later that year de Cosmos refused to address a cabinet meeting until Trutch left the chamber, setting a precedent that is still upheld. Colonial lieutenant governors were not known for impartiality, having been directed by the British government to act not just as the queen's ambassadors, but also as agents of Whitehall policy. De Cosmos's stance reduced the gubernatorial post to the quaint sinecure it is today.

De Cosmos claimed he was "the first British Columbian to advocate the introduction of responsible government into the colony; the first person to recommend a union of the colonies of Vancouver Island and British Columbia—and the first to advocate the confederation of British Columbia with the Dominion." He got a taste of his own medicine in 1874 when an angry crowd, associating de Cosmos (who had also been elected as an MP to the House of Commons in Ottawa in 1871) with a rumour that Prime Minister Sir John A. Macdonald was reneging on his confederation pledge to build a railway to Victoria, stood outside the legislature chanting "We'll hang de Cosmos on a sour apple tree." However, he was re-elected MP that year but had to resign his provincial seat due to a change in the law. In Ottawa, his radical nonconformity and

Amor de Cosmos, founding publisher of the British Colonist— *"brilliant editor and clever politician, a hot-tempered batchelor and eccentric"—crossed swords with almost every notable citizen at one time or another. He launched his paper in 1858 with a blistering attack on Governor Douglas and the ruling Hudson's Bay Company establishment.* BCARS C–06116

coolness to cliques—the HBC's "Fort Clique" had been one of a swarm of bees in his bonnet during his early years—kept him out of political inner circles on Parliament Hill. He argued for an elected rather than London-appointed governor general, and advocated Dominion representation at an Imperial parliament. He lost his seat by 225 votes in 1882 after delivering a visionary but apparently disloyal speech in the House of Commons. De Cosmos's swan song was that he saw "no reason why the people of Canada should not look forward to Canada becoming a sovereign and independent state . . . I was born a British colonist . . . I do not wish to die without all the rights, privileges and immunities of the citizen of a nation."

When he returned to Victoria he was snubbed when the governor general visited the city. He shunned public life and was often seen taking solitary walks around town, an enigmatic apparition attired, in the words of George Woodcock, in "beaver hat, impeccable frock coat, and well-polished patent-leather boots, with a cane or umbrella hooked on his forearm ready for self-defence [his barbs had brought him to fisticuffs with Roderick Finlayson, Robert Rithet, Robert Dunsmuir] . . . He became less genial and garrulous, more morose and more liable to lose control under the influence of the wine and whisky that he drank rather freely." His mental state deteriorated and he died in obscurity in 1897 and was buried with little ceremony at Ross Bay. His old foe Helmcken, feeling the chill of his own mortality, wrote to the *Colonist* to criticize the "mockery of honour paid to Amor de Cosmos, whom forty years ago, and thirty after, a large section of the people of Victoria considered a hero, a patriot, who fought for the emancipation, improvement, progress and welfare of the country, less for his own material interests than for fame, honour and glory—even those, and they were not few, who disapproved of his course and opinion, for the most part admired this much. That such a man should have come to this—alas, poor Yorick! such a funeral is neither worth living, nor dying for . . . This is not the first time that a public man, a pioneer . . . has been thus heartlessly treated!

Governments, corporations and the public seem to have no hearts, no sentiment, no memory—callous to all but their own interests or affairs." Helmcken forgot to mention that de Cosmos's political interests had prevented him from living up to his assumed name. The lover of the universe had opposed Chinese immigration and Native land claims.

·⇐ DOMINION CUSTOMS HOUSE ⇒·
1002 Wharf Street

The Customs House in Victoria is now the oldest federal building west of Ontario. It was built in 1873–75 to plans drawn in Ottawa by the Department of Public Works' supervising architect, Thomas Seaton Scott, in a provincial version of the mansard-roofed Second Empire style of mid-nineteenth-century France. The Second Empire style was one of several—Renaissance, Gothic, Greek Revival and others—that were favoured by architects in the Victorian period, and it was adopted by Public Works to create an identity for post offices and customs buildings across the country. In Victoria, the appearance of this obviously federal-style architecture seemed a sign of Ottawa's commitment to confederation promises. (A more elaborately decorated Second Empire style federal Post Office and Customs House, built in the 1880s, once dominated the corner of Government and Wharf streets.)

In 1897, customs officers—whose most demanding routine was to ensure a "head tax" was paid by every Chinese immigrant or sponsor—were besieged by crowds of impatient prospectors battering on the doors demanding licences for entry to the Klondike gold fields. Banner headlines in newspapers across the continent, and in Europe and Australia, reported the discovery of gold after the Alaska steamers *Portland* and *Excelsior* docked at Seattle and San Francisco with returning prospectors aboard. The Seattle Chamber of Commerce claimed there was a ton of gold on board the *Portland*. Within weeks of the news of the "treasure ships" and their fabulous cargo, 1,500 would-be prospectors sailed north.

San Francisco and Seattle promptly announced themselves as gateways to the gold fields, but the most tumultuous effects were felt in Victoria, as thousands of prospectors landed in the city from around the world.

Access to the Klondike was through Alaskan ports, but the gold fields were in Canada's Yukon Territory. Miners' licences had to be bought in Victoria. Equipment and food bought in the city were duty free. The British Columbia Board of Trade, recalling the boom year of 1858, promoted the city as "the quickest, safest, cheapest—and duty saving route" to the Klondike. Shop owners closed down their stores, barbers threw away their brushes, policemen and Royal Navy ratings deserted, ferry crews sailed north and jumped ship. Overloaded steamers sailed from Seattle, Portland and San Francisco. The other local manufacturers and shopkeepers—those who didn't flit to the gold fields—stayed and prospered. The Albion Iron Works quickly produced three models of portable stove. Signwriters were suddenly in demand to paint "Klondike Supplies" on stores that supplied everything a miner would need— bacon, beans, canvas tents, tin pans, stoves, snowshoes, salt, oilskin coats and mosquito nets.

In the winter of 1897–98, 22,000 prospectors climbed the Chilkoot Pass through the Coast Mountains between Alaska and British Columbia. Each of them carried over 1,000 pounds of equipment, much of it bought in Victoria. Over 30,000 gold-seekers eventually reached Dawson City but only half actually prospected for gold, and only one in four found any. A hundred or so panned enough to retire on. Many played out the Klondike lottery in the bars and dance halls of Dawson City, which temporarily overtook Victoria as the largest Canadian city west of Winnipeg. Even the architect Francis Rattenbury ventured north, with a scheme to run steamers to the gold fields.

Klondike characters Alexander "Big Alex" McDonald, the "King of the Klondike," who made a fortune buying and leasing claims, "Silent" Sam Bonnifield, saloon owner and gambler, Charles "Arizona Charlie" Meadows, scout, sharpshooter, and showman, Father William Judge,

Catholic missionary and the "Saint of Dawson City," and William Ogilvie, the incorruptible land surveyor who recorded miners' claims yet never made a penny himself, were the talk of Victoria's saloons and bars. The drama and danger of the Klondike washed up every time a ship failed to return from Alaska. In 1901 the Canadian Pacific Navigation Company's *Islander*, steaming down the Lynn Canal at full speed at night, struck an iceberg and sank, killing forty-two people. Her skipper, Captain Hamilton Foote of Victoria, mortified that he had been socializing in the opulent saloon when the steamer rammed the iceberg, refused to be saved and drowned after the *Islander* went down bow first, propellors still turning. Among the passengers were many miners returning from the Klondike with their haul. Rumours of sunken treasure circulated in Victoria's waterfront bars for years, and indeed some gold was found when the *Islander* was raised in 1934.

Any miner so ill informed as to arrive at the Yukon frontier without a licence was denied entry by constables of the North-West Mounted Police, led by an appropriately named superintendent, Samuel B. Steele. He set up Maxim machine guns on border posts on the White Pass and Chilkoot summits to defend Canadian territory and enforce customs duties. Standing beneath a Union Jack by their border post—a tent in the snowdrifts—the Mounties enforced a law that required every prospector to pack a year's supplies into the gold fields. In the manner of James Douglas during the gold rush of 1858, the handful of Mounties, impressively dressed in scarlet tunics under buffalo coats, maintained law and order by courage and steadfast imperial self-confidence. In Dawson City, there was none of the lawlessness of the Alaska town of Skagway, which the miners had to pass through after sailing from ships berthed at Victoria's Wharf Street docks. An English traveller wrote that of all the "tough corners of the globe . . . the most outrageous quarter I ever struck was Skagway . . . It seemed as if the scum of the earth had hastened here to fleece and rob, or . . . to murder." John Muir, the Scottish naturalist, described it as "a nest of ants taken into a strange country and stirred up with a stick." But the most enduring images of the gold rush were penned by a former Victoria bank teller, Robert Service, who romanticized Dawson City's dancing girls, gamblers, sharpshooters, and showmen in his bestselling books of verse, *The Spell of the Yukon* and *The Trail of Ninety-Eight.*

TOP *The boardwalk outside the* Colonist's *Wharf Street office; the forest looms on the edge of the town, c. 1858.* BCARS A–04656 BOTTOM *In 1897, Williams & Co., Clothiers & Hatters, at 647 Johnson Street, was one of many stores that became "Klondike Outfitters" overnight. Crinolines and top hats were replaced with canvas tents and tin pans, salt, snowshoes and portable stoves for prospectors on their way to the gold fields.* BCARS A–00515

·⇐ POINT ELLICE HOUSE ⇒·
2616 Pleasant Street

One of the pleasures of Point Ellice House, built in 1861 on Pleasant Street, is a Victorian garden edged with white picket fencing and shaded by the evergreen boughs of a giant Sequoia tree planted by owner Peter O'Reilly in 1877. The tree is Californian, but the croquet lawn, rose garden and "woodland walk" are typical of English landscape design of the time. Victoria's largest grove of arbutus trees in the garden is one of the few examples of indigenous species among the northern European holly, ivy, laurel and rowan. Like many of Victoria's settlers from the British Isles, the O'Reillys planted the flowers and trees of home. Restoration of the house and garden was helped by a painting by the oft-courted but never-married belle, Charlotte Kathleen O'Reilly, one of the O'Reillys' four children, who maintained the property and kept detailed diaries until she died in 1945.

Point Ellice house gained a reputation for being haunted when a visiting couple were given a tour of the home by a mystery guide. Later, in

POINT ELLICE
HOUSE
VICTORIAN HOUSE & GARDEN
← PARKING ▭

one of the bedrooms, they identified Charlotte Kathleen O'Reilly's dress on display as that which their guide had worn. But if ghosts from the home's early days stepped out the doors and ventured beyond the garden today, they would be in for a shock. Outside the garden, Pleasant Street passes through a semi-industrial zone and terminates at the gates of a scrapyard—a relic, it seems, of the industrial Victoria of sawmills, factories and shipyards built in the area in the 1890s. The house and garden preserve an earlier era when Pleasant Street was lined with salubrious homes set in leafy gardens that sloped down to the shore of Selkirk Water and the Gorge—a long narrow inlet of the Inner Harbour that was a Victorian scenic attraction complete with tidal "reversible falls." The O'Reillys' neighbours included a judge and one-time mayor, a militia lieutenant colonel, a provincial premier and a sea captain.

Peter O'Reilly was born in England, educated in Ireland, served with the Irish Constabulary, and emigrated to Victoria in 1858 armed with a letter of introduction to Governor James Douglas. Letters of introduction were essential calling cards for travellers hoping to join the close-knit upper crust on the extremities of the empire, and O'Reilly's letter resulted in an appointment as the first Colonial Gold Commissioner and

TOP *Point Ellice House was built in 1861 and bought in 1867 by Peter O'Reilly, the first Colonial Gold Commissioner and Magistrate. The O'Reillys' hospitality was well known, especially by officers from the naval station at Esquimalt, who welcomed invitations to the house not so much to glimpse the beautiful garden but to court the equally attractive Charlotte Kathleen, one of O'Reilly's daughters—the centre of attention in this photograph c. 1885. Mr. and Mrs. Peter O'Reilly are seated behind.* BCARS C-03924

BOTTOM *Point Ellice House and garden are a perfect evocation of upper middle-class life in early Victoria. The entrance sign looks like a hand-printed invitation to a garden party.* RW

Magistrate. He settled in Victoria after spells of duty in the Cariboo, became a director of several commercial firms, including Albion Iron Works (one of the company's stoves sits in the kitchen), and was elected to the Legislative Assembly in 1864. He numbered Governor Douglas, Chief Justice Begbie and Bishop Hills among his friends. Douglas thought him "a gentleman of excellent character, high moral worth, an able, active resolute Magistrate."

O'Reilly's wife-to-be, Caroline Trutch, was familiar with British colonial society when she arrived in Victoria in 1861 with her widowed mother, having just travelled in India where her sister's husband was a colonial officer in Madras. Her father too had served the empire, in the West Indies. Her brother, Joseph Trutch, had already settled in Victoria and was Chief Commissioner of Lands and Works, and became the province's first lieutenant governor. Caroline Trutch blended effortlessly into the colonial milieu. Point Ellice, with its conservatory, woodland walk, croquet and tennis lawns and gregarious hosts, became a port of call for the visiting upper class. Point Ellice's most distinguished guests were Sir John A. Macdonald and Lady Macdonald, who called on the O'Reillys when they visited Victoria in 1886. (Letters from the prime minister to Lieutenant Governor Trutch were found hidden in a drawer in the house in 1986.) Point Ellice garden parties attracted the local business and political élites out to play. Royal Navy officers were frequent callers, among them Robert Falcon Scott, who served aboard HMS *Amphion*, and later became "Scott of the Antarctic," and who was said to have lingered in Charlotte Kathleen's charms.

Point Ellice, like most early homes in Victoria, was copied from illustrations published in architectural pattern books. In the mid-nineteenth century, progress overtook the aristocratic practice of architecture. From the 1840s to the 1880s, pattern books helped frontier architects and builders, especially in pioneering towns, keep up with the latest trends. Cast-iron foundries and lumber companies sent out catalogues showing cast or milled accessories—and even complete buildings—that brought mass-produced ornament and instant architecture to the frontier. Architectural and popular scientific magazines printed plans showing the latest commercial and residential styles. Builders and architects adapted these, and Point Ellice (built as a cottage for John Wark's daughter) was designed by John Wright in this way. John Teague designed additions to the home in the Italianate manner after O'Reilly bought the property in 1867. The O'Reillys' rising social status can be read on the gravel carriageway that curves to the front entrance and in the sequence of increasingly elaborate rooms from the lowly kitchen, where a system of bells was installed to summon the servants, to the antimacassared sitting room. The interior, restored to the 1890–1914 period, contains many items that were owned and used by the family. Unusually for a city where there is much enthusiastic fabrication, almost all of the furnishings at Point Ellice are original.

The O'Reilly family maintained the home for one hundred years, a continuous tenure that helped it resist the saccharine interpretations of the "heritage industry." When it became a provincial heritage site, the house was virtually untouched by modernization; in the garden and inside the house, Pleasant Street still lives up to its name. Original blue and gold floral wallpaper can be seen in the main bedroom; early marble block wallpaper is visible in the hallway. A Georgian fireplace and a piano imported from London dominate the drawing room. O'Reilly's pull-out writing desk is open in the library; his bookcases are stocked with the Imperial Dictionary, Public Works Reports, *Baedeker's Northern Italy*, the Bible, and Sir Walter Scott. Bearskins on the Persian carpets evoke Victoria's European sophistication overlaid with the romance of the frontier in a manner that speaks for all the homes of Victoria's nineteenth-century gentry. ✍

INCORPORATED BY ROYAL CHARTER

1862

BANK

OF

BRITISH

COLUMBIA

The Old Town

THE QUEEN IS DELIGHTED TO RECEIVE THE WELCOME GIFT OF
YOUR PRODUCTS, AND SHE HAS ASKED ME TO THANK YOU, AND
ALL YOUR STAFF, FOR YOUR GENEROSITY—*Vice-Admiral Sir
Peter Ashmore KCB, KCVO, DSC, Master of the Royal
Household, HM Yacht* Britannia, *to Rogers' Chocolates, 1983*

GOVERNMENT STREET

WITH fossilized facades glowing with nineteenth-century
Italianate and chateauesque stonework and contemporary
replicas mimicking their splendour, Government Street
reveals much of Victoria's history and personality. In the 1890s it was the
city's premier business address, with enough banks, offices and empori-
ums to keep an army of clerks in the new federal Post Office, an ostentatious French Second Empire edifice that overlooked the harbour at
Government and Wharf streets, sweating as they sorted the city's mail.
The eight blocks north of the Inner Harbour as far as Chinatown was the
city's commercial core. But by 1907, when Francis Rattenbury designed
a local head office for the Merchants Bank of Canada on Douglas Street,

*In 1862, the Bank of British Columbia arrived in Victoria and
pinned a three-foot-high brass plate at its entrance. The bank's
$5 notes, the first issued in the colony, bore equally elaborate en-
gravings of Queen Victoria, a sailing ship, a gold rush miner,
and Britannia.* AUTHOR'S COLLECTION

Government Street's decline was written on the Merchants Bank's Beaux Arts walls. After a disastrous fire in 1910 that consumed the block (where the Eaton Centre now stands) on the east side of the street, many businesses moved east to Douglas Street two blocks away. Government Street's eminence began to erode. The Belmont Building, built as a grand hotel a stone's throw from the Empress, at Government and Humboldt streets, was never opened. An economic slump in 1912 and the First World War postponed completion and the building was later fitted out as an office block. It was the last significant commercial development on the street until the Eaton Centre was built in the late 1980s.

Today there is not a single bank on Government Street (although the historic facades remain). But the sidewalks still bustle with businesses, many of them dependent on summer visitors. Among the souvenir shops with their totem poles and teapots are shops that retain an authentic turn-of-the-century British character. Murchie's coffee shop and tearoom is run by the descendants of John Murchie, a Scottish tea and coffee blender and erstwhile supplier to Balmoral Castle, who established an import and blending business in New Westminster in 1894. The Spode Shop, opened in 1924, is the oldest china shop in the city; its stock is in the style of 1824. Irish Linen Stores has sold linen and lace since 1910 and clothiers W & J Wilson have traded in the city since 1862. George Straith British Importers seemed cut from the cloth of a London gentleman's outfitter when it opened on the ground floor of the Weiler Building in 1917.

Mr. and Mrs. Charles W. Rogers, the founders and makers of Rogers' Chocolates, pose for a formal photograph. Their store, with a marble-tiled entrance vaulted with Art Nouveau stained glass, is a perfect period piece. The interior—opened as a jewellery store in 1903—is delicately decorated with wood and glass display cases and fin-de-siècle Art Nouveau lights that were retained when the couple moved in from across the street in 1916.
BCARS A–09230

·⇐ WEILER BUILDING ⇒·

921 Government Street

The lofty wood-panelled entrance at the Weiler Building, Victoria's first department store, is a remnant of the carriage trade era when John Weiler furnished the city's turn-of-the-century Rockland and Oak Bay homes. John Weiler established an upholstery and furniture company on Government Street in 1862 and built a factory on Humboldt Street in 1884. Four sons, George, Charles, Otto and Joseph, took over the business in 1891. The company manufactured wood panelling, mantles, office and saloon fixtures, and imported furniture, crockery, glass, lamps, ornaments, silverware, linoleum, and carpets from Britain. Weiler's was the store for the well-to-do. Art Nouveau fittings from Tiffany's, New York and Liberty's of London, and fabrics from Morris & Co. were displayed inside a building whose facades were as highly patterned as the Persian carpets Weiler also sold. As well as residential work, the firm fitted out interiors in the Bank of Montreal, the Temple Building and other 1890s commercial blocks. Weiler published a 350-page catalogue for serious shoppers and architects of the day, who could also pop down to the company's workshop, located on James Bay (where the Union Club now stands), to see their furniture being made.

The building, designed by architect Thomas Charles Sorby, was one of the largest timber-framed structures in the province when completed in

The Weiler Building, designed by architect Thomas Sorby, was one of the largest timber-framed structures in the province when it was completed in 1898. It housed Victoria's first and most fashionable department store. The building's highly mannered facade was an advertisement for the Weiler brothers' cabinet-making business—"If we can afford to build such a store, imagine what we can do for your home," their stylish architecture seems to say. RW

1898. Two-foot-thick Douglas fir posts and beams hold up the five-storey emporium, whose floors were served by one of the city's first electric elevators. Generous arched windows allowed daylight to the innermost core to illuminate Weiler's merchandise. Glass blocks on the sidewalk once let the sun filter into the basement vaults. The facades were clad with brick, elaborately arched and corniced in Florentine Romanesque style. Sorby also designed homes for Weiler's customers. "The Laurels," a turretted Queen Anne style residence for merchant Robert Ward, built in 1889 at 1249 Rockland Avenue, gained a glowing writeup in the *Colonist*, which praised its moorish windows and Renaissance fireplace mantles, ballroom, and classical columns. But Sorby failed to secure a more important commission in 1892 when Samuel Maclure was retained by Ward to design his new business block, the Temple Building.

Sorby's other rival was the dreaded Francis Rattenbury. Like Ratz, Sorby was a Yorkshireman, who emigrated to Montreal in 1883 after working as a government architect in the old country. He too had a nose for opportunity and moved to Vancouver when the Canadian Pacific Railway was being completed in 1885. He soon established a thriving practice with the CPR as his main client. He designed the first Hotel Vancouver, was the local assistant architect during construction of the CPR terminus, and built a mansion for the railway's superintendent. He also designed Vancouver's Provincial Court House and Bank of British Columbia. Sorby settled in Victoria in 1888, and in 1892 was one of five finalists in the competition for the Parliament Buildings. But his mock-medieval Flemish proposal lost out to his younger fellow countryman's design. Rattenbury's star rose with the Parliament Buildings and the CPR's Empress Hotel. Not only did he pick up one of Sorby's big clients, he also pinched some of his ideas. It was Sorby who dreamed up an ambitious scheme to fill in James Bay and develop Victoria's Inner Harbour with public architecture and waterfront parks—a civic improvement scheme that Rattenbury drew in 1903 as his own. Ironically Ratz had an office in the Five Sisters Block that Sorby had designed in 1891.

·⟸ ROGERS' CHOCOLATES ⟹·
913 Government Street

Rogers' Chocolates is one of only two stores—E. A. Morris Tobacconist is the other—to retain its original Edwardian cast-iron and glass, marbled and mosaic-tiled shopfront and wood-panelled interior. Originally opened as a jewellery store, Rogers' Chocolates is delicately decorated with glass display cases and Art Nouveau light fittings that have been immaculately maintained since Mr. and Mrs. Charles W. Rogers moved in from across the street in 1916. Here, among the old-fashioned display cases as nowhere else in the city, are the ghosts of Victoria's fin-de-siècle carriage trade's hatted ladies and frock-coated gents. Rogers' Chocolates dates from a time when Government Street was packed with small stores, restaurants and emporia. When the building was completed in 1903 by architect Thomas Hooper, the tenants on the block included a fish shop and fruiterer, an electrical supply store and a jeweller.

Rogers' Chocolates' founder, Charles W. Rogers, was born in Boston. He began trading in Victoria as a greengrocer and importer of candies from San Francisco. In 1885 he perfected his own recipe, still secret, for the now famous Victoria creams. Customers once queued around the block for Rogers's savouries during the hour or so a day when he deigned to open his shop. But his opening hours were the least of his eccentricities: the couple lived upstairs and "Candy" Rogers was frequently seen at work in his kitchen dressed in long johns. Reputedly he visited his bank attired the same way.

This reputation did not deter Vice-Admiral Sir Peter Ashmore KCB, KCVO, DSC, Master of the Royal Household, HM Yacht *Britannia*, who wrote to the store after a royal visit in 1983: "The Queen is delighted to receive the welcome gift of your products, and she has asked me to thank you, and all your staff, for your generosity. I am also to say that, even more than the prospect of tasting your delicious-looking sweets, Her Majesty derives especial pleasure from the good wishes, thoughtfulness and loyalty which prompted your kind present." This graciously pompous communication, which is proudly displayed in a picture frame in the store, could have dated from 1883—a time when the clock in the corner of Rogers' Chocolates shop seems to have stopped.

·⇐ E. A. MORRIS TOBACCONIST ⇒·
1116 Government Street

Morris the Tobacconist, as the shop was known from its Edwardian streetcar advertising in Victoria and Vancouver, has changed little from the 1890s when top-hatted gents and epauletted Royal Navy officers would sail into the shop to buy "Quality Pipes & Requisites" and "House Blend Tobaccos and Havana cigars." One fancies the Dunsmuirs, *British Colonist* editors, magistrates and politicians strolling into Edward Arthur Morris's celebrated shop to buy their baroque-labelled boxes of Romeo y Julieta, Saint Luis Rey, and Montecristo Cuban cigars, and pipes that were (and still are) hand-made in Montreal.

Morris came to British Columbia from London in 1877. He worked as a supplier of dynamite and black powder to mines and railways before settling in Victoria, where he commissioned Thomas Hooper to design his store in 1892. For Hooper, an established architect, the shop design was a small job but one that clearly gave him much pleasure. Morris was prepared to fit out the interior with the finest materials available. Most of

TOP *Government Street, c. 1900. The Bank of BC, the arched facade of the Pemberton Holmes Building, and the mansard roof of the old Post Office and Customs House are on the right; the Weiler Building is in the left middle distance.* BCARS A–03004 BOTTOM *The shop built for "Morris the Pipe Man, Morris the Tobacco Man," purveyor of "Quality Pipes & Requisites" and "House Blend Tobaccos and Havana cigars," is as richly decorated as the labels on the boxes of cigars it sells.* RW

MUNRO'S BOOKS OF VICTORIA

The Dominion Post Office Building and Custom House,
Victoria, B.C.

the building's original features survive—beautifully cut period lettering on the facade, leaded glass on the shopfront and an entrance arch carved from Italian alabaster. Inside a Venetian blackamoor *torchère* in wood and gilded gesso guards the Aladdin's grotto of mirrors and mahogany panelling, glass cabinets and display cases, complete with original cast-iron safe from San Francisco, and a vintage electrolier—an alabaster classical pillar with an ever-ready gas flame for cigar smokers' convenience. One feels that everything an Edwardian gentleman would need, short of Saville Row tailoring, could be obtained here in the days when the local men would meet at Morris's for the latest news and gossip.

·⇐ PEMBERTON HOLMES BUILDING ⇒·

1000 Government Street

The Pemberton Holmes Building was named after Joseph Despard Pemberton, son of a Lord Mayor of Dublin, a surveyor and railway engineer said to have received a bronze medal in the Crystal Palace design competition in 1851. That same year he applied to the Hudson's Bay Company in London and was accepted for the post of Colonial Surveyor

TOP *Munro's bookshop, formerly the Royal Bank of Canada's Neo-classical style main branch, is one of Victoria's best examples of preservation and creative reuse of a heritage building.* RW BOTTOM *When Victoria's first Customs House was built in 1875, its mansard roof and dormer windows brought a provincial French flavour to Wharf Street. The new Dominion Post Office and Customs House, designed in the Ottawa version of French Second Empire style in the 1890s, brought Parisian metropolitan grandeur. Proudly featured on postcards, the building dominated the Inner Harbour at the northwest corner of Wharf and Government streets until its demolition in the late 1950s.* AUTHOR'S COLLECTION

and Engineer. Pemberton drew accurate artistic pen-and-ink maps of the Victoria area for the HBC, and for the colonial goverment to which he was elected as a member of the Legislative Assembly. His "zeal and talent" were rewarded when James Douglas renewed his three-year contract and gave him a salary increase and expenses for a trip to England. With a band of Métis helpers he surveyed the local coastline, the Fur Trade Reserve around Fort Victoria, and outlying areas from Esquimalt and the Cowichan to Nanaimo and Barkley Sound. He laid out the Victoria townsite in 1852, and he surveyed and supervised the construction of its roads, bridges and early public buildings, including Fisgard Lighthouse, Victoria Law Courts and the Colonial Administration Buildings.

In 1860 Pemberton published an influential book in London, *Facts and Figures Relating to Vancouver Island and British Columbia*, in which he wrote that Victoria could rival San Francisco as a Pacific port, and that Britain should establish an imperial line of commerce and communication across Canada to Victoria and across the Pacific to Australia. His work was actually an early proposal for the "All Red Route." By the 1880s, like most early HBC or colonial government officials and politicians (in early Victoria the one job frequently led to the other), Pemberton had joined the business brigade. With his son, Frederick Bernard, he established a real estate business in 1887 that still has an office in the Pemberton Holmes Building, built on the site of the fort where Pemberton began his colonial career. "Polished, gallant and courteous— a fine type of the Irish gentleman of the old school," he also acquired an extensive private estate called Gonzales that ran from the corner of Rockland Avenue and St. Charles Street to the sea. It could be seen from his twenty-room mansion, completed in 1885, where he lived with his aristocratic German wife until he died in 1893.

The Pemberton Holmes Building was one of the most up to date in the city when it was built in 1899. Architects in late-nineteenth-century North America looked to Europe for historical inspiration, and to Chicago—where ten-storey, or taller, stone or brick-clad palazzo-style office blocks used steel frame construction—for innovations. Even on three-storey blocks, a contemporary Chicago-style facade brought the appearance of metropolitan sophistication to smaller towns. The ten-storey Auditorium Building in Chicago, designed by the leading American architect Louis Henry Sullivan, had just been completed, and Thomas Hooper persuaded his client C. H. Vernon to adopt the style. Decorative features on the building's column capitals also allowed Vernon, proprietor of the British Columbia Pottery and Terracotta Company, to display product samples on the facades to advertise his company's decorative wares.

·⇐ TEMPLE BUILDING ⇒·
535 Fort Street

The Temple Building, one of Victoria's architectural gems, was designed in 1892–93 by Samuel Maclure. It was Maclure's first major commission in Victoria, gained through a brother's business connection with the prominent client, merchants Robert Ward & Company. The building is also one of the few commercial buildings Maclure designed in a career noted more for residential work. Maclure was joined in 1900 by an English architect, Cecil Crocker Fox, who had trained under Arts and Crafts designer C. F. A. Voysey. Maclure, who subscribed to the English magazines *Country Life* and *The Studio*, knew of Voysey's reputation and happily hired his pupil. Maclure and Fox, as the practice became known, were highly regarded as the architects of Tudor Revival villas, outstripping even Francis Rattenbury to become the most sought-after society architects in Edwardian Victoria and Vancouver.

Samuel Maclure was born in 1860 in New Westminster, son of John Cunningham Maclure, a Scottish surveyor who had come with an advance party of Royal Engineers to survey New Caledonia in 1858. Maclure's father and his mother, Irish-born Martha (McIntyre) Maclure, settled in the Fraser Valley to farm. Samuel Maclure, the first white child to be born in New Westminster, then the colonial capital, was sent to school in Victoria and worked as a telegraph operator in Yale and Vancouver. He had a talent for drawing and became interested in architecture when he went to art school in Philadelphia in 1884–85, and visited Boston and New York. The Maclure family eventually developed the province's biggest clay and brickworks, but they were not wealthy at the time and young Samuel's studies were cut short. He returned to Victoria and worked for the Esquimalt & Nanaimo Railway, studying architecture and teaching art classes (he was an accomplished watercolourist) in his spare time.

"Sam" Maclure, as he was called, first caught the attention of local society not as an architect of fine villas but because of the manner of his marriage to Margaret Catherine Simpson. The couple eloped, she disguised as an elderly lady as she boarded an evening steamer to the mainland, and married in Vancouver in 1889. Maclure set himself up as an architect in New Westminster and returned to Victoria in 1892. There he

The Temple Building, designed in 1892–93 by Samuel Maclure, is one of Victoria's architectural gems. It was built for Robert Ward, whose business activities included being an agent for six insurance companies, a salmon exporter, a justice of the peace, president of the Board of Trade, pilotage commissioner and British Columbia's Consul for Norway and Sweden. Ward's varied resumé was typical of the networking boosters of the era. The thistle motif on the building is a reference to both Ward's and Maclure's roots; the style was contemporary American Romanesque—a combination of bold form and delicate details. Looking at the structure in later life, Maclure thought he had "beaten the Americans at their own game." He proved something to himself with its exquisite design, so accomplished that he never felt the need to repeat it. RW

opened an office in the Five Sisters Block at the northeast corner of Fort and Government streets. (The building was destroyed by fire in 1910, taking many of the architect's records and drawings with it—and those of Rattenbury and other architects who were also tenants.)

When the Temple Building opened, the *Colonist* called it the "most attractive office building in the province." Maclure even won praise for the design from his professional colleagues—no mean feat in Victoria's architectural community, whose competitive members were not all known for mutual regard. At the third annual meeting of the British Columbia Institute of Architects, the Five Sisters Block's stonework, for example, was described as "coarse" and the Board of Trade Building "factory-like." But the Temple Building, with its terracotta decoration, twin "Scotch" granite columns flanking the entrance, and unusual brick-walled inside stairway, was singled out as "well-designed . . . terracotta detail was made for it, not its facade for the detail." Maclure not only integrated the ornament and structure with ease at a time when lesser architects clumsily applied bits of ornament, but the overall composition, and the foliated terracotta panels and capitals on the neo-Romanesque entrance, show his up-to-the-minute knowledge of the work of American architects H. H. Richardson and Louis Sullivan. Maclure's early work in New Westminster had been based on pattern book designs. The Temple Building commission was his first opportunity to shine and he burst out with a flush of inspiration, skillfully marrying contemporary design ideas he had seen in the United States to Victoria's smaller urban scale.

Samuel Maclure's Temple Building was a creative North American interpretation of a historic European style; the Bank of British Columbia (left) was an elaborate academic copy. Nevertheless, its Renaissance facades, emulating those built for fifteenth-century Florentine merchants, were the finest of their type in the city when the building was erected in 1886. RW

·⟸ BANK OF BRITISH COLUMBIA ⟹·
1022 Government Street

From Montreal to Melbourne, nineteenth-century banks were built in noble classical styles to project an aura of stability, strength and security. Doubtful depositors could look at the Roman columns and Renaissance stonework of Victorian banks and be reassured that their savings would be in safe hands.

No such reassurance adorned British Columbia's first bank, opened by Alexander Davidson Macdonald in a wood frame building at Yates and Wharf streets in 1859. Macdonald's bank was the first in Victoria to print paper money (the Hudson's Bay Company issued tokens or drafts on its London account). Coins circulating in the town were mostly American dollars until 1862, when a British government shipment of £7,000 in sovereigns for the colonial coffers arrived. Fortunately, this was not deposited at Macdonald's bank, which went bust after being robbed of $30,000 one night in 1864. The crime was never solved. Macdonald was suspected but the case against him—that the robbery was a cover for the bank's looming insolvency—was not proven; his alibi was that he had been in the Cariboo at the time. But he abandoned his Italianate villa on Michigan Street to his creditors after investigators closed in. Before a court hearing, he boarded a San Francisco-bound ship off Holland Point and was never seen again.

In the early 1880s, when the Bank of British Columbia's directors decided on a new building in Victoria they commissioned Warren Heywood Williams, a Portland architect, to express their superior status in stone and cast iron. Williams gave them exactly what they wanted— an Italian Renaissance palazzo that would have done the Medicis proud. Like most architects of the time, Williams worked in whatever style a client instructed; when commissioned to design a mansion for Robert Dunsmuir in 1886 he sketched a Scottish baronial folly. The Bank of British Columbia was his first significant commission in Victoria and he had to swallow some humble pie to earn his fee: plans for the building, based on current British fashion, came from the bank's London board-room. The Ionic columned corner entrance, a plethora of pediments, cast-iron "stonework" from Albion Iron Works, and a cornice capped with iron cresting laced with Canadian and British floral motifs, were applied in extravagant layers as workmen erected the elegant facades in 1886. But even the bank's architecture dims in comparison with the fame and financial success of its most eccentric employee—the remarkable Robert Service.

Robert Service was born in England in 1874 and brought up in Scotland where he worked as teller at the Savings Bank of Glasgow. He emigrated in 1894 and worked as a farmhand near Duncan, Vancouver Island, dug ditches and washed dishes in California, and roamed the American Southwest, guitar slung on his back like a medieval minstrel. He landed back at Victoria in 1903 and worked for a short time at the Bank of British Columbia (by then the Canadian Bank of Commerce) on Government Street. An apocryphal tale has it that he slept above the bank vault with a loaded revolver by his side. It was the sort of story he would tell—Service went on to become the bard of the Klondike.

Transferred to Kamloops and then to the Yukon Territory in 1904, he worked as a teller in Whitehorse and Dawson City. He entertained locals with his songs and patter and was encouraged by the editor of the *Whitehorse Star* to "strike the rich paydirt" of the still-warm gold rush days. Service read gold rush stories from the *Star* and the *Klondike Nugget* in Dawson City's Carnegie Library, befriended old prospectors and, in his rented log cabin or late at night in his teller's cage, penned stirring verse and prose in works like *The Trail of Ninety-Eight*. His manuscripts were pinned to the wall in sheets as he wrote—a poetic frenzy that was rewarded with instant success. He sent some poems to Toronto and his first volume went to three printings before his publisher's salesman reached the Rockies.

But "the vagabond of verse" never did trek over the Chilkoot Pass, the treacherous ice-bound route to the gold fields in the winter of 1897-98. He arrived at Whitehorse in comfort on the brand new Yukon and White Pass Railway. His log cabin was built during the Klondike gold rush but he was too late to experience the event himself. Fans of "Canada's Kipling" forgave this poetic licence. Ballads like "The Call of the Wild" and "The Shooting of Dan McGrew" formed an image of the gold rush as enduringly popular as the colonial "Little England" he had left behind in Victoria. Robert Service struck it richer than most miners by romanticizing their experience with legends that are as exaggerated as Victoria's Englishness is false. By the time he resigned his teller's post in 1909, his monthly royalties exceeded his annual salary. He moved to Paris in 1912 and later settled in Monte Carlo, where he died a millionaire in 1958.

·⇐ BANK OF MONTREAL ⇒·
1200 Government Street

Francis Rattenbury's Bank of Montreal on Government Street was built at a time when few architects would use one gargoyle when a dozen would do. His smaller buildings look more like miniature castles than courthouses or banks. The courthouse he built in Nanaimo could be a French chateau; the one in Nelson is more Scottish Baronial. The Bank of Montreal, built in 1896 at the corner of View and Government streets in Victoria, looks like a kindergarten castle.

Rattenbury, who was completing the Parliament Buildings at the time, won a competition to build the Bank of Montreal's Victoria branch in a style far removed from the institution's head office in Montreal, a stately columned building modelled on a Neo-classical bank in Edinburgh. Rattenbury's reputation as Victoria's debutante designer gave him enough credibility to convince the bank that a concoction of castellated parapets, rusticated stonework, foliated friezes and grotesque gargoyles, all vaguely Renaissance and Romanesque in inspiration, would make the bank appear not only fashionably but also historically well dressed. The chateau-style roof placed the building in the forefront of contemporary Canadian architecture; its mock-medieval ornament expressed late Victorian society's penchant for decoration laced with visual metaphor (floral motifs, for example, were intended to symbolize the natural world that booming Victorian cities were becoming detached from). Gargoyles, which were designed to spout rainwater from the gutters of medieval cathedrals and carved with demons to frighten the masses, fostered the illusion that the bank's traditions were somehow rooted in the Middle Ages, an imagined heritage that many institutions founded in the nineteenth century sought to project.

At home, too, bankers and business barons saw themselves as the heirs of feudal lords or Renaissance princes and they commissioned mansions accordingly. In contrast to the mock-medieval manor houses Rattenbury designed for them, and the imperial braggadocio of the Parliament Buildings, his skillful eclecticism at the Bank of Montreal is enjoyably informal. The *Colonist* declared the building a "great success . . . a picturesque outline with massive solidity" and called the interior, with its marble countertops and mosaic floors (now altered, as is the corner entrance), "a magnificent new chamber." The *Colonist*, in the undiscriminating boosterism of the time, thought most new buildings great successes but in this case the assessment was not entirely incorrect. One imagines the architect pirouetting down Government Street with the newspaper's review in his hand. The bank was impressed too, and indulged Rattenbury's whimsy by handing him commissions to design branches in Nelson, Rossland and New Westminster. He executed these with less voguish verve than on Government Street. With its combination of masculine massing and almost childlike delight in decoration, the Victoria bank remains his first and most pleasing chateauesque essay. He reworked the style with considerably more grandiosity, if slightly less charm, at the Empress Hotel in 1908. The Bank of Montreal, like his other minor buildings, reveals an engaging side of his otherwise pompous personality.

·⇐ MUNRO'S BOOKS ⇒·
1108 Government Street

Around the turn of the century, Victorian whimsy was brought down to earth by Edwardian pomposity. Rattenbury's Bank of Montreal was an exception to the rule that banks should look the part—that they should be soberly styled and, preferably, adorned with classical columns. When the Royal Bank of Canada opened a branch on Government Street in 1909, the building was a traditional Neo-classical Revival design. Customers not charmed by Rattenbury's mock-medieval Bank of Montreal could walk down the street and be suitably impressed by the Royal Bank's granite facade and Tuscan columns, and awed by a banking hall that was illuminated from a stained glass dome inlaid with the coats-of-arms of Canadian provinces. They could also be assured that the tellers were prepared to protect deposits—the building, designed by Thomas Hooper, is rumoured to have had a shooting gallery in the basement where staff could train to deal with hold-ups.

Thomas Hooper was one of Rattenbury's main competitors in Victoria. He built more but was less famously rewarded, although he managed to pull the Carnegie Library commission from his rival's grasp and designed many of Government Street's turn-of-the-century facades. Like Rattenbury, he was commissioned to build courthouses around the province, including an addition to the one Rattenbury had designed in

TOP *Looking north on Government Street, c. 1900. Rattenbury's miniature chateau style Bank of Montreal is unmistakable in the middle distance.* BCARS B–03703
BOTTOM *The Hotel Canada bar c. 1900—a time when there were eighty-three licensed premises in Victoria to quench the thirst of a labour-intensive economy that was booming with coal mines, logging camps, salmon canneries, sawmills and shipyards.* BCARS F–02562

*Prettily repainted facades at Market Square hide cul-de-sacs
and nineteenth-century lanes that evoke the area's dense urban
character, if not its former bawdy temptations that attracted
Klondike miners and seafaring men.* RW

Vancouver. Hooper too was English, but served his time playing modest roles while Rattenbury arrived in British Columbia to achieve sudden stardom.

Hooper was born in Devon and immigrated to London, Ontario in 1871 with his parents. He showed early promise as a carpenter and, with ambition worthy of Rattenbury but no formal training, advertised himself locally as an "Architect and Builder." The self-taught Hooper moved to Winnipeg, where his brother was the Manitoba government's supervising architect, and then to Vancouver where he was appointed to the equivalent government post. He settled in Victoria around 1890 but kept up with the latest styles and gained a reputation for adaptability that brought him commissions for churches, office blocks, banks, homes, hotels, libraries and warehouses in Victoria and Vancouver. Typical of the turn-of-the-century breed of frontier architect–businessmen, Hooper sat on company boards and invested in property. At its peak, his practice had twenty staff on the payroll. But an elaborate Beaux Arts office block planned for Government Street in 1914 was cancelled when French financial backers pulled out. Hooper's company had already prepared drawings for the project and never recovered from its loss. He moved to New York in 1915 and returned to Vancouver to retire in 1927. Hooper's Neo-classicism, fashionable in 1909, was not appreciated in later years when the Royal Bank was modernized. When the banking hall was converted by Munro's Books in the 1980s, long-hidden Corinthian capitals, marble floors and Neo-classical plaster trim were revealed and restored with respect for Hooper's original design. Contemporary wall hangings and coloured glass reflect turn-of-the-century traditions of craftsmanship without resorting to pastiche.

·⇐ DRIARD HOTEL ⇒·
View Street (Eaton Centre)

When French-born restaurateur Sosthenes Driard bought Victoria's St. George's Hotel in 1872 and changed its name to his own, he inherited a building that was reputed to be the best hotel north of San Francisco. The hotel—and the popular restaurateur's name— were purchased in 1875 by another Frenchman, Louis Redon, later president of the Victoria Electric Light Company. Redon planned a massive seven-storey, 225-room block where "everything will be entirely modern ... rooms with bath-rooms attached, call and answer electric bells, electric and gas lights, and, in fact, everything that modern ingenuity has invented for comfort." The new Driard was built in 1892 by John Teague in big-city style with fashionable American Romanesque Revival facades to match the best in Seattle and San Francisco. It was renowned as "one of the handsomest adornments to the city" and "one of the finest hotels on the western seaboard." When Prime Minister Sir John A. Macdonald and Lady Macdonald visited Victoria in 1886 to open the Esquimalt & Nanaimo Railway, the Driard, rather than draughty Government House, was where they chose to stay.

Emily Carr remembered the interior as "all red plush and palm trees," the setting in 1903 of a debate that would seal the hotel's fate. When Alderman Lawrence Goodacre, a Victoria butcher, moved that the city discuss with the Canadian Pacific Railway "the erection of a tourist hotel at James Bay and to grant certain lands and exemptions in consideration thereof," the Driard's days as a grand hotel were numbered. In 1904, on the leather sofas among the palm trees in the Driard's lounge, Sir Thomas Shaughnessy of the CPR negotiated his Empress Hotel deal with Mayor George Henry Barnard and other city bigwigs. The Driard was outclassed when the Empress opened in 1908, and it lost its well-to-do clientele. So did nearby brothels—a report to the city police committee in 1886 noted fourteen brothels in and around the Driard Hotel, most on

Broad and Broughton streets and most with well-connected madams, all in all employing thirty-eight "girls."

The hotel was damaged in the fire of 1910 that started in "Spencer's Arcade" on Government Street and spread to several blocks nearby. Ironically the owner of the arcade, David Spencer, a Welsh immigrant who had opened a stationer, bookstore and lending library in the arcade in 1882, bought the Driard and rebuilt it as a department store (the fore-runner of a retail empire that was acquired by Eaton's in 1948). While the structure survived the great fire of 1910, it fared less well after the arrival of the Eaton Centre in the 1980s, Victoria's most conspicuous collision between the present and the past. The original Driard, along with sever-al other turn-of-the-century facades, was demolished and reassembled in the Eaton Centre's heritage theme park architecture. A plaque on the Driard's fragments on View at Broad Street identifies the past that the Eaton Centre erased.

·⇐ MARKET SQUARE ⇒·
560 Johnson Street

Most of the Old Town's buildings were erected in the late nineteenth century when Vancouver Island's economy was booming with canneries, coal mines, sawmills and shipyards. When Francis Rattenbury's Parliament Buildings were being raised to reign serene and separate on James Bay, the maze of alleys behind the Victorian facades that line Johnson Street and Pandora Avenue (formerly Cormorant Street) between Government Street and the waterfront, was chock-a-block with sawdust-floored bars, gaudy hotels and bordellos. Boisterous boomtown facades, capped with Classical-style tin-plate cornices, line Market Square's streets like Dawson City dancing troupes—a flamboyance that contrasted with their owners' respectability. The turretted Milne Block, designed by Thomas Hooper and opened at 546–48 Johnson Street in 1891 as the Empire Hotel and Restaurant, was owned by Scots-born

Alexander Roland Milne, collector of customs, registrar of shipping, and controller of Chinese immigration for the Port of Victoria. Like many pillars of society, Milne invested in the property market and put his name on the building's brick facade so no one would forget his passing. But of the gold rush of 1858, only street names remain. Alfred Waddington, who erected the city's first significant commercial building in 1858, surfaced the muddy lane he owned with wooden blocks for customers' convenience. Shops in Waddington Alley, between Yates and Johnson streets, included a butcher, baker, fish shop, grocer, milliner and bootmaker.

Waddington Alley, the first paved city street (the wooden blocks have been restored), was not the only example of Waddington's initiative. Few citizens could claim to have been educated in Paris and at German universities, as Waddington had. Born in London in 1801, he was the son of an English cotton mill owner and worked at his family's mills in England and France before globetrotting to Brazil and California. He became a partner in a San Francisco wholesale business before he ventured north to Victoria in 1858. In Victoria, he proposed visionary schemes to develop the colony. His book *The Fraser Mines Vindicated* was an attempt to revive the town's fortunes when gold fever temporarily cooled. He was a member of the Legislative Assembly from 1861 to 1862, wrote other books and pamphlets and bombarded newspaper editors with letters—and was often dismissed as just "Old Waddy" on his hobby horse. Yet he was one of the first to suggest a transcontinental railway. In 1864 he promoted a wagon road (and potential railway route) to the Cariboo gold fields from Bute Inlet that became a *cause célèbre* when Natives killed the construction crew.

From the courthouse at Bastion Square, and through Market Square to Chinatown, alleys still run through city blocks. Prettily repainted facades hide cul-de-sacs like Paper Box Arcade, a nineteenth-century-style passage in the old Victoria Box & Paper and Grand Central buildings on Johnson Street. At Market Square, galleries and arcades recreate the Old

Town's dense, Dickensian urban character—if not its former bawdy temptations that provided recreation for Klondike miners and seafaring men. The Oriental Hotel at 560 Yates Street, designed in 1883 by John Teague in Victorian Italianate style, had a belvedere from where captains could watch their vessels in harbour and where a beacon, lit to guide ships to anchor at night, led their crews to the hotel bar. The Occidental Hotel at Wharf and Johnson streets boasted a fireplace in every room and a saloon verandah where Klondike miners could nurse their dreams and drams. Many of Market Square's buildings had saloons on the ground floors, like the former Grand Pacific Hotel at Johnson and Store streets, built in 1879 by Carlo and Giocomo Bossi, Italian entrepreneurs who built several of the square's original buildings. The Brown Jug Saloon, which stood at the southeast corner of Fort and Government streets, dazzled denizens with gilded mirrors and a mahogany bar, said to be the longest north of San Francisco—a statistic that did not impress the local temperance society. The group had already survived an embarrassing setback at its first meeting in 1862 when the chairman arrived drunk. However, where the temperance society failed, by example or persuasion, the provincial government succeeded by prohibition. Between 1917 and 1921, one hundred city drinking establishments closed and few reopened. The port's industry, wholesaling and warehousing activity also declined in the 1920s. Ironically, Market Square's courtyard is dominated by a huge trussed canopy made with timbers recycled from the defunct Victoria Machinery Depot shipyard. Nothing, however, remains of the Market Square site's former topography or inhabitants: a Chinese shantytown, built on stilts, once clung to the edges of the Johnson Street Ravine, a shallow gorge carved out by a stream that ran between Johnson and Cormorant streets. ❦

中華會館

朱汝珍書

CHINESE CONSOLIDATED BENEVOLENT ASSOCIATION

Chinatown

WE CAN REMEMBER ONE ALLEY WHICH WAS BARRED BY A GATE
. . . UNDERNEATH THIS WAS A VERY NOTICEABLE STAIN, AND A
GRUESOME STORY ACCOUNTED FOR IT. A CHINESE PURSUED BY
AN ENEMY HAD STUCK HIS HEAD OUT . . . ONLY TO HAVE IT
CHOPPED OFF . . . IN OUR IMPRESSIONABLE AND CREDULOUS
DAYS, THE MEMORY OF OUR HORROR . . . IS STILL VERY VIVID
TO US—*article in the* Victoria Times, *1951*

FAN TAN ALLEY

CHINATOWN is the source of more myths than any other neighbourhood in Victoria. The area's compressed architecture and narrow lanes give visual substance to decades' worth of rumours of secret passages and escape routes. Fan Tan Alley had so many doors that suspects chased by police could quickly vanish into hidden inner courtyards. An account in *Chambers Journal* in 1911 claimed: "underneath Chinatown is a perfect maze of secret passages designed for the escape of the white and yellow gamblers . . . since the Chinese own all the land on which they build, the authorities can do nothing to prevent this burrowing, with all its dangerous possibilities." But the "tunnels,"

Chinatown's architecture is a blend of Chinese and western features. The pagoda-like Chinese Imperial School (now the Chinese Public School), built in 1909 at 636 Fisgard Street, is overlaid with Gothic and Italianate touches. RW

uncovered in the 1950s and supposedly used for smuggling, are relics of Victorian storm drains, and many of Chinatown's buildings were built by retired Hudson's Bay Company employees Roderick Finlayson, William John Macdonald and other European landowners. At the peak of expansion in 1910, only half the lots in the district were Chinese-owned.

During the gold rush of 1858, when hundreds of Chinese immigrants arrived from California and China, Hudson's Bay Company traders in Victoria suddenly found North America's largest Chinatown after San Francisco being built on their doorstep. The Chinese joined the flood of European, Canadian and American miners, adventurers and camp followers in the Cariboo gold fields. Chinese merchants moved from San Francisco, set up businesses in Victoria and prospered within their community. In 1862, Kwong Lee & Company, "Importers and Dealers in all kinds of Chinese Goods, Rice, Sugar, Tea, Provisions," became the HBC's biggest competitor. By 1910 Victoria's Chinatown had grown to cover six city blocks and had almost 3,500 residents and over 150 businesses. There were two theatres, a hospital, three schools, two churches, five temples—and over a dozen opium factories, numerous gambling dens and long-established brothels (in 1886 Police Chief Bloomfield estimated there were one hundred Chinese prostitutes on Fisgard Street).

Chinatown in the nineteenth century—bounded by Pandora Avenue and Store, Herald and Douglas streets—was to European residents a mysterious "forbidden city." Fan Tan Alley (named for Fan Tan, a betting game played with a cup and buttons) had, like cities in China, gates and watchmen at each end to keep outsiders at bay—and to cause the police delay when they conducted their periodic raids. The watchmen at their peepholes could pull ropes and drop heavy doors in place to block the lane and give gamblers time to escape by jumping out windows, disappearing through trap doors and dashing over the rooftops. But in 1915 the constabulary, armed with axes and iron bars, broke into the "Oriental Club" and nabbed 147 people, a record catch intended to demonstrate police and municipal officials' rectitude and resolve. Few non-Chinese

Victoria residents admitted to entering the brothels, opium dens or gambling rooms of Chinatown's wynds and courtyards, although opium was smoked by whites as well as Chinese.

Edwardian-era political rivalry in China led to "Tong Wars" between secret societies in overseas Chinatowns; a Chinese government minister was assassinated in Victoria in 1918. But the city's Chinese community never turned their discontent on the ruling but remote British imperial elite in their Rockland villas. They even erected processional arches, as white neighbourhoods did, to celebrate visits by royalty and governors general—a practice that was not untinged by self-interest. Victoria's 1889 city directory listed fourteen opium factories that processed 90,000 pounds of raw opium each year, for local consumption or to be smuggled to the United States or shipped to Hong Kong. Victoria's opium factories made considerable profits for the city in taxes and for the opium merchants. Until the Dominion government banned the sale and possession of the drug in 1908, "opium dealer" was a legal if not respectable occupation. And, as the British merchants who ran Hong Kong had discovered, it was a profitable one: few Victoria dealers blinked when visiting city hall to pay the biannual licence fee ($250 in 1886).

For a brief time in the early 1880s, when the Canadian Pacific Railway—and Chinese agents in San Francisco and Hong Kong—recruited approximately 10,000 Chinese to work on the transcontinental line through the Rockies, there were more Orientals than whites in Victoria. During winter lulls in construction many of the Chinese labourers were laid off, and drifted back to Vancouver and Victoria where they eked out an existence doing odd jobs—if they could find any work at all. After the CPR was completed in 1885, the lot of the "Celestials," as they were called, did not improve. In Victoria the provincial government refused to help, claiming: "the Dominion Government insisting that the exigencies of the Canadian Pacific Railway rendered the presence of these Mongolian hordes indispensable, the duty of providing relief for these starving people now fairly devolves upon that Government through whose intervention the unhappy necessity has arisen." Neither Ottawa, nor the CPR or its subcontractors who had shipped in the Chinese workers in the first place, offered any help. Unemployed Chinese railway workers, the unsung heroes of Canadian nation-building, had to rely on families and friends in Chinatown for help.

·⇐ CHINESE BENEVOLENT ASSOCIATIONS ⇒·

On the map, Chinatown was cheek-by-jowl with the European city, but socially it might as well have been in Canton. Victoria was a two-tier society in the nineteenth century—the whites upstairs and Chinese and Native Indians in the servants' quarters. Benevolent associations protected Chinese immigrants from hostile host societies. The associations, which represented different clans, organized social clubs, business associations, cultural organizations and schools—social work, in effect, from cradle to grave. The Chinese Consolidated Benevolent Association in Victoria, for instance, ran a school, a hospital and a Chinese cemetery at Ross Bay, and later Oak Bay. Above all, these groups helped immigrants, few of whom could speak English, to negotiate the complexities of a foreign society.

Their buildings were the most elaborately designed in Chinatown. The area's architecture displays a blend of western architectural features and Chinese recessed balconies and tiled overhangs. The Lee's Benevolent Association building, completed in 1911 at 614 Fisgard Street, and the pagoda-like Chinese Imperial School, built next door in 1909, are examples of compatibility in architecture that was not echoed behind the social

Lee's Benevolent Association, built in 1911 at 614 Fisgard Street, is decorated with a Portuguese colonial gable and Romanesque arches along with Chinese tilework and recessed balconies, a distinctive Chinatown style that is derived from Chinese and colonial architecture in Macao and Hong Kong. RW

THE LEE'S BENEVOLENT ASSOCIATIO

facades of the time. These buildings were not designed by Chinese residents but by Victoria's British and Canadian architects. The Chinese Consolidated Benevolent Association, which represented all of the neighbourhood's clan groups, commissioned John Teague to build its headquarters in 1884–85. With ground floor shops, the association's offices above, and a school and temple on the top floor, the building was typical of mixed-use Chinatown architecture. The facade is preserved but the original appearance, with wooden balconies built out over the sidewalk, was altered after an 1890s fire prevention bylaw required that the balconies be removed.

The cramped living and working conditions the Chinese population had to tolerate were the result of ingenuity as much as of the prejudice and poverty that kept them behind the gates of Fan Tan Alley. Several buildings, like the block at 1905 Government Street, were given "cheater storeys," a characteristic feature of Chinatown architecture in Victoria and elsewhere. Hidden mezzanines were squeezed between the ground and second floors so that property taxes could be evaded. After wooden slums on Pandora Avenue were replaced in the 1890s with tenement buildings, some of which survive at both ends of Fan Tan Alley, a bylaw was passed to further reduce overcrowding. The city sent the police to raid the area to levy fines on Chinese caught sharing rooms—but did nothing to improve the conditions or mitigate the economic causes of the problem. In 1893 the Consolidated Benevolent Association instructed those arrested to plead guilty and go to jail rather than pay the $10 fine.

A Chinese family in Victoria c. 1880. In 1858, Chinese were among the flood of miners to the Fraser River gold fields and Chinese merchants from San Francisco opened businesses in Victoria; in 1862, Kwong Lee & Company, "Importers and Dealers in all kinds of Chinese Goods, Rice, Sugar, Tea, Provisions," was the Hudson's Bay Company's main rival.
BCARS C–05473

After the next raid, so many people ended up in jail that the association was able to accuse the police of violating the overcrowding rule. Those charged were released and the bylaw was conveniently forgotten by both sides.

·⇐ CHINESE IMPERIAL SCHOOL ⇒·
636 Fisgard Street

Faded Edwardian advertising signs hint that Chinatown was not entirely an economic or social ghetto: "Wilson Bro's Wholesale Grocers, Sue War Laundry, Coristo Biscuits, Old Chum Tobacco, Tong & Co., Drugs & Groceries," play typographic tricks on walls exposed by demolition. Victoria's bourgeois families retained Chinese servants, had their finery cleaned at Chinese laundries, and bought vegetables grown by Chinese farmers. Property ownership in Chinatown was not exclusive to either group: the warehouse at the southeast corner of Fisgard and Store streets, built in 1898 by a returning Klondiker-turned-property developer, was purchased by a local Chinese man and then bought by Francis Rattenbury in 1909.

Contact between the communities, however, was limited by prejudice and the English class system that also kept white workers in their place. In 1892 all Chinese passengers arriving on the *Empress of Japan* were quarantined at Esquimalt when the ship's doctor diagnosed one Chinese person with smallpox. But the disease was inadvertently spread by white passengers who were allowed to disembark. In the early 1900s the Victoria school board, responding to the bigotry of some white parents, segregated local Chinese children and ruled that Chinese-born students would be barred from city schools unless they could speak English—notwithstanding that they needed to go to school to learn how to do so. The Chinese Consolidated Benevolent Association's riposte in 1909 was to build its own school for children rejected by the public system. With its pagoda roof, tiled eaves and temple finials, the Chinese Imperial

School is the most "Chinese" building in Chinatown. It is also the one with the most western motifs: Italianate cornices, Gothic trefoils and lancet windows give the school a quasi-Christian air—quite appropriate as many Chinese joined Methodist, Presbyterian and other Christian churches, bridging the cultural divide more effectively than the school board was willing to do.

The Chinese Imperial School was renamed the Chinese Public School after the overthrow of China's ruling dynasty in 1912. Dr. Sun Yat-Sen visited Victoria in 1911 while fundraising for the Chinese Nationalist League; hand-coloured photographs of him, looking ever-youthful, are still displayed in shop windows, as if the era of revolutionary intrigue still exists in upstairs rooms. Sun Yat-Sen was tolerated in European and North American diplomatic circles, but ordinary Chinese workers in Victoria's shophouses and laundries, and the servants in the city's affluent homes, were kept firmly in their place. Some homes had a "Chinaman's room" for the cook, houseboy or gardener, although most servants returned to tenement rooms in Chinatown at night. Sunday afternoon was their only time off.

Chinese labourers were accused of stealing white men's jobs and were denied employment on public projects. A "Workingman's Protection Society" was formed in Victoria in 1878 for "the mutual protection of the working classes of British Columbia against the influx of Chinese, and the use of legitimate means for the suppression of immigration." But it was the Chinese who were the foot soldiers of the local economy: at the Wellington mine, owned by the coal baron Robert Dunsmuir, 700 Chinese workers were employed as white miners' assistants to do the dirty work and Chinese navvies laid the tracks of the Esquimalt & Nanaimo Railway (as well as the CPR on the British Columbia mainland). Anti-Chinese feeling led to an Asiatic exclusion law and a head tax on new immigrants that prevented Chinese men from being joined by the families they had worked to support. In an inflationary prejudice the head tax of $50, imposed in 1885 on every Chinese immigrant, was increased to $100 in 1900, and to $500 in 1903. British Columbia lobbied Ottawa to invoke an exclusion act in 1898, but was unsuccessful. Supreme Court Judge Henry Pering Pellew Crease argued against Chinese exclusion not because it was racist but because "the wail of the housewife would sweep through the land, and find a very decided expression in every husband's vote at the polls." Middle and upper class families in Victoria had grown to depend on Chinese servants who, according to one resident, did "twice the work," and were "always sober, and fairly honest."

Victoria's Chinese found an unexpected ally in Judge Matthew Baillie Begbie, whose attitude toward them was the same as it was to all who appeared before him. He opposed provincial and Dominion anti-Chinese legislation and played the subversive where legality allowed, taking special pleasure in exposing the absurdity of cases brought before him. In 1884, when a Chinese laundry owner appealed against a bylaw declaring wash houses (all of which were run by Chinese) a public nuisance, Begbie pronounced the bylaw prejudicial, concluding: "butchers' shops . . . with greasy and bleeding carcasses lumbering the sidewalks and infecting the air . . . stables with their muck-heaps several yards high . . . pregnant with pungent and misalubrious gases [were more offensive] than anything that can be alleged against these wash houses." He scoffed at an 1874 proposal to tax Chinese men's pigtails: "There would be a very simple way of excluding every Chinaman from the Province, by imposing a universal tax, not limited to any nationality, of one or two thousand dollars per annum for a licence to wear long hair on the back of the head; or to exclude Russians by a licence to wear a beard, or Jews by a licence to eat unleavened bread."

> *A faded Chinese laundry sign on the side of a Herald Street*
> *warehouse evokes the toil of the nineteenth-century domestic*
> *servant's routine. Victoria's middle class depended on Chinese*
> *labour to keep their overdecorated homes clean and their*
> *clothes crisply starched.* RW

*Victoria's 1889 city directory listed fourteen opium factories that
processed 90,000 pounds of raw opium each year for local consumption—or to be smuggled to the United States or shipped to
Hong Kong. Victoria's opium factories made huge profits for
opium merchants and generated tax revenue for the city. Fan Tan
Alley was once the local centre of this trade.* RW

Nevertheless, the Chinese Exclusion Act was finally passed in 1923.
New immigrants, and wives and children of men already in the country,
were denied entry. In 1931, only about 12 percent of Chinese in Canada
were women. Chinatown was home for an aging male population, who
sought solace and recreation in the dozen or so melancholy gambling
clubs of Fan Tan Alley. Between 1923 and 1947, when the act was re-
pealed, only eight Chinese immigrants were allowed into the country.
Residents of Chinatown were taxed but denied the right to vote until
1947, when the government was shamed by Chinese-Canadian soldiers
returning from the Second World War.

On either side of Fan Tan Alley's claustrophobic passage, the doors
and brick walls that once hid a warren of opium dens and gambling clubs
open onto souvenir stores. Few of the herbalists, apothecaries, laundries
and other respectable businesses remain on Fisgard Street. To see the
Man Yuck Tong herbalist shop, one of the first in the country when it was
established in 1905 at 544 Fisgard Street, requires a visit to the Royal BC
Museum where the shop and its jars of palliatives and cures, obtained
when it closed in the 1980s, have been reassembled. Down the alley,
beyond the Fan Tan Cafe—one of the city's last traditional noodle
shops—the clatter of mah-jong players in the remaining social clubs, and
the clip-clip, snip-snip in a dimly lit barbershop are the only traditional
sounds to echo from the former Chinese ghetto. ✑

Around Town

A PERSON UNFAMILIAR WITH THE MARVELOUS PROGRESS OF
CIVILISATION . . . SHIPS OF COMMERCE, LADEN WITH EXPORTS
. . . INDUSTRIES, WELL GRADED STREETS . . . PUBLIC AND
PRIVATE BUILDINGS, WOULD SCARCELY BELIEVE . . . ALL THESE
THINGS ARE THE CREATION OF A LITTLE MORE THAN TWENTY
YEARS—*Capt. Newton Henry Chittenden, Victoria 1882*

CITY HALL

WHEN the first mayor of Victoria, Thomas Harris, was elected in 1862, he inherited a town in which, according to the *Colonist* the year before, "the gutters in the main street are at times choked with putrescent filth," and liquor was "cheaper than water." At the first council meeting, at the police barracks at Bastion Square, Harris and his councillors drafted bylaws that banned almost anything that moved. A Committee of Nuisances was formed to deal with "bawdy houses, stray pigs, effluent, and disagreeable stenches." Slaughterhouses, tanneries, distilleries and "other offensive trades" were to be fined—if not moved beyond the city boundary; dumping "rubbish, filth, ashes or offal" on city streets or into the harbour was prohibited; there was to be

St. Andrew's Presbyterian Church plays a dour Scottish tune that bursts into sudden architectural rhythm in its rose window, baronial turrets, Romanesque brickwork and Baltic-style crow-stepped gable. RW

no discharging of firearms; and carriage drivers were required to restrain their horses to a speed limit of eight miles per hour.

The bumptious Harris was soon seen leading his committee on walk-abouts to investigate complaints. The *Colonist* announced that the election of Harris was "another step in the progress of civilisation." If this was not a sarcastic comment, it should have been. Council's first ordinances were written with such verbosity as to be completely unintelligible. Attorney General George Hunter Cary, "shallow beyond belief; conceited beyond conception; untruthful and unscrupulous; devoid of correct governing principles," had made such an "abominable botch of incorporating the city," that the wording of the Act of Incorporation prevented city council from legally raising taxes. Nuisances remained even after city hall paperwork was put in order—in 1884, R. P. Rithet ran for mayor with the slogan that the city "must be drained of its filth or it will be drained of its wealth and populace."

Yet Victoria was also a city with a cricket team and a race track at Beacon Hill Park (where Mayor Harris spent his spare time as president of the jockey club). The city directory noted a townscape "adorned with five churches, two belonging to the Church of England, one Roman Catholic, one Wesleyan, and one Congregational," and that "a Jewish synagogue and a Presbyterian church are in the course of construction." Solidly built Italianate brick buildings had replaced many of the false-fronted wooden structures that had been thrown up during the 1858 gold rush boom. Metropolitan gentlemen's attire—frock coats, top hats and bowlers—was the fashion not just in church but also at city hall and in the legislature as politicians tried to shake off their frontier ways. The *Colonist* used a feminine metaphor to comment on the first election, writing that the town "added several inches to the length of her petticoats and donned crinoline and pantalettes for the first time in her life." But city council's fancy dress was not matched by its accommodation, nor by the solidity of its furniture: Mayor Harris and his merry men met in the courtroom at the police barracks and jail, and Harris, who weighed in at

300 pounds, demolished the mayoral chair when he tried it for size. Harris, an Englishman, was well known as the beefy proprietor of "Queen's Meat Market," Victoria's first butcher shop. One local wag thought the mayor would be "remembered for his proportions rather than his policies." Harris liked to describe himself as a "humble trades-man," but he was not humble enough to balk at leading bailiffs to evict striking miners from their homes at Robert Dunsmuir's Wellington colliery in 1877, when he was the sheriff of Vancouver Island

Victoria City Hall, 1 Centennial Square, is the oldest surviving municipal hall in BC and was built to replace offices on Broad Street. It was Mayor Roderick Finlayson's personal project and he saw it through, after being elected in 1878, with the resolve that he had demonstrated running Fort Victoria for the Hudson's Bay Company. Public opinion was against spending money on a permanent new building, although city council had made do with temporary premises since 1862. Finlayson carried his council with him and held an architectural competition, which was won anonymously by John Teague with a design that the *Colonist* called "Anglo-Italian . . . yet not deficient in dignity." This did not impress the ratepayers who, after Finlayson laid the foundation stone in 1878, protested and interrupted construction forcing Teague to live up to his competition *nom de plume*, "Work and Win."

When it opened, the building accommodated a council chamber, committee rooms, surveyors' quarters, police court and jail. It was enlarged in 1881 and added to in 1891, having survived an embarrassment in 1884 when the city was sued for an unpaid legal bill. Mayor J. W. Carey, who refused to approve the bill, was barred by the bailiff. Judge Begbie directed that city hall's contents be auctioned, but local politicians and businessmen rode to the rescue—to the disappointment of citizens who already had their eyes on choice items. Had the auction taken place after the bell tower was raised in 1891, the prize lot would have been the city's newest, biggest and best-travelled clock, which arrived from England after being mistakenly shipped to the state of Victoria, Australia.

City hall seen from the Maynards' studio balcony c.1891. John Teague, Victoria City Hall's architect, gave the town much of its distinctive character with Italianate business blocks, warehouses and homes. BCARS F–01303

·⇐ VICTORIA PUBLIC MARKET ⇒·

John Teague was born in Cornwall and settled in Victoria in 1862 after gold-seeking in California and the Cariboo. He worked as an engineer for the Royal Navy and began his architectural career by designing naval buildings at Esquimalt. An energetic frontier architect, he had no professional training. But in early Victoria he had little competition. He opened an office in Trounce Alley and went on to give the growing mid-nineteenth century town much of its distinctive character. His trademark style was Victorian Italianate, which he applied with consistency if little imagination to buildings as varied as city hall, warehouses and offices around Market Square and Chinatown, hotels and churches, as well as homes for Judge Begbie, James Dunsmuir and other members of the ruling class. Even in later years, Teague was able to hold his own among more youthful competitors.

In 1891, assisted by Andrew Maxwell Muir, he was commissioned by the city to design Victoria Public Market to be built on Cormorant Street (Pandora Avenue) between Government and Douglas streets. The market was intended to help farmers compete with Chinese growers who travelled into the city and sold fresh produce door-to-door. But the building, far from being a cash cow for the farmers who had lobbied for it, became a civic white elephant. The galleried interior was fitted out with sixty shops and farmers' produce stalls, watering troughs, cattle pens and stables. But the "Oriental peddlers" and other merchants were well established. Despite the Esquimalt & Nanaimo Railway bringing produce to the nearby Store Street station, opened in 1888, the market was never fully let for its original purpose. In 1889 the fire department

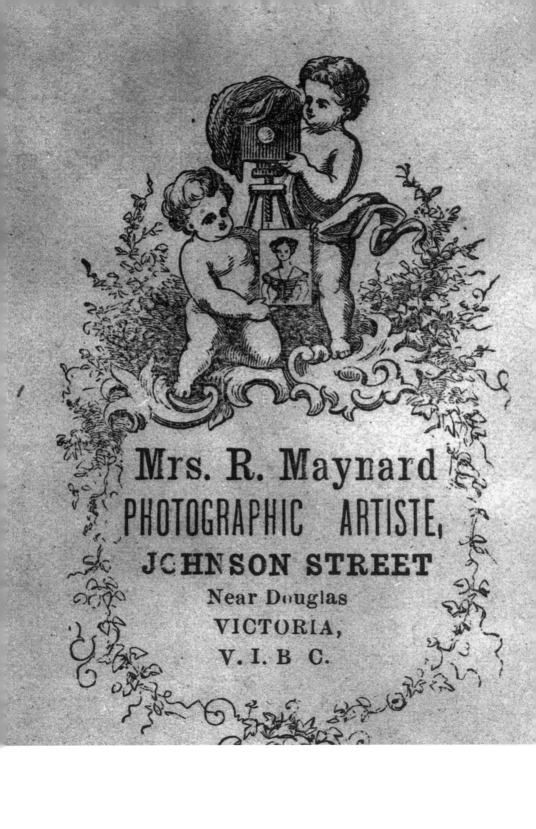

Mrs. R. Maynard
PHOTOGRAPHIC ARTISTE,
JOHNSON STREET
Near Douglas
VICTORIA,
V. I. B C.

moved in, followed by a regiment of garrison artillery and other unintended tenants. One newcomer to the city reported: "All I wanted was to get some fresh eggs and a few vegetables, but the farmers were not in evidence. I found a portrait painter's studio, a real estate agent, the Sanitary Inspector, and the most ghastly of all things—the public morgue." When the building was mooted, one alderman mused: "Perhaps it should be designed so that it can be used as a railroad station, in case it proves a failure as a market." With heavy ornamental iron gates, brick and granite arched facades and a two-storey iron and glass roof supported on cast-iron columns, the building looked the part when the western half of it was leased to the Victoria and Sidney Railway between 1901 and 1914. When the market was demolished in 1959 to make way for a new civic centre, the only stall-holders left were a baker, a candy store, a fishmonger and a poultry shop.

Centennial Square, the civic centre that replaced the market, and which would have pulled down Teague's city hall had it been fully implemented, was intended to be a focus for civic life. A fashionable example of 1960s British-style civic planning, it was optimistically praised as a "radiating urban beautification plan" complete with an Elizabethan garden copied from Hampton Court and a fountain whose defining symbol is a circular parapet said to represent Queen Victoria's crown. Bricks from the old market, originally imported from Britain, were recycled to partly

Hannah Maynard's carte-de-visite *was similar in style to her studio's Neo-classical painted backgrounds that suggested life in the colonies was just like home. When she opened* "Mrs. R. Maynard's Photographic Gallery," *at the corner of Douglas and Johnson streets, she had to overcome social conventions of the time: the* Colonist *reported that* "Mr. Maynard *frequently pretended that he had taken the pictures, whereas in actual fact it was his wife who had done the job."*
BCARS E–09402

pave the square. Also preserved is the McPherson Playhouse, originally a vaudeville theatre opened as the "Orpheum" by Alexander Pantages, the Greek immigrant who built North America's largest chain of music halls after working as a cook in Dawson City. Restoration preserved the facade on Government Street and the Edwardian decor in the auditorium—a gilded grotto of plaster cherubs, cartouches, marbled Tuscan columns, acanthus leaf mouldings, harps and mandolins.

·⇐ MAYNARD STUDIOS ⇒·
723 Pandora Avenue

Hannah Hatherly was born in Cornwall in 1834, was married in 1852 and emigrated to Ontario that year with her husband Richard James Maynard, a sailor and apprentice bootmaker. In 1858 he shipped out for Panama and the Fraser River gold fields while she stayed in Ontario with their children and worked for a local photographer. He returned to fetch her, and in 1862 the Maynards and their four children settled in Victoria. While Richard Maynard went off mining on the Stikine River and then set up a boot and shoe store on Douglas Street, Hannah Maynard opened "Mrs. R. Maynard's Photographic Gallery" at the corner of Douglas and Johnson streets. She had to overcome social conventions of the time: the *Colonist* reported that "Mr. Maynard frequently pretended that he had taken the pictures, whereas in actual fact it was his wife who had done the job . . . until Victoria got used to a woman photographer." She later moved her studio to her husband's Douglas Street shop under a sign that read "Maynard's Photographic Gallery, Boot and Shoe Store." Their life together turned out to be as unconventional as the sign on the shop.

Over the years, Hannah Maynard taught her husband the rudiments of photography. In 1868 he took their eleven-year-old son Albert on a photographic trip up the Cariboo Wagon Road to Barkerville. In 1873 he sailed on the gunboat HMS *Boxer*, the first of several expeditions north to record Native people and their villages for the Department of Indian

Affairs. In the 1880s he was hired to record construction work on the Canadian Pacific Railway, a documentary commission that suited his eye for landscape. The couple rarely travelled together, although in 1879 they sailed on the *Princess Louise* "with a party of 40 other ladies and gentlemen bound on an excursion around Vancouver Island," and in 1888 she accompanied him to the Queen Charlotte Islands, taking along cumbersome equipment and a portable darkroom. But her métier, at which she excelled in a way that eclipsed her husband's wilderness landscapes, was studio portraiture.

The walls of their Victoria studio were lined with painted backdrops and architectural props, a nineteenth-century theatrical artifice designed to make bourgeois subjects feel as if they were still in their plush James Bay and Rockland homes. The Neo-classical scenes painted with foliage, Tuscan columns and balustrades were a contemporary attempt to give the new art of photography a traditional veneer of oil painting. City business barons and their wives were seduced by the classical associations of Hannah Maynard's studio sets; less wealthy sitters were flattered by the illusion of sumptuous decor they could never afford at home; explorers, pioneers and tourists preferred to pose with rifles, bearskins and rugged romantic landscapes.

Hannah Maynard's portraits of Native street peddlers and skivvies were honest and direct, unlike the sentimental souvenir images of "noble savages" that became popular as the continent was settled and tribes conquered. Those Indians unwilling to assimilate with white society found their images purloined and sanitized. Portrait photographers from Winnipeg to Dawson City posed tourists with tame chiefs; Indian names and imagery were appropriated to advertise products of white industrial society. On his trips to the Queen Charlotte Islands in 1884 and 1888, Richard Maynard photographed Natives and their villages with sympathy and candour, but he also had a commercial interest. The Maynards, like all photographers who responded to the Victorian hunger for colonial curiosities and foreign scenes, printed stereoscopic views for sale.

In the nineteenth century, almost all professional photographers were men. Hannah Maynard was an exception, as was her more personal work. She experimented with double exposure and montage—techniques few photographers tried at the time. During 1881–85, annual "BC Gems"—cheek-by-jowl cutout heads of local babies and children—were sold as novelties in Victoria and published in the *St. Louis Practical Photographer*. The magazine, a regular publisher of her work, thought her "one of the most industrious and persevering ladies we have in our business. She stops at no impediment, in our Art, but is a regular go-ahead, even beating our Yankee girls two to one in photography." She followed the "gems" with surreal family tableaux and mordant "living statuary," achieved by coating her subjects' features with white powder. These bizarre images, created after the death of her youngest daughter from typhoid in 1883, were too much for her fans at the *St. Louis Practical Photographer*. The magazine thought them of the "freak order," far removed from her 1870s *carte-de-visite*, cutely decorated with two cupids and a box camera and the legend "Mrs. R. Maynard, Photographic Artiste."

Richard Maynard died in 1907; Hannah in 1918. When she retired in 1912 she told the *Colonist*: "I think that I can safely say with every confidence that we photographed everyone in the town at one time or another." This was no idle claim. From 1887 to 1892 she was the official photographer for the Victoria police; prisoners, prostitutes and swindlers

Richard Maynard and Newton Henry Chittenden pose for Hannah Maynard in the Maynards' studio in 1884. Chittenden was an adventurer who travelled around British Columbia in the early 1880s and, like most visitors to the city and virtually all residents, he called on the Maynards to have his portrait taken. More than any other local photographers, the couple recorded nineteenth-century Victoria and its citizens in all their finery and pretension. BCARS C–08862

were escorted to her studio from the city jail. The Maynards' photographs of moustached members of city council, businessmen, store owners and their premises, Royal Navy ships and their crews at the Esquimalt dockyard, wilderness vistas, Beacon Hill Park, and the homes of the well-to-do amounted to approximately 15,000 glass plate negatives and prints now in the collection of the BC Archives in Victoria. The studio, which the Maynards bought in 1892, still stands at 723 Pandora Avenue just east of city hall. On its second floor are luminous windows and a door that opened onto a balcony, from where the pair could gaze upon the town that they photographed so well.

·⇐ CARNEGIE LIBRARY ⇒·
794 Yates Street

Andrew Carnegie was born in Dunfermline, Scotland in 1835 and emigrated to America with his family in 1848. They settled in Pittsburgh where Carnegie began work as a "bobbin boy" in a textile mill. He moved to a telegraph office, then a railway company, and through enterprise, shrewd investments and efficient use of manufacturing technology, especially in iron and steel, he rose from rags to riches—much the way that Robert Dunsmuir did on Vancouver Island.

Carnegie never forgot his roots or the family's hardship during the 1840s before they left Scotland. As a boy he was chased out of a private Dunfermline estate; he later bought the land and gave it to the town—along with parks, libraries and public swimming baths. While there are countless bequests from nineteenth-century capitalists lingering in museums and art galleries around the world, many business barons, like the Dunsmuirs, hung on to their loot. Carnegie was an exception. After he sold his industrial empire he didn't just give some paintings to the local

A grotesque carving inspired by European medieval architecture guards the entrance to the Carnegie Library. RW

museum, he gave most of his fortune away. The first Carnegie Library was built in Dunfermline in 1881. By the time Carnegie died in 1919 he had funded over 2,800 libraries around the world. His motivation was to bring "sweetness and light" to the "monotonous lives of the toiling masses." But his most important legacy was the quixotic notion that the wealthy had an obligation to give back to society what they had gained. In 1902 Carnegie offered $50,000 to Victoria for construction and endowment of a library. But city council debated whether or not to apply for what was perceived as an American's tainted cash—Carnegie's philanthropic reputation had been tarnished by a strike while he was absent from his mills in 1892.

The architectural commission too provoked controversy when the city decided, at the suggestion of some local architects, to select one of their group by secret ballot. Francis Rattenbury was not among them and he wrote a stinging letter to city council implying impropriety. Rattenbury suggested a competition be held—although, as the *Colonist* pointed out, he had previously opposed a contest being held for the new Government House. After his success with the Parliament Buildings, he felt he was the best-qualified designer for every major city project. He certainly showed more vision than city hall when he sketched a Beaux Arts library building facing the harbour directly north of the Empress Hotel. But the city chose an undistinguished former brewery site at Fort and Yates streets. "Ratz" retired from the fray and the competition was won by one of his rivals, Thomas Hooper.

Hooper's building was opened in 1906 and carried less plumage and was considerably smaller than Rattenbury's library design. But it echoed the blend of Neo-classicism and Romanesque Revival that Rattenbury had used for the Parliament Buildings. The Carnegie Library's eight-foot-high classical columns cut from single blocks, medieval carving, rusticated stonework, coloured Art Nouveau glass and Romanesque arched entrance conspire to suggest that Hooper had not been entirely uninspired by his rival's work.

·⇐ HUDSON'S BAY COMPANY DEPARTMENT STORE ⇒·
1701 Douglas Street

When the Hudson's Bay Company was founded by a group of London traders in 1670, its Royal Charter from King Charles II rang with the stirring words "The Governor and Company of Adventurers of England trading in to Hudson's Bay." The HBC explored the North American continent from the St. Lawrence River to the Pacific coast, and built trading posts from Labrador to Russian Alaska, and California to the Sandwich Islands. From its base at York Factory on Hudson's Bay the company built a continental trading empire, importing British products to exchange for furs which were exported to its London auction house on an almost industrial scale. Up to 1870, when it surrendered much of its territory to the Dominion Government and lost its trading monopoly, it controlled 40 percent of the land in the country. Until 1970, when head office moved to Winnipeg, its board of directors still met at Beaver House in the City of London.

In the nineteenth century, the HBC produced leaders of the calibre of James Douglas and Donald Alexander Smith, also a Scot, who rose from fur trader in Labrador to become governor of the HBC, president of the Bank of Montreal, director of the Canadian Pacific Railway and Canadian High Commissioner in London. With a London board appointed from the top echelons of British society, the HBC, one of the great imperial trading names, was run rather like an old boys' club. But the company's fur traders—and those of the competing North West Company of Montreal—were mainly Scottish and French Canadian, the former recruited from the crofting and fishing communities in the Highlands and Islands of Scotland, the latter from isolated settlements in Quebec. They administered their territory as if it were a feudal empire: even in the 1970s HBC factors in isolated fur trading posts paternalistically controlled the distribution of government welfare cheques and treaty money to the Indians.

On Vancouver Island, farms run by the Puget Sound Agricultural Company (an HBC subsidiary) gradually replaced the fur trade in Victoria. From Fort Victoria the HBC exported salmon, cedar shingles, potatoes and cranberries, and provisioned whaling ships at Honolulu and Royal Navy vessels at Esquimalt. A second fort was built at Nanaimo when coal was discovered in 1852. In 1846 Berthold Seeman, a naturalist on HMS *Herald*, had noted that the HBC sold "tools, agricultural implements, blankets, shawls, beads, and all the multifarious products of Sheffield, Birmingham, Manchester and Leeds . . . offered at exorbitant prices. There being no competition, the company has it all its own way." Such was the dominance of the HBC over remote settlements in the Canadian northwest that resentful settlers translated the company's acronym as "Here Before Christ." For Indians, who were paid low prices for pelts whenever there was a slump in the European market for beaver hats, it meant "Hungry Belly Company." American competitors thought the HBC a "Hated British Company."

When Chief Factor James Douglas became governor of the united colonies of Vancouver Island and British Columbia in 1858, his resignation from the company marked the end of an era. Fort Victoria was sold during the gold rush property boom, and as the frontier receded, trade diversified from furs, farming and shipping to hardware, consumer goods and property management. A store was built on Wharf Street below Bastion Square in 1859 (where its stone retaining walls can still be seen), and the fort was demolished and its site auctioned as building lots.

To attract development to the edge of downtown, the HBC began to build a palatial new department store on newly widened Douglas Street in 1914. It was designed in the metropolitan manner that the company had begun to project, but stood half-empty until completed after the First World War. The HBC directors had sent Edmund Burke, a Toronto architect, to London to look at Selfridges Department Store, the most up to date in the empire when it was begun in 1907. When Burke returned, he designed the Victoria store in Selfridges' image—a Neo-classical design that swaggers with Edwardian confidence. Burke's columns, cornices and facades lavishly covered with decorative terracotta (cast from the same moulds that were used to make the facade ornament on the company's stores in Calgary and Vancouver of the same period), brought big-city braggadocio to town.

The HBC's department stores were an attempt to adapt to changing times. The fact that the company was responding rather than leading, as its eighteenth-century explorers had done, was a symptom of its decline. The company had ignored manufacture and sales; despite the fashionable demand for beaver hats in the Georgian gentlemen's shops of London's West End, the HBC never made a single beaver hat. The company's romantic self-image spared its staff such lowly labour. Peter Skene Ogden, a chief factor on the coast in the nineteenth century, once wrote to Governor George Simpson: "You are I presume fully aware that the Fur Trade and Civilisation can never be blended together and experience teaches us the former invariably gives way to the latter." Douglas voiced the same sentiment and would be dismayed at how true it has turned out to be. Today the HBC's closest connection with its past is a line of outdoor clothing bearing the label "Northern Spirit." The real spirit of "the Bay"—the company's Northern Stores Department's fur trading posts—was sold in 1987 to pay down corporate debt. Ironically the buyer, a Finnish company, renamed the profitable department the North West Company, the name of the HBC's fur trade rival that it had absorbed in 1821.

One former HBC director condemned the sale of the trading posts with words that could have been Douglas's own: "Only unpardonable cowardice and incompetence could lead the Canadian owners of this great historic company to throw away these jewels in its crown. The Company now abandons the Canadian North; it severs generations of a trusting and respectful relationship between native peoples and traders—it deletes the words and discards the heart of its historic name: Company of Adventurers." Inside the Victoria store, amidst displays of modern merchandise, only one authentic reminder of the HBC's fur trading days is still sold—English woollen "point blankets," so called because their primary-coloured stripes and sewn-in scale indicated barter value in exchange for pelts.

The directors of the Hudson's Bay Company sent Toronto architect Edmund Burke to London to look at Selfridges Department Store, the most up to date in the empire when begun in 1907. When Burke returned, he designed the HBC's Victoria store in Selfridges' image—a Neo-classical design that swaggers with Edwardian confidence. RW

·⇐ BAY STREET ARMOURY ⇒·

The Bay Street Armoury, between Douglas and Blanshard streets, was built in 1914–15 by the federal government to replace the Menzies Street drill hall, a brick building dating from 1874 that still stands behind the Parliament Buildings. The Armoury's designer (and local militia man), Colonel William Ridgeway Wilson, was born in China and trained as an architect in Liverpool and London. He showed unexpected flair by casting the main entrance in the style of a Moorish medieval fortress—a swerve from his conservative Gothic Revival mode seen at the Church of St. John the Divine, built in 1912 at 1611 Quadra Street.

The Armoury, whose appearance recalled the equally crenellated old colonial police barracks and jail that stood in Bastion Square, seems incongruous now, but it was built in an era when architects emphasized their designs to express their function: banks boasted Greek columns to declare their liquidity and solidity; business barons' homes were built like feudal estates; government buildings were buttressed with the stonework of the Roman Empire. The Armoury, complete with medieval-style portcullis, also looks its part. Warfare and imperial military service never seemed so noble and boyish a calling as they do here.

Like similar buildings across the country, the Armoury marked the increase in Canadian military assistance to the Empire following the Boer War. In 1899 when the Boer War began, 10,000 loyal citizens lined the wharves of the Inner Harbour and sang "Onward Christian Soldiers" as twenty-six British Columbia volunteers embarked for Vancouver and South Africa (the mining town of Ladysmith was later named by James Dunsmuir for the relief of the siege of Ladysmith, South Africa in 1900). Few in the jingoistic crowd were informed about the issues that provoked the war. Even fewer at the Inner Harbour send-off chose to think about a controversial anti-imperial editorial that had run in the *Victoria Times* in 1898, condemning Lord Kitchener's response to the uprising in the Sudan. The editor wrote: "Great Britain is waging one of those dirty little stock exchange wars of hers along the Nile, and her soldiery are butchering the inhabitants . . . with a diligence any slaughter-house employee might envy . . . 'victory' of the British and Egyptian troops over the dervishes [is] as bloody and disgusting a story of murder as we have ever read." But the commanders of Bay Street's buttressed, castellated

TOP *Officers of the BC Brigade of Garrison Artillery pose as if in the officers' club, c. 1886 (the painted backdrop and floor reveals this as a studio photograph). While the troops manned Victoria's coastal defence batteries in dreary isolation at Fort Rodd, life for the officers in Victoria was as relaxed as the picture shows; the coastal batteries never fired an angry shot.* BCARS A–06533

BOTTOM *James Douglas organized Victoria's first militia in 1855. Along with Royal Marines based at Esquimalt, it was the backbone of the colony's defence in the mid-nineteenth century. The militia included an all-black brigade, the Victoria Pioneer Rifle Corps, formed in 1860 and nicknamed the "Africa Rifles." Its recruits were mainly Americans who arrived during the 1858 gold rush.* BCARS C–06124

redoubt, one of the largest of its type in the country, would not have been wounded by this account of the Battle of Omdurman at a time when Canada accepted its allegiance to the empire—and its architectural follies—as readily as soldiers of the queen obeyed their orders.

·⊂ MISSIONARIES & CHURCHES ⊃·

Visitors sailing into the Inner Harbour in the late nineteenth century might have wondered if the panorama they saw—a skyline bristling with spires and bell towers—was less the result of Rattenbury's "Imperial Garden of Eden" and more a vision of Christianity firmly planted: there were churches of every kind and architectural style. From 1873 until 1913, a Sunday closing rule was observed despite occasional opposition. One letter-writer, however, complained to the *Colonist* in 1910 that citizens' attention to the Garden of Eden was taken more seriously than attending sermons: "Go around our city any Sabbath and you will see the residents cultivating gardens, mowing the lawns, trimming the shrubs, flowers and fruit trees, repairing buildings and painting fences . . . such habits are religiously immoral, and religion being the foundation of morality, it would appear that our moral standard is very low."

Church missionaries never doubted their moral standards or purpose. While their city colleagues erected Gothic Revival churches and congregations pottered in their gardens, missionaries of all denominations were toughing it out on the northwest coast to bring Christian ways to Native cultures that, from their standpoint, seemed barbarous, primitive and pagan. Missionaries learned indigenous languages and spared no midnight oil in spreading their propaganda: a copy of St. John's Gospel translated into Tsimshian in 1889 by Bishop William Ridley of Caledonia is still displayed in a glass case in Christ Church Cathedral. Victoria was the port where missionaries from Europe disembarked, the port from which they sailed for Indian villages up the coast, and the port to which they would return on leave or to consult with their bishops. No visitor looked upon the city's spires with quite the same feeling of reassurance as the missionary on a steamer's deck after a long coastal posting.

Roman Catholic Bishop Modeste Demers's intention, when he arrived in Victoria in 1852, to civilize the "poor children of the forest" was typical of the benevolent condescension dispensed by the Oblates of Mary Immaculate, who established a mission at Esquimalt in 1858, and the Sisters of St. Ann in Victoria. But the mutual curiosity of early encounters gave way to suspicion and conflict. The Church of England's "Society for the Propagation of the Gospel in Foreign Parts" was unambiguous in its theological and imperial quest: when the Anglican Church Missionary Society arrived in Victoria in 1857 it was determined to "overthrow the dark spiritualism and plant instead Christian truth," and "change the natives from ignorant bloodthirsty cruel savages into quiet useful subjects of our Gracious Queen."

Indian children were taken from their parents and forced to attend residential schools, the first of which was opened by the Roman Catholic Church in 1861 at Mission, BC. In the 1880s the Department of Indian Affairs' policy was to assimilate the Indians into a white society which few desired to join. Some missionaries criticized government policy but failed to see their own behaviour as equally presumptuous. Driven by conviction that often became arrogance, they discredited the Indians' potlatch ceremony and other traditions essential to tribal self-confidence and community stability. Above the pulpit in the church at Metlakatla Mission, a frontier Gothic piece of town planning designed to save the Indians from booze and perdition, Father William Duncan of the Church Missionary Society strung a huge banner across the nave ordering his flock: "THOU SHALT CALL HIS NAME JESUS. HE SHALL SAVE HIS PEOPLES FROM THEIR SINS."

Duncan came to Victoria from England in 1857 as the Anglican Church Missionary Society's pioneer, stayed with Dean Cridge for three months, before launching himself into the "lonely grandeur" of the north coast. He first founded a mission at Fort Simpson, a Hudson's Bay Company trading post, but in 1862 he set up his own commune at Metlakatla, in the words of traveller Newton Chittenden, "for the purpose of greater isolation . . . where he had gathered about 1,000 . . . and through firm Government and faithful secular and religious training raised them from barbarism to the condition of civilised people." Metlakatla Mission was "a neat village of about 150 houses, beautifully situated upon the Tsimpsheean peninsula . . . a large, fine church and school-house . . . a store, Salmon Cannery, and Sawmill."

Duncan's messianic discipline and radical social philosphy were tolerated by the church until he fell out with Bishop Ridley over church procedure and, like a Moses of the Northwest Coast, took his flock to Alaska. When Duncan "found . . . a great want of suitable hymns for the heathen," in the church's books, he composed his own. On one occasion in Victoria he persuaded Judge Begbie to return four convicted Natives to his care rather than have them confined in jail, a request that had less to do with the Indians' welfare than with Duncan keeping his power and control over them. And yet, when he left for Alaska he did not have to force the Natives to follow. Many Indians adopted to the missionaries' new ways. At Metlakatla, Duncan attempted to establish an economically self-sufficient community engaged in fish canning, spinning, weaving and handicrafts. For a while he succeeded, but ultimately his Utopia was flooded by the cheaper factory-made products that flowed up the coast from Victoria, San Francisco and Vancouver.

Less strident than Duncan, but no less self-righteous, was Methodist Thomas Crosby, ordained in Victoria in 1880. Crosby was born in Yorkshire in 1840 and emigrated with his parents to Ontario in 1856. He moved to Victoria in 1862, taught at Nanaimo Methodist School and began a coastal mission by dugout canoe. Images of Crosby paddling up the coast in all weathers and drifting alone into every desolate fjord linger as a montage of his remarkable resolve. With his wife, he ran the Fort Simpson mission from 1874 until 1897 and obtained a ship, the *Glad Tidings*, a 71-foot steam schooner built for him in 1884 by William Oliver at New Westminster. Oliver, a Clydeside ship's carpenter not unknown in the taverns of Wharf Street, became Crosby's Man Friday and loyally sailed north after fitting the ship with a steam engine in Victoria. During his career Crosby built churches, schools and mission houses in fourteen coastal communities. Five United Church mission ships were named after him, the last of which was retired in 1993.

Like his colleagues, Crosby instructed the Indians to destroy their totem poles, abandon their communal lodgings, move into European-style dwellings and worship in Gothic churches. Missionaries insisted that the Indians give up their sacred poles and masks as proof that they had become good Christians. Crosby was aware that the changes he introduced were severe, but pronounced: "I cannot have anything to do with the old ways. The dance, the potlatch, et cetera. It is all bad." In their effort to convert the Indians to Christianity, missionaries made them dispose of their ceremonial relics, and collaborated with collectors in removing them. Crosby became a collector himself, an activity that has since blemished his reputation. While he ostentatiously burnt some of the Tsimshian people's poles, he assembled a collection of tribal treasures in the 1880s during his voyages up and down the coast, and sold most of them to a Pennsylvania oil mogul in 1908.

Few churchmen of the time acknowledged or even recognized the loose moral ground they stood on, but some outrages could not be ignored. When the collector George A. Dorsey shipped twenty-two boxes of coastal Native possessions to Chicago from Victoria in 1897, the Reverend J. H. Keen wrote to the *Colonist* to expose "the rascal's . . . wholesale plunder . . . Bones and other things have been removed whole-sale . . . the perpetrators had not even the grace to cover up their excavations." Native nations are now campaigning to have the items returned, and the activities of Crosby and other missionaries and collectors have returned to haunt clergymen, museum curators, and the heirs to nineteenth-century private collections. Few can agree on whether artifacts were given away, bought or stolen; the Anglican Church returned five artifacts in its possession to the Nisga'a people in 1993, but only after it proposed selling them to pay for church renovations—which caused a furor in Victoria.

IN 1859 THE CHURCH OF ENGLAND appointed the Reverend George Hills as Bishop of British Columbia to administer parishes on Vancouver Island and the mainland. Hills found Victoria gasping after being struck by gold fever, and he was able to exercise more authority than his predecessors who had been mere chaplains at the Hudson's Bay Company fort. Hills was supported by an endowment from Baroness Angela Burdett-Coutts, an English aristocrat and banking heiress who funded churches throughout the empire, but her money did not offer him immediate comfort when he arrived in Esquimalt in 1860. He had to trudge through knee-deep mud to Victoria, where he was greeted coolly by Governor James Douglas. Undaunted, Hills buckled down to his first task, to erect a church and clergy house. Baroness Angela Burdett-Coutts's fund had already paid for a church but the building, manufactured in London in cast- and corrugated-iron sections for shipment to the colony, was still en route when Hills arrived, and he settled for the Dean Cridge's frame church, built in 1856 on Church Hill. This burned to the ground in 1869 and was replaced in 1872 with a wooden Gothic cathedral that became a landmark for mariners. It also became the setting for the schism between

The Reverend George Hills, seated in his rectory in an appropriately Gothic-style straight-backed armchair, c. 1874. Even the fireplace screen is decorated with a religious scene. Hills, who built a wooden Gothic cathedral in 1872 on Church Hill to dominate his parish, found his architectural efforts rivalled by William Duncan of the Church Missionary Society. St. Paul's Anglican Church, which Duncan completed at Metlakatla in 1874, held 1,200 worshippers—more than any church in Victoria at the time. BCARS G-03832

*St. Andrew's Roman Catholic Cathedral was designed by
Montreal architects Perrault & Mesnard and dedicated in 1892.
The pair never set foot in Victoria. But their High Victorian
Gothic essay, with its soaring 175-foot steeple and elaborate
polychrome decoration, captured the spirit of the age and the
ambitious city over which it rose.* RW

Hills and his assistant Dean Cridge that led to a breakaway church being
formed in 1874.

As well as sending Hills a church, Baroness Burdett-Coutts sponsored
the British Columbia Emigration Society's bride ship *Tynemouth*, which
brought eligible young ladies to populate the colony. Angela College,
built in 1865 as an Anglican girls' school and very English "ladies'
deportment academy," was named in the baroness's honour. The red
brick house was designed by John Wright in the Anglican Church's hallmark Victorian Gothic Revival style and the building, at 923 Burdett
Avenue, was bought by the Sisters of St. Ann in 1959. Angela College
and similar brick buildings in Victoria look as if they have been shipped
from the streets of London (English bricks, Scottish granite and cast iron
were imported to Victoria as ship's ballast until the 1870s, when brickworks were established in the city and quarries were opened on the
coast).

When the Bishop's "Iron Church" was unloaded in 1860, it was erected at the corner of Douglas and Fisgard streets. The prefabricated structure was dismantled in 1912 when the site was sold to the Hudson's Bay
Company for its grand new department store. The Iron Church's pieces
were salvaged and recycled by local homeowners and its organ inherited
by St. Paul's, Esquimalt. Proceeds from the sale of the site paid for the
Church of St. John the Divine, an elaborate replacement designed by
Colonel William Ridgeway Wilson at 1611 Quadra Street. Wilson stuck
to well-trodden ground during his architectural career, with the notable
exception of the Bay Street Armoury. When the equally conservative

Anglicans commissioned him to design the new church in 1912, Wilson re-created an image of mid-Victorian England: the church's offset copper steeple and brick and stone polychrome effect echoed the High Victorian Gothic style fashionable in Britain thirty years before.

CHURCH DENOMINATIONS chose building styles that reflected their religious, cultural and geographical origins, as well as prevailing architectural taste. Scottish Baronial and German Romanesque decoration and commemorative stained glass windows do their best to relieve the dour demeanour of St. Andrew's Presbyterian Church, at Broughton and Douglas streets, designed by the well-named English architect Leonard Buttress Trimen in 1888. Trimen also designed several notable homes in a brief career. Victoria's first Tudor Revival villa, Ellesmere, at 1321 Rockland Avenue, built for merchant James Angus in 1889, was his calling card; Ashnola, a rambling, now demolished Jacobean mansion built in 1891 for Emily Dunsmuir, one of Robert Dunsmuir's daughters, was his posthumous fame (he died in 1891). The Angus home's Tudor style paved the way for Samuel Maclure, Victoria's best-known residential architect, who exploited the style's cultural references just as church architects adapted their buildings to religious ones. Coincidentally, Maclure met his wife-to-be, Margaret Simpson, at St. Andrew's where her stepfather, Reverend Macleod, was the minister.

ST. ANDREW'S ROMAN CATHOLIC CATHEDRAL, dedicated in 1892 at 740 View Street by Dutch-born Bishop John Nicholas Lemmens, was designed by Montreal architects Messrs. Maurice Perrault & Albert Mesnard. Remarkably sensitive to the milieu of a place they had never seen, the Montreal designers adapted thirteenth-century French Gothic style to Victoria's nineteenth-century British setting, an architectural entente that created the city's most elaborately decorated religious building and one that, despite its mélange, is the most gracefully proportioned. The rose window, deep set in the French facade; the soaring 175-foot steeple patterned with polychrome tiles in nineteenth-century English manner; the chateauesque north tower crested with cast iron, and stone coursing on the brickwork—all happily blend English and Continental High Victorian Gothic fashion. The offset effect of the tall steeple and shorter north tower was intended not only to be "picturesque" but also to imitate the unfinished appearance of many European medieval cathedrals. The overall design was based on a church the architects had built at Vaudreuill, Quebec.

The interior glows with stained glass and resonates to the sound of a Casavant organ installed in 1907. Massive plaster-covered wooden and cast-iron columns hold up the fan-vaulted ceiling and the balcony. The superb stained glass windows feature biblical scenes and figures and were crafted in Toronto and Portland. The ebullient Assumption window, installed in 1892, was made by the Royal Bavarian Art Institute, Munich. St. Andrew, whose sculpture was originally mounted outside above the rose window, is featured in glass behind the altar whose ceiling, until liturgical changes were invoked in the 1960s, was painted midnight blue and sparkled with a myriad of gilt stars. A new altar—whose design would be repudiated by the missionaries of the nineteenth century—blends Christian and Native themes and imagery. The past is now fossilized in the crypt where the remains of Bishop Modeste Demers, his successor, Archbishop Charles John Seghers, and Father John Jonckau, a pioneering priest, are interred.

METROPOLITAN METHODIST CHURCH rises up from the corner of Quadra Street and Pandora Avenue in a startling sequence of bartizans and baronial turrets. The architect Thomas Hooper visited cities in eastern Canada and the United States during the early 1890s and applied to this church much that was fresh in his mind when he returned. Hooper introduced contemporary Richardsonian Romanesque to the city. The style was named after Henry Hobson Richardson, the American architect who revived and reinterpreted medieval church architecture of Provence and tailored it to nineteenth-century America. Richardson worked in Boston and Chicago in the 1870s and 1880s, where he designed churches and commercial buildings. His style was characterized by heavily rusticated stonework, medieval carved column capitals, cavernous arched entrances and rhythmic arched windows. Hooper's spiky version of it introduced a fairy-tale silhouette of Loire chateau/Scottish Baronial towers and turrets as a fanciful foil to the Romanesque rustication. The interior's curving gallery, supported on cast-iron columns manufactured by Albion Iron Works, is illuminated by a coloured glass rose window shipped from London, Ontario. An organ from Quebec was installed in 1910 above Renaissance wood panelling.

If Victorian Gothic was the prevailing British Imperial style then Richardson established the American one. Imitations in his manner sprang up across the continent, bringing robust urbanity to frontier settlements and grandeur to eastern cities. When the competition to design Victoria's Parliament Buildings was judged in 1892, several elaborate plans in the Richardson mood were unrolled from the submitted portfolios, including Francis Rattenbury's winning design.

TEMPLE EMANUEL, at Blanshard and Pandora, was designed by John Wright in the antique Romanesque style that was favoured by the Jewish faith. The temple (the oldest surviving synagogue in Canada and the oldest church of any denomination in continuous use in BC) was seen as a symbol of Victoria's growing social sophistication when it was begun in 1863. The St. Andrew's Society, the French Benevolent Society, the German Choral Society, the Masonic Lodge and Mayor Harris were present when Colonial Chief Justice Cameron laid the foundation stone. The *Colonist* thought that the ceremony, led by the band of HMS *Topaz*, evidence "by all classes of our community [of] hearty goodwill and brotherly feeling" The temple served Victoria's growing community of around one hundred Jews, most of whom had emigrated to the US from Europe, and who had come north from San Francisco during the 1858 gold rush. Some were British-born: Victoria's second mayor, Lumley Franklin, was the son of a Liverpool banker; his brother, Semlin, became the first Jewish member of the Legislative Assembly. Most came from Germany and eastern Europe as headstone names and places—Leiser, Franck and Lezack; Odessa, Saxony and Bavaria—at the Jewish Cemetery testify. The cemetery, opened in 1860 on a leafy plateau at Fernwood Road and Cedar Hill Road, is the oldest of its kind in the province.

·◁ QUADRA STREET BURIAL GROUND ▷·

No site in Victoria has quite the palpable spirit of the past as the old Quadra Street burial ground on the north slope of Church Hill, where Bishop Hills built his first cathedral. Here, along formal pathways and among mature trees and faded obelisks, are the ghosts of old Victoria. During the gold rush of 1858, the original pioneers' burial ground outside Fort Victoria was sold, partly because the land was more profitably used for buildings but also because the buried bodies were being unearthed by stray dogs and foraging pigs. Governor James Douglas had the remains disinterred, among them those of his former lieutenant Charles Ross, and re-buried at a new cemetery on Quadra Street. Ross was later joined by the colony's first Chief Justice, David Cameron, and HBC poineer John Wark.

Gravediggers at the Quadra Street burial ground were rarely unemployed. Many of the European pioneers were already middle-aged when they moved to Victoria: Douglas was forty when he founded Fort Victoria in 1843. Burials averaged one a week until 1873, by which time the cemetery was full. A new site at Ross Bay was opened that year; the Quadra Street burial ground was fenced off and all but the tallest tombstones were consumed by tangled undergrowth. In 1909 the city voted to turn the neglected site into a public park. Slightly off the beaten track, it remains a surprising space whose nineteenth-century Neo-classical memorials, and the adjacent Gothic hulk of Christ Church Cathedral, lend the old burial ground the atmosphere of an English churchyard or a hidden Parisian necropolis.

Although burials ceased in 1873, the ashes of Dr. J. S. Helmcken were placed by his wife's grave in 1920. There are more recently erected memorials to Royal Navy sailors based at Esquimalt from 1846–68, and to members of the Canadian Scottish Regiment who were killed in the First World War. But a patina of moss, lichen and decay laps the older granite and sandstone monuments that still stand. Their weathered typography is, in some cases, as eroded and obscure as inscriptions in ancient Rome. Few remember the anonymous Chinese who were consigned to a corner of the graveyard, or Thomas Pritchard, native of Abergavenny, Wales, died 1883, whose Neo-classical tomb's crumbling sandstone is decorated with ecclesiastical Gothic script and an ornamental pineapple, an exotic embellishment of the time. A stone obelisk bearing a masonic compass and set square marks Andrew Phillips, native of Arbroath, Scotland, died 1870, now unknown. Never known were three newborn children buried in 1860, 1861 and 1862 by their "fond and forlorn mother," Ellen Carroll. Victoria is old enough, just, to have such melancholy buried beneath living memory.

·⇐ CHRIST CHURCH CATHEDRAL ⇒·
900 Quadra Street

When the bell-ringers practise in the gloaming, seventy-one spiral steps above Christ Church Cathedral's shadowy buttresses, the sounds of medieval London thunder over rooftops, bounce around corners and

Stained glass panels in Christ Church Cathedral illustrate secular and religious life in early Victoria. The architecture panel shows the cathedral being planned—with the completed building outside the window (top left). RW

RCHITECTUR

echo down lanes across the city. No aspect of Victoria's Englishness is more convincing than the peal of Christ Church Cathedral's bronze bells, replicas of those at Westminster Abbey. Eight were installed in 1936; Queen Elizabeth II and the Duke of Edinburgh attended a ceremony when two more were installed in 1983. Cast at the Whitechapel Bell Foundry, makers of Big Ben's chimes, the bells were so heavy that hoists from Yarrows shipyard at Esquimalt were needed to raise them and their supporting steel girders up to the belfry. The biggest bell weighs one and a half tons.

It took thirty years before Christ Church Cathedral received the bells that would match its status as the Episcopal Seat of the Bishop of the Diocese of British Columbia. Plans for the cathedral were unveiled in 1896 when a design by architect John Charles Malcolm Keith was chosen after an international competition. Keith's delight at winning the contest was deflated when, after he moved from Seattle to supervise the work, he found that the church couldn't afford to start construction. Laying the first stone was delayed until 1926, and even then the building went up in fits and starts only when funds were available. The first service took place in the nave in 1929. The west front's twin towers were not completed until 1954; the apse was only finished in 1994 with the installation of a momentous stained glass window (by Christopher Wallis, an English artist who also designed the main window at Government House). Keith's other ecclesiastical commission of the time, a Gothic Revival design for the First Presbyterian Church, at 1411 Quadra Street, was also bedevilled by delay. The contractor went bust and services had to be held in the church hall until the main building was completed in 1915. Keith also designed Fisgard Street police station, built in 1920 in English Edwardian Neo-classical style.

Christ Church Cathedral's lofty Gothic Revival interior, based on medieval English religious architecture, was intended as a symbolic connection with the old country. RW

Keith, a clergyman's son, was born in Nairn, Scotland in 1858, and trained as an architect in Inverness and London before emigrating to California. Keith's design for Christ Church Cathedral (for which he was made Fellow of the Royal Institute of British Architects) was based on medieval Gothic cathedrals in France and England—particularly Durham and Lincoln (which he knew from his schooldays)—and was intended to be equally monumental. Steel-reinforced concrete columns clad in stone, Gothic arches, rib-vaulting, and exterior flying buttresses were built to support a massive square central tower that would have risen 185 feet above the nave, had it been built. But the money ran out and Victoria was denied not just a monumental tower but a leaning one as well—examination of the cathedral's foundations in the 1980s, when the apse was being built, revealed that the ground would have shifted beneath the tower's weight. Nevertheless, Christ Church Cathedral is a striking building despite the missing tower. The solidity of the stonework, the inscriptions around the walls in the typographic style of medieval illuminated manuscripts, the flying buttresses and the Gothic Revival interior with soft stained glass illumination gave the Anglicans the symbolic connection with the old country that was intended.

The windows surpass even those in the Parliament Buildings in variety and quality. The rose window was designed and made in London. The north aisle windows, illustrating the twelve apostles, were made by James Ballantine of Edinburgh. Those on the south aisle, by an English artist, J. E. Nuttgens, show figures in church history from biblical and Roman times to seventeenth-century England, and were exhibited at the Royal Academy before being sent to Victoria in 1929. Lively vignettes in smaller panels above both aisles illustrate secular life and work; those on the north aisle, in Arts and Crafts style, illuminate life in turn-of-the-century Victoria with images of the Fur Trade, Exploration, Mining, Engineering, Poetry, Law, Lumbering, Farming, Architecture, Art, Industry and Fishing. The more formally styled south panels show Literature, Medicine, Science, Astronomy, Music, The Sacred Ministry,

College and School. The windows also commemorate the local worthies who paid for them. The pulpit was carved from a 500-year-old oak felled in Sussex for the purpose. The wrought-iron choir screen, reputedly designed by Sir George Gilbert Scott, came from Westminster Abbey. The chapel's bishop's chair was given by St. Paul's Cathedral. Arthur Foley Winnington Ingram, the Bishop of London who had raised funds toward construction, accepted an invitation to lay the foundation stone, which was salvaged from the previous cathedral built across the street in 1872. The old cathedral's portable organ, shipped around Cape Horn in 1862, stands in the Lady Chapel. Military flags hang in the cathedral—a graphic illustration of the concord between the English church and state that provided the moral force to guide British imperialism through the nineteenth century. The seven lancet windows on the west front represent Anglican dioceses in Palestine, India, China and Japan.

A more famous hand than the Bishop of London's laid a stone in 1929 when, as the *Colonist* reported, "the RT. HON. Winston Churchill and his party visited Christ Church." The "superintendent of the work suggested to the British ex-Chancellor that, since he held a union card, the masons would be very pleased if he would lay a stone in the north-west tower . . . Mr. Churchill's answer was immediately to shin up the ladder and get to work. Remarking that he 'found the mortar a little stiff,' Mr. Churchill used the level in the true professional style and well and truly laid the stone." But the most charming aspect of the somewhat chilly building is the story of the robin that flew in during construction and made a nest among the half-built columns. The masons waited until the bird's brood had hatched and, in the manner of their brethren who anonymously carved the elaborate details on the medieval cathedrals of Europe, they later fashioned an image of the bird and its nest on the nave's southeastern column capital. ✒

Rockland & Oak Bay

NEVER, EVEN ON ITS BEST DAYS, [HAS IT] BEEN A COMFORTABLE
PLACE . . . DRAUGHTS PENETRATE ALL PARTS . . . FIRES IN ALL
ROOMS FAIL TO OVERCOME THE COLD AND DAMP. . . IN THE
SELECTION OF A SITE FOR THE GUBERNATORIAL MANSION ALL
OTHER CONSIDERATIONS WERE SACRIFICED TO VIEW AND
SITUATION—*The* Colonist's *opinion of Cary Castle, 1888*

ROCKLAND

AFTER Captain Henry Bailey Ella, a native of London, came
to Victoria in 1851 as First Officer on the Hudson's Bay Company vessel *Norman Morrison* with settlers to the colony, he
stayed on and helped chart coastal waters for the Admiralty. Ella built
Wentworth Villa in 1862 at 1156 Fort Street, a grandly named but modest
home that was one of the first built on upper Fort Street. Ella's villa, built
with California redwood, was designed in Picturesque Gothic pattern
book style by John Wright (who had used a pattern book for Point Ellice
House and the Carr House around the same time). When the house was
completed, Ella and his family had a clear view from their verandah, west
to the town and south toward Beacon Hill and the sea, across a patchwork

*Businessman Biggerstaff Wilson knew only one way to express
his perceived status when he commissioned a home from society
architect Samuel Maclure. An English manor house was what
he wanted, and in 1905 that is what he got.* RW

landscape of moorland, Garry oak meadows, dairy pasture and scattered homes. Upper Fort Street remained a small residential cluster until James Douglas's neighbouring Fairfield Estate was sold and subdivided into ten-acre properties in the 1880s. Rockland, as the area became known, developed as an exclusive residential suburb. In 1885 Robert Dunsmuir set the district on an upward course when he commissioned Craigdarroch Castle for the top of what soon became Victoria's Knob Hill—a status that was confirmed in 1903 when Samuel Maclure collaborated with Francis Rattenbury to build a new Government House nearby. Above St. Charles Street, the city's poshest properties even had their own water tower, erected in 1909 and styled like a classical folly.

Rockland was where the fortunes made by mining moguls, coal field conquistadors and railway rulers were spent; where department store dukes, nouveau-riche brewery and biscuit barons, and Union Club members chose to stay. Regent's Place, an Italianate villa at 1501 Fort Street, was built in 1885 for David Williams Higgins, a newspaper publisher, tramway company director and member of the legislature. Ellesmere, at 1321 Rockland Avenue, was designed in 1889 in Tudor style for James Alexander Angus, a Scottish merchant and brother of Richard Angus, the CPR and Bank of Montreal executive. Illahie—designed by Samuel Maclure—was built in 1907 in the style of an Elizabethan mansion at 1041 St. Charles Street, for Charles Fox Todd, heir to the Horseshoe Brand Salmon cannery. The house at 1005 St. Charles was designed in 1910 for Simon Leiser, a German-born coffee, spice and grocery merchant. Rockland's residents prospered in different ways, but they arrived at a unanimity of taste in the homes they built.

Many of Victoria's early homes were designed from pattern books, the most influential of which was written by an American landscape architect, Andrew Jackson Downing, who transposed the English "picturesque" fashion for quaint Gothic and Italianate cottages and villas set in natural landscapes to North American settings. The design that inspired Wentworth Villa's pitched roof, delicate Gothic tracery, bargeboard ornament and bracketed single-storey porch was illustrated as a "Cottage in the English, or rural Gothic Style" in Downing's *Cottage Residences* published in 1842. Similar books had been published in London. Downing distilled their message and guided American and Canadian architectural taste for half a century. For $50, builders could receive a Downing plan by mail. Downing hoped his book would be "a precursor of more varied and complete works from others," and his work was imitated by other publishers and manufacturers—if not to the standards he set. By the 1890s his ideas were being mass marketed as homes for the hoi polloi. In the 1860s Victoria's architects and builders had been able to sell Downing's Tuscan villas and English cottages as being fit for the gentry. But by the 1890s the discriminating classes who moved to Rockland were more sophisticated in their taste. What the nouveau riche wanted were architect-designed homes that would confirm their British identity—and in Samuel Maclure, not Andrew Downing, they found their style and their man.

·⇐ WILSON HOUSE ⇒·
1770 Rockland Avenue

In the nineteenth century, architectural styles were chosen not just as an expression of social status or aesthetic taste but also for their association with culture and ideas. Roman works were copied in the United States as exemplars of a society noted, as ancient Rome was, for government and civic pride; Greek architecture signified stability, liberty, law and order; Gothic symbolized religion and learning; Renaissance represented trade. The same themes were explored and exploited by architects in Victoria and throughout the British Empire, but with more debate and ultimate confusion. Gothic and Classical architecture vied with each other in a mid-nineteenth-century "battle of the styles" that resulted in Gothic or Renaissance railway stations, carpet factories, textile mills and town halls whose appearance depended more on fashionable whim than symbolism.

These ideas, in all their variety, filtered down to residential architecture. A banker or business baron like Biggerstaff Wilson in Victoria wanting to project a cultivated or aristocratic image would commission an Italianate or Tudor Revival home. A more idiosyncratic owner, like Captain Jacobsen in Esquimalt, might choose a sugary Second Empire villa and insist on decorating it with the imagery of his trade. Rockland's Italianate, Georgian and Dutch Colonial, Craftsman, Swiss Chalet, and Arts and Crafts homes reflect the turn-of-the-century freedom to use style for its own sake.

In Victoria, no style achieved the popularity of Tudor Revival and the preferred practitioner was Samuel Maclure. Maclure built so many houses in Edwardian Victoria that anything with Tudor timbering tends to be ascribed to him by local real estate agents: when they advertise "Maclure style" properties everyone knows what they mean. By one estimate, he designed over 500 houses, many of which still stand; he even designed workers' cottages at Clayburn in the Fraser Valley, the site of his brothers' brickworks. Of the 500 homes perhaps 10 percent were top-notch. Many of them were built in Rockland, none more characteristic of his oeuvre than Biggerstaff Wilson's home.

Biggerstaff Wilson's father was William Wilson, an English gold rush pioneer merchant who ran a store that still stands at Trounce Alley and Government Street. Biggerstaff Wilson worked for the Bank of British Columbia, inherited money from England, married the daughter of the owner of the Victoria Phoenix Brewery, and ran a cold storage company. When he commissioned a new home from Maclure he knew only one way to express his social status. An English medieval manor house was what he wanted, and in 1905 that is what he got. The house is Victoria's finest expression of Tudor Revival, by the architect who made the style his stock in trade. The building is more than just another of the "little bits of Old England" so dear to the city's heart. Maclure took the worn-out, transplanted late-Victorian revival style and used it for more than just nostalgic fancy dress to satisfy his clients' dreams of living to the manor born. He managed to breathe new life into its hackneyed halls. Canadian architects could avail themselves of the latest Arts and Crafts fashions or William Morris wallpaper pattern by subscribing, as Maclure did, to British journals like *The Studio*. But what the *The Studio* could not teach was instinctive use of space. Maclure was a master of space and volume, particularly when designing grand central halls around which all rooms were arranged. He had a passion for picturesque rooflines and portes-cochère. But he also had more talent than contemporary copyists. When he moved away from his Tudor Revival mode, designs influenced by the English Arts and Crafts movement, Californian Craftsman style and the early work of Frank Lloyd Wright, put him in the mainstream of progressive contemporary design.

Francis Rattenbury also designed houses for clients in Rockland, but he never matched Samuel Maclure's consistent popularity, although he too could be playfully experimental (one of Rattenbury's more adventurous residential designs, built in lively Arts and Crafts style in 1900, still stands at 1745 Rockland Avenue). Both Rattenbury and Maclure had a feel for the picturesque landscape settings of the homes they designed, and they used wood and stone in harmonious response—a balance that the architectural writer Andrew Jackson Downing called a "happy union between the locality or site, and the style chosen."

·⇐ ART GALLERY OF GREATER VICTORIA ⇒·
1040 Moss Street

The Victoria Art Gallery's collections are exhibited in contrasting buildings—the Spencer House, a nineteenth-century villa, and an adjoining modernist gallery. If the new gallery were built today it would probably be designed in fake heritage style. But in 1958, when it was begun, the notion that modern buildings should look the part was widely accepted. The art gallery is one of the few sites in the city where old and new coexist in honest architectural harmony. The small gallery is a treasure—not only for the way the layout blends old and new; North American and European paintings and furniture give an insight into local collectors' and wealthy homeowners' taste at the turn of the century; in the grounds there is an unexpected, almost secret, mossy garden decorated with a Shinto shrine.

Built in 1889 in Italianate style, but boasting a baronial galleried hallway, the villa's architectural foibles were the result of an unlikely team: Elmer H. Fisher, a Scottish immigrant, and English-trained William Ridgeway Wilson. Fisher moved to Seattle, where he was immediately successful as a metropolitan architect, and left the less talented Wilson to complete the job. Wilson's work was good enough for the villa to be a suitable temporary residence for the lieutenant governor after Cary Castle burned down in 1899. Originally built for Alexander Arthur Green, a local English banker and Wells, Fargo agent who had moved to Victoria from the Australian gold fields, the house was bought by David Spencer, the local department store owner, in 1910 and donated by his daughter to the gallery in 1951. The grounds once stretched from Fort Street to Rockland Avenue. The villa retains many oddly matched features: the wood-panelled baronial hall, complete with a fireplace decorated with Minton tiles illustrating the legend of King Arthur; rooms hung with Victorian salon paintings; Palladian windows; and a rooftop belvedere. The quirky interior gives the gallery the personality not of an exclusive institution, but of an eccentric club that meets for tea in the dining room to discuss the latest acquisitions. In addition to European work the gallery is noted for its extensive collections of Asian art, Native prints and carvings, and drawings and paintings by Victoria's most famous painter, Emily Carr.

Emily Carr, born in Victoria in 1871, was brought up in middle-class English manner in an Italianate house her merchant father built on Government Street. The pattern book property, where Carr spent her childhood playing in her father's fairy-tale English garden, seems far removed from the moody vivid paintings of totem poles and the coastal rain forest that she created in later life. Cast as the city's rebellious artist, struggling and ignored for much of her life, she has become as much a cultural icon as the totem poles that she painted. She has also been enrolled in the eccentrics' hall of fame, admired as having been a friend of the Indians when they had none among white society.

Carr's published memories of childhood are titled *The Book of Small*, "Small" being how she remembered herself. She was the youngest of five sisters but broke away from her family's Jane Austen expectations to study art in San Francisco during 1890–93. After she returned to Victoria she taught art to local children but the town's bourgeois society, with its nostalgia for a pre-industrial England that had long since changed, stifled her creative development. She later observed bleakly that her critics "had transported their ideas at the time of their migration, a generation or two back. They forgot that England, even conservative England, had crept forward since then." She resented the commonly held attitude that the Canadian wilderness was not worth painting and that the only place to study art was London or Paris. Nevertheless, she left for London in 1899, lodged with a friend's sister she called "Aunt Agatha" and attended the Westminster School of Art, a traditional institution that gave her a grounding in technique, if little else. On a holiday visit to Ucluelet in 1899 she had been stirred, and was later obsessed, by the brooding West Coast scenery and mystical culture of remote Indian settlements—terra incognita to her London tutors. She took her illustrations of coastal Native life to Frederick Warne, publisher of the Beatrix Potter books, but was turned down. Her view of the old country as "tame, self-satisfied and meek" was confirmed and the prospect of repressed married life either in England or at home was rejected.

Fin-de-siècle London was an imperial capital at the height of its prestige, but it was not an artistic one. For aspiring painters of the day, Paris was Europe's city of culture and enlightenment. Carr had been told that London was where Canadians went to have their "crude colonial ways given an English polish." But she was no more impressed by this than she had been by her father's genteel anglified Victoria. She felt more at home in the arboretums and exotic palm houses of Kew Gardens or on painting trips to the countryside than jostled by crowds at Piccadilly Circus, or mourning at Queen Victoria's funeral in 1901. Carr witnessed the event but was unmoved by the procession of attendant European royalty: "Kaiser William with his furious moustachios," and "mouse-like queens no one had ever heard of" gliding by as London's population "groaned and wept."

She returned to Victoria in 1904 and lived in Vancouver from 1906 to 1910. While saving for a trip to Paris she gave art lessons to schools and societies. She was a founding member of the British Columbia Society of Fine Arts, but did not last long teaching at the "Ladies' Art Club" from whose snobbish company she was happy to be dismissed. Compared to the Ladies' Art Club, the Native art she saw in Alaska, which she visited with her sister Alice in 1907, was an unpretentious and powerful reflection of her own personality. After a cruise up the coast she announced that she would "come up every summer among the villages of BC and I shall do all the totem poles and villages I can before they are a thing of the past." The totem poles were "real art treasures of a passing race," and she made several trips producing a series of vigorous watercolours of Indian villages.

In 1910, accompanied by Alice, Carr took the train to Montreal and sailed to Europe. She studied in Paris and painted in Brittany during 1910–11, tutored by the Scottish artist John Duncan Fergusson. While Carr was hardly the sophisticated café-culture bohemian, she absorbed enough post-impressionism to bring a freshness to her work. But she received scant recognition when she exhibited and sold only some slight but vividly coloured works of local scenes when she returned. She was dismayed by the prevailing public taste. Vancouver's citizens were just as provincial as Victoria's when it came to appreciating contemporary art. Carr's loose French sketches were scoffed at as children's work. She made a painting trip to the Queen Charlotte Islands in 1912. But her subject matter, Indian totem poles and northern forests, was not understood by a society reared on Victorian Highland scenes, which saw the aboriginals only as a wretched people. Her attempts to convey Native spirituality to the society that was trying to destroy it were ignored. She offered works for sale to the provincial government. These were declined on the advice of anthropologist Dr. Charles Frederic Newcombe who judged that Carr's artistry, "too brilliant and vivid to be true to the actual conditions of the coast villages," distorted their value to the Provincial Museum as objective topographical and cultural records.

Carr suffered a crisis of confidence after Newcombe's official rebuff. Her paintings were unacceptable as anthropological records and her new Franco-Scottish Colourist style had been dismissed as infantile. Like the Indians, she had been completely marginalized. The following year she opened a boarding house at 646 Simcoe Street on her father's old property, intending to use one room as a studio. Much to guests' alarm, she hung her paintings of totem poles in the dining room. "Grotesque monsters" was one comment in the visitors' book, although two Indian-style eagles she painted on the woodwork inside are now protected as a provincial heritage site. She devoted more time to her menagerie of pets than to her guests, or to her painting—she hardly touched a paintbrush until 1927, when she was approached by Eric Brown of the National Gallery in Ottawa who asked for fifty paintings for an exhibition on West Coast art and offered Carr an expenses-paid trip east. He also arranged for her to meet members of the Group of Seven, who shared her fascination with the northern Canadian landscape.

The attention and encouragement she received in 1928 plunged Carr into a turmoil that, on trips up the BC coast in the 1930s, resulted in an avalanche of mature work. Sketching on location, she captured Native imagery not as contemporary museum curators did by preserving the artifacts in glass cases, but with an intuitive sense of Natives' spiritual and physical world. Recalling one dream-like trip to the Queen Charlotte Islands, she wrote: "Tanoo, Skedans, and Cumshewa lie fairly close to each other on the map, yet each is quite unlike the others when you come to it. All have the West Coast wetness but Cumshewa seems to drip, always to be blurred with mist, its foliage always to hang wet-heavy. Cumshewa rain soaked my paper, Cumshewa rain trickled among my paints . . . totem poles were dark and colourless, the wood toneless from the pouring rain . . . moss-grown, dilapidated . . . rain turned their dust to mud . . . strong young trees were richer perhaps for that Indian dust . . . Our boat headed for the sea. As we rounded the point Cumshewa was suddenly like something that had not quite happened."

Carr's vivid journals were acclaimed when published, and *Klee Wyck*, her first book, received a Governor General's Award in 1941. She exhibited regularly at the Vancouver Art Gallery, which holds a large collection of her work, and attracted attention at the Tate Gallery, London. But throughout her career her home town proved arid ground. Even in the 1930s, by which time her work had been exhibited and praised in Toronto and Ottawa, she failed to receive her due. Victoria had no patrons who responded to the originality and quality of her work. When Provincial Secretary S. L. Howe commissioned a series of murals to decorate the rotunda in the Parliament Buildings in 1932, he chose the safe, unimaginative brushwork of the government's publicity artist George Southwell rather than Carr's fierce talent.

Little, it seemed, had changed since the *Colonist* had mocked modern

*Emily Carr, one of Canada's best-known painters, c. 1939.
Carr saw a gloom-laden beauty in the tangled dripping forests
and sudden sunbursts of the West Coast. Natives remembered her
as one of the few white people to take an inquisitive rather than
acquisitive interest in their culture. In her studio, or on painting
expeditions, she escaped from the chintz and teacups of her
English upbringing in James Bay. The title of the painting in
the background, "Sunshine and Tumult," sums up both her
personality and her career.* BCARS D–06009

art in 1912: "Gentle reader, are you a post-impressionist, a futurist, a cubist, or anything of that kind? We have been looking at some pictures that are described as belonging to these schools, and have reached the conclusion that either the people who painted them are crazy, or we are." Only a paper in a city like Victoria could have made such comment; only a city like Victoria could have moulded and, paradoxically, sustained an artist like Emily Carr. After a lifetime of emotional struggle, including curmudgeonly correspondence with gallery owners after her talent had been finally recognized, she died in 1945 in St. Mary's Priory, a Catholic home for senior citizens, now the James Bay Inn. She is buried beneath a modest marker in Ross Bay Cemetery, along with the respectable citizenry who ignored her work when she was alive.

·⇐ CRAIGDARROCH CASTLE ⇒·
1050 Joan Crescent

When Robert Dunsmuir hired Warren Heywood Williams of Portland, Oregon—whose previous effort in Victoria had been a faux Renaissance palazzo for the Bank of British Columbia—to design Craigdarroch Castle, the architect responded with an extravagant pile of whimsy designed to recall the baronial architecture of his client's native land. Legend has it that Dunsmuir promised his wife, Joan, a castle if she left Scotland with him in 1850. But locals who watched the rusticated retreat being built above the town understood its true meaning. Like peasants scoffing at their landlord's pretension, they dubbed it "Dunsmuir Castle" when it was completed in 1889 on the city's highest hill.

In 1885 Robert Dunsmuir, an Ayrshire coal miner who became the wealthiest man in the province, set Rockland on a fashionable course when he commissioned Craigdarroch Castle to remind him of his native Scotland on Victoria's highest hill.
BCARS D–03608

Robert Dunsmuir was a small-town Ayrshire coal mine manager who left Scotland in 1850 on a three-year contract with the Hudson's Bay Company to prospect for coal on Vancouver Island. When his contract expired he worked as a freelance manager for the HBC and then as mine superintendent for the London-based Vancouver Coal Mining and Land Company, which bought the HBC's operation in 1862. He resigned in 1869 after, it is said, tottering home from a binge at a local saloon and stumbling across an extensive coal seam near the sea north of Nanaimo. Convinced he had struck it rich, Dunsmuir made secret test bores, borrowed money from San Francisco moneylenders, and built a wagon road to transport the coal and a dock to load it.

Coal was the fuel of the nineteenth-century British Empire, and in 1870 Dunsmuir sold his first 65 tons to the Royal Navy. After a test on HMS *Boxer*, his coal was judged superior to his former employer's product. One ship's captain later said he would "steam halfway around the world" for it. Esquimalt was a coaling station as well as a base for the Royal Navy, and Dunsmuir's Wellington seam rivalled even Welsh coal for quality. The Admiralty in London became the first customer to help make his fortune. Still short of money, Dunsmuir took on partners, including Rear Admiral Farquhar, Commander at Esquimalt. In 1875 he signed a crucial deal to supply coal to the Pacific Mail Steamship Company, San Francisco. He expanded his port, bought a steam locomotive from Philadelphia and increased his work force. By his hard work, flinty character and good luck, and by the labour of his employees, he became the wealthiest man in the province, if not always the most well-liked. Eventually he capped his career with a seat in the provincial legislature. In its heyday, the Dunsmuir family's industrial empire included

Craigdarroch's American architect designed what he thought a Scottish Baronial home should look like. He certainly captured the moody romanticism of the time. Craigdarroch looks as if it leapt off the pages of a novel by Sir Walter Scott. RW

Legend has it that Robert Dunsmuir promised his wife, Joan, a castle if she left Scotland with him in 1850. He asked his architect to carve a Shakespearian epigram for her in Craigdarroch's hall: "Welcome ever smiles and Farewell goes out sighing." But Robert Dunsmuir was never welcomed at his hearth—he died before Craigdarroch was completed. It is his widow's doleful presence that permeates the castle's empty rooms to this day.

the Wellington and Cumberland coal mines, steamships, railways, iron works, sawmills, a quarry, and press and property investments.

Craigdarroch's architect designed what he thought a Scottish Baronial home should look like. He certainly captured the moody romanticism of the time. Craigdarroch looks as if it leapt off the pages of a novel by Sir Walter Scott. While Scottish Baronial broadly describes the spirit of the place, Scotch broth might best describe the home's eclectic style. The conical turrets and chateau-style slate roof blend sixteenth-century Scottish Baronial and French Loire styles; the decorative ironwork on the balconies is a typically Victorian embellishment; the rusticated stonework and arched windows are Richardsonian Romanesque; the irregular tall chimneys hark back to Tudor England. For good measure, there is a hint of Renaissance Italy in the columned porch that extends as a loggia halfway around the home. Williams died a few months after construction started and his partner, Arthur L. Smith, was left to make sense of the plans—a dining room door opens onto a four-foot drop—and to put the Scotch granite columns, sandstone and granite from Dunsmuir's quarries, and marble tiles from San Francisco in the right places.

Inside, beyond Craigdarroch Castle's porte-cochère and Minton-tiled vestibule, the hallway and salons establish the mansion's baronial pretension. The grand hall's stone fireplace, bronze bas-relief Highland scene, and stag and ram's heads trophies on the wood-panelled walls could be in a Scottish hunting lodge; the drawing room is lavishly plastered in Regency style; the library, dominated by a carved fireplace bearing the epigram "Reading Maketh the Full Man," is illuminated by Tiffany-style stained glass aglow with Scottish bluebells, thistles and hollyberries. The hall staircase is quite astonishing. The stairwell, with inglenooks on the landings where the servants would surreptitiously sit and catch their breath as they climbed, rises through four storeys to the full height of the home. Every surface of this giddy ascent is covered in what appears to be hand-carved wood panelling that would not disgrace the sumptuous Canadian Pacific Railway magnates' mansions in Montreal. Dunsmuir's baronial conceit, however—what poet John Betjeman, describing late-Victorian follies in England, called "ghastly good taste"—was an enjoyable sham. The stair's wood panelling was manufactured by Andrews and Company of Chicago, which from 1885 to 1895 employed 500 men in four factories where machines "churned out acres of fine panelling and marquetry flooring" to be dispatched by railway boxcars across the continent to glorify office lobbies, railway stations, churches and mansions. Craigdarroch, for all its fine stone carving and craftsmanship is, in this evocation of aristocratic life, the quintessential Victorian capitalist's fantasy—a mail-order ancestral home.

Although the town's older aristocracy thought the Dunsmuirs *arrivistes*, and feigned indifference toward the family's allure, Craigdarroch was the setting for society weddings. In 1891, when Jessie Sophia Dunsmuir, sixth daughter of Robert and Joan Dunsmuir, was married to Sir Richard John Musgrave, the *Victoria Times* found the occasion "the most fashionable and brilliant in Victoria's history . . . the body of Christ Church Cathedral was filled with invited guests, while hundreds of ladies, and dozens of gentlemen not so highly honoured, crowded the aisles, the churchyard and the streets. There were six bridesmaids. Twenty young lady friends and companions of the bride acted as her maids of honour. In the afternoon Sir Richard and Lady Musgrave, after the mystic knot had been tied by the Rev. Canon Beanlands, received between 200 and 300 of their friends at Craigdarroch Castle, the home of the bride, the fashionable company spending several hours in the palatial residence and its beautiful grounds. The band of HMS *Warspite* was present to enliven the proceedings . . . during the evening the newly wedded pair embarked on the steamer *Lorne*, which had been specially prepared for their accommodation, and which enjoyed the honour of conveying them to Vancouver. At the terminal city a private car will be taken for the east, en route to the ancestral home of the groom in Ireland."

Dunsmuir died in 1889 and left his entire fortune to his wife Joan, who promptly began to spend it on a trip to Europe while the castle was being completed. She lived in the mansion until she too died, in 1908. Today, polite lady guides inside recount how Joan Dunsmuir sat day after day, eighty-seven steps up in the turretted belvedere, alone with her thoughts and the local newspapers. These she perused for society gossip about her two sons, who had disputed the will; to seek eligible bachelors for her brood of daughters; and to stay well enough informed to run the family empire.

Robert Dunsmuir had risen from a $5-a-week HBC miner to lord of a commercial empire worth $15 million when he died. But his heirs, in the words of the Dunsmuirs' biographer Terry Reksten, "went from promise to obscurity in three generations." Craigdarroch's contents were sold at a spectacular auction in 1909. The estate, which extended from Fort Street to Rockland Avenue, was subdivided and the castle sold by lottery after the heirs could not agree who should keep their father's baronial folly. The lottery-winning land speculator went bust. In 1919 the house was reopened by the Prince of Wales as a military hospital for returning First World War soldiers. It was later occupied by a college and a music conservatory until the Craigdarroch Castle Historical Museum Society and the City of Victoria secured its future as a heritage site. The society has restored the home and refurbished it in original style, not without reverence for its original owner's achievements: Dunsmuir, the self-made man, would consider society's interpretation of these his due.

Robert Dunsmuir once said, "I have never allowed any man to get the better of me if I could help it, and I never go into any undertaking unless I can control it." In 1882 he was elected to the provincial legislature while tendering to build the Esquimalt & Nanaimo Railway, a political hot coal that the Dominion government was anxious to build to fulfill the Confederation promise of 1871. In 1883 he concluded the deal of the decade when he was granted a subsidy of $750,000, a land grant of two million acres and all mineral rights for building a railway seventy-five miles long. He seemed destined for high honours. But he was accused of treason after he made an injudicious remark in the legislature, which some members interpreted as support for annexation by the United States, and his chances of the expected knighthood were destroyed.

At Dunsmuir's funeral in 1889 the press reported that "the streets were thronged with people from every part of the province who had come to pay their last respects to the man who had done so much to promote the best interests of their common home." Funeral marchers assembled outside the Parliament Buildings, a host that included a military band, a miners' band, Wellington miners, St. Andrew's and Caledonian Society men, naval officers, politicians and friends. An estimated 12,000 people, half the city's population, witnessed the procession, which took half an hour to pass St. Andrew's Kirk on its way to Ross Bay Cemetery, where the "man of iron will and gigantic intellect used for the benefit of his fellow men," as the *Colonist* obituary chimed without irony, was buried.

Other commentators, and many of Dunsmuir's miners, thought his interests were exclusively his own. The first HBC miners, and many of their successors, were British and they brought their trade unions and labour activism from home (American trade unionists also worked in the Dunsmuir mines). Part of Dunsmuir's legacy was labour discontent which simmered and boiled over in a series of bitter strikes during his son James's reign. The clan's reputation was sullied: Dunsmuir mines eventually employed 3,000 miners who, in one activist's opinion, Dunsmuir "thinks . . . should be slaves." In 1876 the San Francisco steamship company that was his best customer reneged on its contract. Dunsmuir reduced wages rather than lay men off. The miners went on strike, but with no union they were forced to accept his terms. A more serious dispute began in 1877 after miners accused their employer of tampering with the weigh scales (miners were paid according to how much coal they dug), and bailiffs were called in to evict the strikers from the company shacks they rented. In a later strike, troops were sent to maintain order.

British Columbia's socialist politics have their roots in the Dunsmuir coal seams and the family's exploitation of the workers. The Dunsmuirs employed their countrymen, but came to prefer east European and Chinese labourers who were less likely to organize resistance. When the miners protested against low wages and squalid working and living conditions, Dunsmuir brought in strikebreakers from the waterfront bars of San Francisco. In his early days Dunsmuir was a decent employer and paid his men well, but he ran the mining communities on almost medieval principles of serfdom. Robert Dunsmuir's home was a castle in more ways than one.

·⇐ GOVERNMENT HOUSE ⇒·
1401 Rockland Avenue

Victoria dozed off around the turn of the century behind a half-timbered veneer of privilege and nostalgia that was not entirely the fabrication of the town's tourist trade. The city attracted an army of British residents, memorably described by a former *Victoria Times* reporter as "the remittance men, the old China hands, the burra sahibs of the Indian civil service and their mem sahibs, the retired Malayan or African policemen, the former tea planters from Ceylon and the rubber planters from Borneo . . . the ex-merchants of Hong Kong and Shanghai and Bombay . . . gunboat commanders who knew the road to Mandalay . . . battier British, those who regarded themselves as the chosen race . . . the élite of Victoria BC," a time when well-born citizens "acquired the English accent without ever having set foot in England."

Nowhere in Victoria were acquired and actual English accents more shrill than in the salons of Government House, the rambling residence of the queen's official representative, the Lieutenant Governor of British Columbia. The vice-regal appointee's duties no longer include dealing with wars, Indian affairs, foreign treaties and other momentous affairs of state, as they did when Governor Anthony Musgrave helped steer the colony into Confederation in 1871. Musgrave was the last Governor of British Columbia required to act with an imperial statesman's guile and determination. A Historic Sites and Monuments Board plaque in the rock garden at Government House summarizes Musgrave's colonial career: "Imperial Civil Servant . . . Governor of Newfoundland (1864–69) . . . B.C. (1869–71) . . . under his devotion B.C. entered the Dominion on July 20. 1871 . . . knighted in 1875, subsequently held vice-regal office in Natal, South Africa, Australia, Jamaica, and Queensland where he died." After Musgrave, the gubernatorial post became a provincial government rather than a London Colonial Office appointment. Opening flower shows and other minor social events are typical activities in the lieutenant governor's contemporary daily round, a recreational role accompanied by the panoply but not the power of imperial office that now seems somewhat Ruritanian. When he visits the Parliament Buildings he appears attired in plumed-hatted, gold-braided nineteenth-century fashion, preserving the illusion that the sun has not quite set on the British Empire.

The original residence was built by George Hunter Cary, the first Attorney General of the Colony of Vancouver Island, who was dispatched from England in 1859. Cary chose the bleak, blustery hilltop site and planned a private home befitting his status. But he had to scale down his architectural ambitions after his "Never Sweat Mine" in the Cariboo failed to provide enough funds. Before financial ruin brought the creditor to his door, Cary erected a three-storey, battlemented Norman keep and a porte-cochère. From this vantage, he could look down upon the town where he was ridiculed and twice arrested—for disorderly conduct while galloping across the James Bay bridge and on the Fort Street footpath. The irascible Cary was never afraid to throw down the gauntlet. Begbie thought "his rage and despair something almost frightful to see— if they were not also comical." Helmcken's diagnosis was that Cary was "not overburdened with the ordinary ideas of right and wrong . . . genius and madness in him were closely combined." After being dismissed by Douglas, Cary returned to England where he died insane.

When Arthur Kennedy arrived as Colonial Governor in 1864, and found no official residence prepared, he bought Cary's "queer architectural intrusion on the wild landscape." In 1865, after vacillating over the expense, the government purchased the property as the official vice-regal residence (a factor in Victoria being chosen as the colonial capital in 1868) and hired the architect John Wright to add two wings and a central hall in French Norman style. The castle did not impress Kennedy's successor, Governor Frederick Seymour, who thought the building "damp, bleak . . . an unsightly pile," and who chose to reside at New Westminster. One member of the government observed "woodpeckers and rats were destroying the plastered walls." These appear to have been absent in 1876, during the week-long visit by Governor General Lord Dufferin, whose wife, the Marchioness of Dufferin, politely noted: "The house is very nice and comfortable: there is a good ballroom, small drawing room, large billiard room, and excellent bedrooms. We have a Chinese cook who is, I grieve to say, highly British, having cooked for six Governors, but he is very good in his homely style; Ah Sam is his name . . . I have a very comfortable sort of housekeeper, a housemaid with a Chinaman under her, our own four servants, and a coachman and a gardener," the latter helped by prisoners from Victoria's jail. One morning in the ballroom, Lady Dufferin was surprised to find "six prisoners, with chains to their legs and an armed man standing over them, polishing the floor."

The *Colonist* thought Government House had "never, even on its best days, been a comfortable place . . . The wind whistles through numerous cracks and crevices in the walls; the roof leaks in spite of constant patching; cold draughts penetrate all parts. Fires in all rooms fail to overcome the cold and damp of the atmosphere. In the selection of a site for the gubernatorial mansion all other considerations were sacrificed to view and situation." Nothing now remains of Cary's Norman folly, except the situation he chose. Cary Castle burned to the ground in May 1899. The *Vancouver Province* ran an epitaph that summed up its style and status: "This picturesque old pile, of all and no styles of architecture, was one of the most historic as well as one of the oldest residential buildings in British Columbia."

Cary Castle's name and baronial style lived on in a more comfortable and architecturally distinguished replacement built by Victoria's two leading turn-of-the-century architects, Francis Rattenbury and Samuel Maclure. Rattenbury, who had friends in high places, submitted a design to the provincial government hoping to gain the commission. He declined to enter an architectural competition that had been organized by W. C. Wells, Commissioner of Lands and Works. Then he outmanoeuvred the Vancouver winners by persuading Wells to let him review the proposed design, which had already been criticized by an anonymous architect in a letter to the press. Rattenbury claimed the cost estimate of the winning entry was inaccurate, and threw enough doubt on it that the Vancouver team was paid off and Rattenbury was asked to undertake the new building's design and construction. Anticipating accusations of impropriety he suggested another architect be chosen, while he would supervise the project, and recommended Samuel Maclure. Maclure soon fell ill—suffering, one imagines, from the effects of dealing with his

TOP *Government House's decor was the talk of the town when the public were given a preview of the completed building in 1905. The pièce de résistance was the ballroom designed by Samuel Maclure that was decorated with stylized Native imagery by artist James Bloomfield. Francis Rattenbury—who else?—was responsible for the mansion's overall design.* BCARS D–03031

BOTTOM *Government House was almost totally destroyed by fire in 1957. All that survived was the stone porte-cochère (seen in this picture) that had been designed by Rattenbury for Lieutenant Governor James Dunsmuir in 1909. It was the only part of the old building that could be saved and it remained in place when the present Government House was built behind it.*

AUTHOR'S COLLECTION

A STONE BOUNDARY MARKER SET BY THE ROYAL ENGINEERS 1859–60 AS PART OF THE ORIGINAL SURVEY OF GOVERNMENT HOUSE GROUNDS AND FAIRFIELD FARM.

insufferable partner—and Rattenbury finished the building himself.

Rattenbury's design was an amalgam of the old Cary Castle and the Arts and Crafts/Elizabethan Revival phase he was toying with at the time; the building looked like a scaled-up version of his own Oak Bay home. Maclure is thought to have worked on the interior design, commissioning stained glass and stencilled decoration from Henry Bloomfield and Sons, New Westminster, the province's leading stained glass manufacturer. Persian carpets, ottomans, antique tables and chairs, tapestries, brass jardinieres and other furnishings, ordered from London by Weiler Brothers and Spencer's store, were the talk of the town when the public got a preview of the completed building in 1905. The pièce de résistance was the ballroom, a galleried hall decorated with cryptic stencilled images of Native chiefs and themes. Rattenbury's cost control throughout his career was unreliable, but his bills were accurate to the last penny. When Government House was finished, at double the estimated cost, he was plunged into a predictably acrimonious post-mortem. He was accused of improper procedure when ordering materials and of tiling his kitchen at Oak Bay with marble meant for Government House. Rattenbury was outraged. "I emphatically deny the charges made," he responded, "and on my part claim they are slanders, maliciously and knowingly made by the arbitrators for the purpose of discrediting me in the eyes of the Government and the people of British Columbia." The

The most historic stone at Government House is a marker in the garden placed by the Royal Engineers who surveyed the hill in 1859–60. Visitors can wander in the gardens but the residence is only open once a year—on New Year's Day—when the public are permitted a glimpse of the stately home. For the rest of the year, Government House guards its exclusivity. Hopes of a royal audience are dashed by a notice at the entrance that cautions: "Please be advised that the guest book serves as a record of our visitors and not as the basis for invitations." RW arbitrators included rival architects Thomas Hooper and Andrew Maxwell Muir, who had coveted the commission themselves. Muir's opinion of Ratz was well-known. In 1903, he had written to the *Colonist* saying that Rattenbury "has done more local work . . . than any other man . . . The truth is, he is anxious for the almighty dollar, aye, more so than many of his professional brethren, who if they had made as much by a fortuitous set of circumstances, rather than by pre-eminent ability, would have retired long ago." Rattenbury was forced to appear in front of a Parliamentary committee but he batted his way off the sticky wicket, although not without a cloud shadowing him as he left.

Throughout the building's life the vice-regal residents fashioned their own improvements. Lieutenant Governor Sir Henri-Gustave Joly de Lotbinière, the first to occupy the new premises planted ornamental trees in the gardens. In 1909 his successor, James Dunsmuir, added a stone porte-cochère based on Rattenbury's original drawings. Not all lieutenant governors and their wives took to Victoria's specifically English way with gardens. George Randolph Pearkes had to rescue the grounds from neglect in the 1960s. BC's first Chinese-Canadian Lieutenant Governor, David Lam, laid out an English rose garden with arbours and pergolas in 1991. In complete contrast to this formality, the grounds slope south toward Ross Bay in a wild tangle of Garry oaks and glaciated rocky outcrops that is inaccessible to the public. The stunted natural landscape would still be recognized by the Royal Engineers who, in 1859–60, made the first survey of the area and left a boundary marker that is still in place below Government House's flagpole.

For the most part, the gardens were the inspiration of the third Lieutenant Governor, Thomas Wilson Paterson, who commissioned a plan from G. K. McLean, a Vancouver landscape architect. McLean's winding driveways, rock gardens, ponds, perennial borders, lawns and arboretums, all in the picturesque style of Beacon Hill Park, remain largely unchanged. The rose gardens, rowan trees, rhododendrons, Douglas firs, English oaks, London planes, camellias, copper birches and heather-covered outcrops are firmly embedded in the era of turn-of-the-century British horticulture. Paterson, a Scottish railway contractor, politician and lieutenant governor from 1909 to 1914, also erected the stone wall and iron fence on Rockland Avenue to keep stray cattle from nibbling his rosebuds. The iron fence was made in Vancouver, based on a design submitted by Morris & Co., London, who suggested bronze gates and coat of arms, the latter supplied by Tiffany Studios, New York.

The vice-regal residents were briefly shaken by protest after the sinking of the *Lusitania* in 1915. Troops were posted after a mob threatened to rattle the gates because Lieutenant Governor Francis Barnard's wife was the daughter of a local German brewer. But the Chatelaine's German ancestry did not deter the Duke and Duchess of Connaught or the Duke of Devonshire and Prince Arthur from enjoying the Barnards' hospitality in 1916 and 1918. Nor was the Prince of Wales bothered by Lady Barnard's German roots when the Barnards accompanied him to lay the foundation stone for Queen Victoria's statue in front of the Parliament Buildings in 1919—Victoria herself was half German, although her heirs changed the dynasty's name from Saxe–Coburg–Gotha to Windsor in a public relations coup during the First World War.

Government House's finest hour came in 1939, when King George VI and Queen Elizabeth arrived on a royal tour that began at Quebec City and proceeded by train through the Rockies to Vancouver. When the steamer *Princess Marguerite*, escorted by four Royal Canadian Navy destroyers from Esquimalt, arrived with the royal couple at Victoria, bonfires were lit on Beacon Hill, the searchlight on the Causeway Garage swept the evening sky, and a gun salute bellowed across the harbour. One hundred thousand people lined a fifteen-mile processional route to the Parliament Buildings. The 5th BC Field Regiment played "God Save the King" on the front lawn as the royals entered the buildings by their exclusive route to the Legislative Chamber, where they praised the province's "impressive contribution to this great Dominion and to the British Commonwealth of Nations."

At Oak Bay, a thousand school children scattered flowers in the path of the monarchs' entourage. At the Empress Hotel, 250 invited guests attended a luncheon where the king gave an address that was broadcast around the Empire. At Beacon Hill Park, he presented the royal colours to Esquimalt's naval detachment while the loyal crowd of 25,000 people accompanied the Naden Naval Band in "Rule Britannia." At Government House, the queen was regaled by "45 Men of Angus," local residents all born near Glamis Castle in her native Scotland, and then she was driven to Hatley Park for a picnic and a walk in the Dunsmuir estate's Japanese and Italian gardens. At night, fireworks illuminated Beacon Hill Park. Out in the darkness of the Strait of Georgia, warships and coast guard cutters fired off salutes at sea, the last local flashes of an empire that had sustained Victoria's strategic importance for one hundred years.

Rattenbury's Government House was destroyed by fire in April 1957. Lieutenant Governor Frank Ross, his wife, seven maids and the cook who sounded the alarm, fled the blaze in their nightdresses as the building "bloomed like a huge scarlet camellia." No one was injured, but the building was burned out except for half a dozen chimneys and the porte-cochère. The lieutenant governor and his staff stayed in suites in the Empress Hotel until Government House was rebuilt. Born in Scotland, Ross had liked the building's style and discovered a set of Rattenbury and Maclure's turn-of-the-century blueprints, which guided the reconstruction to ensure that the regal taste for granite walls and wood-panelled interior design rose from the ashes. The new reinforced concrete structure that opened in 1959 was decorated with a veneer of 1899. The drawing room is a replica of Maclure's Georgian Revival salon. Life-size royal portraits greet visitors across the oak-panelled entrance hall; there are oil paintings of colonial governors and lieutenant governors; four vast canvases by G. Horne Russell on the grand staircase celebrate the empire-building Grand Trunk Pacific Railway; the stair's stained glass window, fitted in 1990, is an iridescent tapestry of regal crests, monograms and medallions. The ballroom, with its parquet floor, viewing gallery, chandeliers and luminous hilltop outlook seems, like the building and the lieutenant governor's post, to be completely detached from reality—an echo of Belle Epoque role-playing; an architectural Gilbert and Sullivan operetta.

·⇐ OAK BAY ⇒·

In Oak Bay, British accents are spoken in speech, stone and sport. Windsor Park's cricket pitch, overlooked by half-timbered homes, is an image of village England more perfectly preserved on the Pacific coast than in the old country. Oak Bay Avenue may not be narrow enough to fit in an English village, but its tea rooms and antique shops do their best to foster that illusion. The district's bracing braes, sandy bays, golf links and seaside promenades could be on the Firth of Clyde; the Royal Victoria Yacht Club, in name at least, emulates the blue blazers of Cowes. The Oak Bay war memorial's desolate site on the edge of Uplands Park can seem at times as melancholy as the cliffs of Dover. The very name Oak Bay sounds stoutly Anglo Saxon, as is the municipality's reeve—an old English term for mayor. The district's social priorities were summed up in 1914, when *The Week*, "The official organ of the Victoria Real Estate Exchange and of the Royal Victoria Yacht Club," announced: "In spite of War's alarms and the dislocation of teams consequent on the departure of so many of our local cricketers for the front, the committee of the Pacific Coast Cricket Association has decided to go forward with their annual tournament."

The first white settler in Oak Bay did not play cricket. John Tod was a retired Hudson's Bay Company factor. Tod was born in 1792 in Dumbartonshire. He left Scotland for York Factory and a career with the HBC, rose to the position of Chief Trader at Fort Kamloops in 1841, and served on the first Vancouver Island Legislative Assembly. He bought an estate, Willows Farm, in 1850 and built a house, with help from French

Canadian carpenters from Fort Victoria, where he lived with his Native wife. Tod's home (at 2564 Heron Street), and the Helmcken House, are the oldest in the Victoria area. Now hidden deep in suburbia, the Tod house is said to be haunted. Sceptics shivered when a skeleton was discovered in the garden in 1952 and identified as the remains of an Indian woman. Tod was said to have fathered ten children by almost as many Native wives.

Tod's ghosts were joined in the 1880s by Victoria's bourgeoisie who built shady summer cottages among the pines and Garry oaks on its beaches and coves. In 1891 the Oak Bay Land and Improvement Company was formed to develop the area as a resort and garden suburb. The Victoria Electric Railway Company's Fort Street tram line was extended to the sea in 1891, and Oak Bay's summer cottages began to be replaced by permanent homes. The streetcar company laid out playing fields at Oak Bay Park, now Windsor Park. In 1892 the Victoria Golf Club opened its links, conveniently reached by the tramway's "golfer's special." On Beach Drive the following year, the London-owned Mount Baker Hotel, a watering hole for upper-crust Canadian and colonial travellers, opened its doors. It was the finest on the island, substituting for burned-out Government House when the Duke and Duchess of York were on a royal tour in 1901, but it too was destroyed by fire the following year. Rattenbury designed a successor, the Oak Bay Hotel, which opened nearby in 1907.

When the London-based British Columbia Electric Railway took over the line in 1897, its local office (in Rattenbury's Bank of Montreal) published a "Tourists' and Visitors Guide to Victoria" recommending evening concerts at the Mount Baker Hotel after a day out visiting the Parliament Buildings and Beacon Hill Park. The guide also suggested ocean docks "where steamships . . . from the Golden Klondike, the Sandwich Islands, Australia, Japan and China, may be seen," and Esquimalt, "the station for Her Majesty's Navy in the North Pacific . . . capable of docking the largest battleship in the British fleet." Tram passengers could also admire Oak Bay's English-style homes, many designed by architects Francis Rattenbury and Samuel Maclure, who built villas on the seashore for themselves and their clients. Maclure's home was demolished in the 1960s, but Rattenbury's still stands.

"Ratz" was elected to Oak Bay Council when the district was incorporated in 1906. He declared that it was one of the loveliest residential areas he had seen and formed a "Beauty Committee" to maintain its garden city character. Prospect Place and San Carlos Avenue, near his own home at 1701 Beach Drive, were owned and laid out by Rattenbury to this end. He developed a perceptive sense of urban and landscape design that can be traced to his English training at Lockwood and Mawson. In 1897 he had written to the *Colonist* regretting the removal of trees that partly obscured his Parliament Buildings: "It makes me heartsick to see each tree as it falls. It is so rarely that an architect is fortunate enough to have the opportunity of erecting a large building amongst the delicate traces of woodland scenery."

On his travels in Europe, he noted the need for zoning, planning and building controls if Victoria and its surroundings were to remain "the beauty spot of Canada." He had been taken by leafy, decoratively lit lakefront promenades in Switzerland and he thought Victoria could achieve the same. But except at the Inner Harbour his plans were largely ignored. (Mayor Alfred James Morley proposed rebuilding Pandora Avenue as a boulevard all the way to Oak Bay but only managed to commission Victoria's ornamental street lamps—christened "Morley's Folly" in 1910 after their cost became known.) While the city was keen to promote tourism, it also clung to its declining late-nineteenth-century economy. Beyond Rattenbury's imperial enclave around the Empress Hotel, the Inner Harbour was lined with slowly rusting industries. In Oak Bay Rattenbury's thoughts on town planning were more welcome. Council purchased several headlands for public parks, and Windsor Park was bought from the BCER in 1922. Oak Bay become one of the first municipalities to adopt the Town Planning Act to control the area's buildings and appearance. Rattenbury's ideas, and self advancement, led him to the Uplands Company, which appointed him consultant architect for the swish suburb to be laid out on the site of the HBC's Uplands Farm.

The Town Planning Act did not allow the municipality to deal with the cemetery established by the Chinese Consolidated Benevolent Association in 1903 after part of the Chinese section of Ross Bay Cemetery was swept into the sea by storms. Chinese Point, between Gonzales and McNeill bays, became a controversial issue as Oak Bay developed in the Edwardian era and in the 1920s. Nearby homeowners objected to the graveyard. The town council tried to close it but, since it had been in use before the district was incorporated in 1906, lawyers advised council that the Chinese had every right to maintain the ground. They continued to dig up their deceased every seven years, storing the bones in the bone house to await shipment and reburial in China. The graves were then reused. The bone house became a temporary resting place for boxes of bones from across the country, but filled up when the fifth seven-year shipment was stranded by the Second World War. The graveyard filled up too; there were over a thousand graves by the time the cemetery was abandoned to wildflowers and curious children in 1950.

TOP *The Uplands estate was planned as a garden city suburb in 1909 with gracious homes and leafy boulevards—but the project never lived up to the promise of the estate's palatial gates. Even Francis Rattenbury's magic touch could not save the scheme from the economic depression that hit the province in 1912.* RW BOTTOM *Oak Bay's scenic coastline and views of the Olympic Mountains lured city dwellers to build weekend cottages by the sea. In 1907 Rudyard Kipling wrote: "If they care to lift up their eyes from their almost subtropical gardens they can behold snowy peaks across blue bays, which must be good for the soul." Turn-of-the-century taste for romantic landscapes was reflected in the painterly postcard images of the time.* AUTHOR'S COLLECTION

ian Range (Seen from Foul Bay,) Victoria, B.C.

·⇐ UPLANDS ⇒·

Oak Bay has been so thoroughly and pleasantly suburbanized that it is difficult to imagine the days when the Hudson's Bay Company farmers, who cleared and settled its wilderness, had to ward off local Natives for whom the farm's cattle were a tempting source of food. Charles Bayley, who ran Uplands Farm in the 1850s, complained: "Window glass unknown, some used oiled paper instead. Furniture none, round logs for seats, bunks for bedsteads, deer, bear and sheep skins for carpet, bugs innumerable, fleas without limit. Four miles from the fort and our only protection shotguns and dogs." James Douglas reported to London in 1854 that the Cadboro Bay Farm (Uplands) had been attacked and one farmer assaulted before the Indians were chased away. Even the farm's proximity to Fort Victoria offered little hope of rapid reinforcement. What did deter the Indians was Douglas's implacable resolve to track down and bring to trial any of them who ignored the law. Those who watched the HBC's activities at Cattle Point were not tempted to interfere. A waterfront park and picnic grounds now soften the point that was bleak and windswept when snorting, half-drowned animals were driven ashore in the nineteenth century.

Overlooking Cattle Point, Uplands Park—named for John Upland, one of the HBC farmers—is a prickly, unmanicured landscape scattered with gnarled Garry oaks and infested with the blazing yellow gorse that homesick pioneers introduced from Scotland. In complete contrast, the nearby Uplands estate, bounded by Cadboro Bay Road, Beach Drive, and

Francis Rattenbury embellished his nostalgic English Arts and Crafts style home in Oak Bay with Tudor pretension as his architectural reputation and social standing rose. Glenlyon School, which took over the house in 1935, did not entirely erase his ghost. A collection of his plans, now in the BC Archives, was found in the attic in 1978. RW

Uplands Park, is a reassuring world of Tudor Revival and Italianate homes, sheltered leafy gardens and ostentatious beachfront property. Uplands Farm was bought in 1907 by Winnipeg and Victoria developers and laid out in 1909. It was sold to the Compagnie Franco-Canadienne in 1911 who formed a subsidiary, Uplands Limited, to develop the suburb. To promote the estate's exclusivity, prospective residents were required to spend a minimum $5,000 building their dream manors.

Uplands was never completed quite as planned, but sprawling mansions such as Riffington at 3175 Beach Drive, a Tudor manor house built in 1913 to a design by Vancouver architect Philip Julien, show what was intended. Spiffy Riffington was owned by Hubert Wallace, a shipbuilder whose family began building ships in Vancouver in 1894 and who bought Yarrows, Esquimalt in 1946. The home's aristocratic architecture, intended for the whole of the Uplands estate, was visualized by Rattenbury, the consultant architect in 1909. But when the First World War began, only nine homes had been built, and by 1930 only thirty-four had been completed—some rumoured to have been built and paid for by bootleggers who ran rum from Oak Bay's coves to the United States during prohibition. But even the smugglers could not afford the Edwardian architecture favoured by the estate's pre-war developers, and the unbuilt lots were filled with 1950s ranch-style bungalows.

Uplands may have been half-built but its layout and design came with an impressive cultural and social pedigree. The landscape architect was John Charles Olmsted of Olmsted Brothers of Massachusetts, sons of Frederick Law Olmsted, the designer of Mount Royal Park, Montreal, and Central Park, New York. Olmsted the elder visited England in 1850 and returned to the United States impressed by the aesthetic and social benefits of parks that he had seen. He planned Central Park in 1858 with his English partner, Calvert Vaux, with wooded meadows, curving pathways, avenues and architectural follies that set the tone for urban parks across the continent. Victoria's Beacon Hill Park is an example of the English style that Olmsted embraced. His nineteenth-century garden suburbs, laid out with tree-lined streets that curved round the contours of the land, were the model on which Uplands was based. Olmsted's apogee came in 1893 when he landscaped the grounds of the World's Columbian Exposition in Chicago. The exhibition's Neo-classical landscaping and gleaming Roman architecture influenced grand civic projects in North America, and made Rattenbury's Parliament Buildings in Victoria— although largely derived from British sources—very much in step with the times.

Charles Olmsted's plan for Uplands, with its pillared gateways, Neo-classical street lamps, a main axis on Midland Way, winding avenues and much foliage, is also an example of the "garden city" ideal—a Utopian notion to allow people the benefits of city life close at hand while living in a semi-rural paradise. The idea originated in England in the nineteenth century as an alternative to overcrowded cities but it was exploited to offer bankers and businessmen a retreat from their industry and commerce. By the time the idea reached Victoria, which had already evolved as an informal garden city, the concept had been corrupted by realtors peddling snobbery—"all the beauties of nature and comforts of modern civilisation to the aristocratic new residents who are yearly settling in Victoria," as the Uplands Company's publicity enthused.

Middle class domestic bliss in a beautiful suburban setting was the Uplands ideal and it is one of the last North American examples of this late-nineteenth-century planning. Uplands Park was to have been only the southern half of a larger suburb until the company sold the land in lieu of taxes in 1946. The estate's street plan is now as confused as the architecture. Midland Way's boulevard and circular intersections look imperial on the map but on the ground turn out to have been a delusion of grandeur. What was meant to be a suburban Champs Élysées expires in the tousled undergrowth of the park. There is something surreal and satisfying about Uplands' stymied snobbery. The pillared stone gateways on Uplands Road and Beach Drive that announce the area's intended privacy and privilege mark the real estate empire that never was.

·⇐ RATTENBURY RESIDENCE ⇒·
1701 Beach Drive

In 1898, a few months after the Parliament Buildings had opened, Francis Rattenbury married Florence Eleanor Nunn, daughter of a former British Indian Army captain who had settled in Victoria in 1862. If Rattenbury thought he had gained a partner who would participate in the social whirl of the most prominent architect in the province, he was mistaken. Florence had enough grit to accompany him on an unexpected honeymoon in the summer of 1898 over the Chilkoot Pass, where his primary interest was to chart a route for his Bennett Lake and Klondyke Navigation Company—he sent progress reports to the *Colonist* which printed them with enthusiasm, as if they had been received from an explorer in darkest Africa. He even named one of his steamers after Florence in an attempt to make her feel part of his professional life. But after they returned, she preferred to potter around in the garden of the Oak Bay home, Iechinihl, which he began to build the following year.

For the next few years, Rattenbury could justifiably strut about the town with a cosmopolitan air—in 1905 he made business trips to London and New York. But in 1906, he encountered his first setbacks. At the peak of his triumph at the Empress Hotel, he resigned as the CPR's architect, ostensibly over a dispute about interior design, for which the wife of the railway's hotel superintendent in Montreal had been hired. Ratz played the temperamental artist if he was not given complete control of his projects. He preferred to work alone, and habitually fired off outrageously pompous letters to clients if they interfered with his designs. He was quite prepared to tout for work, alternating arrogance with obsequious flattery, as when he addressed Premier Walter Scott of Saskatchewan.

Scott was about to announce a competition for new legislative buildings in Regina in 1906, and Rattenbury tried to pre-empt the competition by suggesting that he was the only architect who would be willing to move to Regina to supervise the work. Hoping to be appointed without further ado, he wrote: "In case the great honour of designing your new Parliament buildings were entrusted to me, I am so situated at the present time, owing to various large buildings that I am now erecting all being close to completion . . . that I could and would be delighted to come and live in Saskatchewan and study the conditions on the ground . . . I am sure we could erect Buildings that would utilize the site to obtain a magnificent result . . . worthy of the great future of the province." Rattenbury undertook to make no charge for initial plans and assured the premier that, if he was not satisfied, he could take the product back to the store and buy another brand. The architect concluded: "I think, however, that from the experience that I have had in similar works . . . that I need not fear that such action would be found necessary." But in 1907 a competition was held, which Rattenbury lost to Edward S. Maxwell of Montreal.

By then, Rattenbury may have regretted leaving the CPR. He had seen better prospects with another transcontinental line, the Grand Trunk Pacific Railway, which planned a northern track to the Pacific coast. The GTP would arrive on the coast at Prince Rupert, where it would connect with steamship services to the Orient—routes that were planned to compete with the CPR's Empress liners sailing from Victoria and Vancouver. Rattenbury's ego was inflated by the prospect of grand urban design for the brand new city the railway would build and he drew up plans for a bombastic Beaux Arts terminus and a colossal chateauesque railway hotel. But they were never built. Returning from a business trip to London to raise cash, GTP potentate Charles Melville Hays chose to sail on the *Titanic*. He and his vision sank with the ship. Although the railway was completed in 1914, the outbreak of the First World War consigned Rattenbury's hotel and train terminus to the provincial archives, where the drawings can still be seen. The value of his land along the railway line plunged.

Fees for the Parliamentary Library eased him through the First World War. Dismayed by the failure of the GTP, which declared bankruptcy in

1919, and trapped in an unhappy marriage, Rattenbury found his interest in architecture waning. His marriage ossified and would come to an acrimonious end. But at the Empress Hotel, while celebrating the commission for the Crystal Garden in 1923, the fifty-six-year-old Rattenbury was, as his former colleague Samuel Maclure later put it, "bewitched" by Alma Pakenham, a wartime heroine and *arriviste* twice married and thirty years his junior. He surreptitiously visited her house in James Bay, where she lived as an apparently respectable piano teacher with her young son, but later made no secret of their trysts after gossip reached Mrs. Maclure, who had earlier befriended Alma but was more sympathetic to Florence.

Rattenbury might have retained his reputation had he been discreet, but locals drew the line when the couple began to appear at the theatre after Florence had refused Rattenbury a divorce. Simmering with frustration, as she too was, he tried every base tactic short of murder to dispose of her and pointedly entertained Alma at Iechinihl. The Rattenburys were finally divorced in 1925. But when Florence moved to a home of her own at 1513 Prospect Place—designed, ironically, by Samuel Maclure—she insisted it be within sight of Iechinihl, which she brooded over until she died in 1929. Rattenbury and Alma married but were ostracized by local society. His buildings were still admired but his career was in ruins. When Percy Leonard James, the associate designer of his two last works, the CPR Steamship Terminal and the Crystal Gardens, sought credit for both, Rattenbury had few friends left to contradict the claim.

What stories buildings tell. Rattenbury's Oak Bay home presents a postcard image of old England, a scene of peace and contentment. For a time, the Rattenburys were at ease here with their two children, their croquet and their garden parties. The home's Indian name Iechinihl—"a place of good things"—seemed initially to bless the property. In the garden by the seashore, when long summer shadows creep up in the gloaming, Ratz's ghost will come up, whisky in hand, and touch you on the shoulder. "How about this?" it will say, unfolding a sketch of some romantic project far away. Glenlyon School, which took over the house in 1935, did not dispel the architect's ghost. A collection of his plans, now in the provincial archives, was found in the attic in 1978.

Rattenbury was never satisfied. He kept adding mock Tudor gables to the back of the house, spoiling its modest Arts and Crafts personality, much as his growing self-importance erased whatever charm he had once had. Rattenbury designed smaller buildings, including some Arts and Crafts-influenced homes. His own, with its rustic stone, leaded glass, patterned shingles and picturesque gables, is still the most attractive. But while his travels made him aware of the Arts and Crafts, Art Nouveau and avant-garde developments in Europe, he never broke new ground. He lacked Maclure's adventurous sense of interior space. He flattered his clients' taste for ostentation where Maclure cultivated restraint as a measure of good taste. He lacked the patience to attend to details and was more comfortable wielding a flamboyant brush than a precise pen. But he had an instinctive ability to mellow his baronial bent with coziness and charm, and he designed a string of minor banks and courthouses that now seem picturesque follies.

Looking at his buildings and unrealized projects, one is left with the rather melancholy impression that, along with the Empire it celebrated, Rattenbury's talent was ultimately unfulfilled. Opportunity in the colonies was there for the taking—Rattenbury would have been lucky to land the Parliament Buildings prize in the old country. Architectural historian Alan Gowans has written that the Parliament Buildings were a "lifeless variant of the Natural History Museum in South Kensington." Rattenbury never escaped the styles of 1890s that appealed to his provincial patrons' nostalgia. He played safe, if entertaining, games with late Victorian styles, fully embracing his clients' old-world tastes but limiting the development of his own. He was one of the legion of able British architects who prospered building colonial works from Sydney to Singapore, and Madras to Montreal. Like many aging empire builders, he retired to England in 1929, accompanied by the notorious Alma. But he was unknown and unfeted in his native land. In a bizarre turn of events he was murdered by his chauffeur, who was also his wife's paramour, in an Agatha Christie setting in Bournemouth where he and Alma had settled. The "Villa Madeira" case caused a sensation in 1935, making not only the front pages of the Bournemouth *Echo*—"All Night Queue for the Villa Murder Trial . . . Sensational Allegations by the Prosecutor . . . Retired Architect's Death . . . Chauffeur accused of Murder"—but the *Times* of London. The case packed out the public viewing galleries in the Old Bailey and was the inspiration for a play, *Cause Célèbre*, by Terence Rattigan. But for his well-publicized demise, Rattenbury would have ended his days in obscurity. A reporter at the Old Bailey trial described the disillusioned architect as "just another retired colonial with a few interesting stories to tell."

·⇐ ROSS BAY CEMETERY ⇒·
Fairfield Road at Memorial Crescent

Ross Bay was named after Charles Ross, the Hudson's Bay Company chief factor who supervised the construction of Fort Victoria in 1843. Opened in 1873, Ross Bay Cemetery is the city's largest and most characteristic nineteenth-century necropolis, but it is not the oldest. The Quadra Street burial ground was opened in 1858 and the Jewish cemetery in 1860 on Cedar Hill Road. There was also a small burial plot in the grounds of St. Ann's Convent. Ross Bay Cemetery was planned with picturesque winding carriageways, avenues and artful vistas flanked by random plantings. Victorian society, which had manuals for everything, was guided to the grave by *On the laying out, planting, and managing of Cemeteries*, published in London in 1843. The author, John Claudius Loudon, was convinced that cemeteries should be "scenes not only calculated to improve the morals and the taste, and by their botanical riches to cultivate the intellect," but also should "serve as historical records." At

Ross Bay, row upon row as they line the leafy pathways, are the carved tombstones of the city's Victorian elite, as elaborate as the glistening black hearses and plumed horses that took them there. Loudon also thought a cemetery should be "a school of instruction in architecture, sculpture, landscape gardening." Were he to visit Ross Bay, he would not be disappointed.

Twenty-seven thousand people are buried at Ross Bay. The domain of the dead can be gloomy when autumn fog drifts in accompanied by doleful hoots from Trial Island lighthouse, invisible offshore. But spectres are likely to be members of the local Old Cemeteries Society poking around the headstones that stand like a petrified population. Every Victorian funerary adornment and inscription is here: from the "Last Anchorage" of Captain J. W. Troup of the CPR to the majestic monument to Governor James Douglas, "Knighted by Queen Victoria." Robert Paterson Rithet's tomb was designed to look like a Romanesque mausoleum; that of the Helmcken family is in Egyptian style. Robert Dunsmuir lies under a huge grey granite pedestal. Many of the epitaphs echo with Victorian sentiment and sanctimony. Lawyer and politician Charles Edward Poole, according to his guardian angel, was "A Just Man Made Perfect." Granite books open at appropriately inscribed pages, urns overflow with festoonery, and Neo-classical muses bestow cultural graces on those who may not have been particularly enlightened when alive. Emily Carr, "Artist and author, lover of nature," rests in the company of Victoria's pioneers, provincial premiers, lieutenant governors, nobs and reprobates. Here are Hudson's Bay men Roderick Finlayson, John Wark and Kenneth Mackenzie, along with Amor de Cosmos, John Teague, Peter O'Reilly and William Joseph Pendray. Sisters of St. Ann are buried beneath neatly arranged white crosses. Military memorials, commissioned by the Ottawa branch of the Imperial War Graves Commission, London, are laid out in orderly ranks.

No name at Ross Bay received greater commemoration than that of James Douglas, 1803–77, who was buried beneath one of the largest

As in life, so too in death, all Victorians had their allotted places. At Ross Bay Cemetery the dry ground was reserved for the ruling classes; the shoreline was assigned to Chinese, Natives, indigents and smallpox victims. Many of the epitaphs echo with Victorian sentiment and sanctimony. Lawyer and politician Charles Edward Poole, according to his guardian angel, was "A Just Man Made Perfect." RW

memorials, a giant Neo-classical red granite block, topped by a stylized Celtic cross and enclosed by an ornate cast-iron fence. Douglas's funeral was the most elaborate in the city until the death of Robert Dunsmuir in 1889. A steamer was chartered from New Westminster to bring mourners to Victoria; a sixty-carriage, mile-long procession lumbered from Douglas's house to Ross Bay, via the Reformed Episcopal Church where Bishop Cridge conducted the memorial service. The guns of HMS *Rocket* boomed across the harbour; the city's church bells pealed; schools and shops closed. Pallbearers included Douglas's old friends Judge Begbie and Roderick Finlayson. The tribute in the *Colonist* concluded: "No history of the province can be written without Sir James Douglas forming the central figure around which cluster the stirring events that have marked the advance of the Province from a fur-hunting preserve for the nomadic tribes to a progressive country of civilised beings, under the protection of the British flag and enjoying a stable and settled form of government." Douglas had a penchant for panoply but his friend Judge Begbie asked to be buried beneath a simple wooden cross with the words "Lord be Merciful to Me a Sinner," thought too plain by his colleagues who erected a large granite monument instead.

Victoria's establishment wished to be seen as important in death as it had been in life. Echoing the English class system, the cemetery's trustees assigned religious denominations and social groups to a hierarchy of stone and situation. Presbyterians were kept apart from Catholics; Anglicans were separated from Methodists. All occupy the high ground

HIS LAST ANCHORAGE

IN LOVING MEMORY OF
CAPTAIN JAMES WILLIAM TROUP
BORN FEB. 5, 1858, PORTLAND, ORE.
DIED VICTORIA, B.C. FEB. 20, 1931

TO·THE
MEMORY
OF·THOSE·WH
DIED·FOR·KIN·
AND·COUNTR
IN·THE
GREAT·WAR
1914 ··· 1919

1939 ··· 194

TOP *An elaborate Mediterranean-style marble headstone carved with garlands and bas-relief medallions marks the grave of stonecutter and merchant Carlo Bossi, a native of Lombardy.* RW
BOTTOM RIGHT *The typography on Ross Bay Cemetery's monuments is as varied as the architectural styles—Celtic, Neo-classical, Greek Revival, Gothic, Egyptian and Romanesque. Roman type was chosen for its classical elegance and nobility; contrasting neo-Gothic lettering on the war memorial is crude but effective. Around the turn of the century there were about one dozen monument works in Victoria that produced carved markers as well as general architectural carving.* RW
BOTTOM LEFT *The "Last Anchorage" of Captain J. W. Troup of the CPR is an individualistic gravestone carved with the imagery of the deceased's former occupation.* RW

they had been accustomed to in life. "Aboriginals and Mongolians," as the cemetery trustees described Indians and Chinese, were allocated rough land on the shore. In this inferior section, the *Colonist* routinely reported, coffins were washed out to sea by winter gales and it was only after bones began to fetch up on the beaches that a seawall was constructed in 1911. The epitaph of John Dean, 1850–1945, a failed city mayoral candidate, had the last word on life's iniquities and compensations: "It is a Rotten World, Artful Politicians are its bane. Its saving grace is the artlessness of the young and the wonders of the sky." He might have added that whatever they did in life, the saving grace of Victoria's elite, their sentimentality aside, was that they summed up their achievements with idealism and artistry. Ross Bay seems more like a sculpture garden than a city of the dead. ✌

Out of Town

CHARMINGLY PICTURESQUE . . . PINE AND OAK COVERED SHORES
AND ROLLING HILLS . . . THE DISTANT VIEW IS ONE OF EXCE-
EDING GRANDEUR, COMPRISING THE LOFTIEST PEAKS OF THE
OLYMPIC AND CASCADE MOUNTAINS—*Capt. Newton Henry
Chittenden, describing Victoria, 1882*

ESQUIMALT & NANAIMO RAILWAY

BRITISH COLUMBIA joined Canadian Confederation in 1871, after
the Dominion Government promised to "secure the commence-
ment . . . within two years from the date of the Union, of the
construction of a Railway . . . to connect the Seaboard of British Columbia with the Railway system of Canada; and further, to secure the completion of such Railway within ten years." When the Canadian Pacific
Railway was completed in 1885, after years of scandal, debate and often
difficult construction, the western terminus was Vancouver. The journey
to Victoria had to be continued by ferry, not over bridges at the north end
of the island, to connect with the Esquimalt & Nanaimo Railway,
Vancouver Island's own disconnected part of the transcontinental route.
Prime Minister Sir John A. Macdonald visited Victoria and drove the last
spike at Shawnigan Lake, north of Victoria, to open the E&N in August

*A spectacular wooden trestle on the Esquimalt & Nanaimo
Railway, c. 1900. Scenically, the E & N was likened to a
miniature CPR when the line opened in 1886.* BCARS D-05599

1886. The transcontinental railway was a nation-building dream for Macdonald, the Glasgow-born first Canadian Prime Minister, and he had, somewhat prematurely, named Esquimalt the terminus in 1873. This seemed to be confirmed by the "Carnarvon Terms," a review of the 1871 compact, adjudicated by the British Colonial Secretary, Lord Carnarvon, who authorized the E&N. The route was surveyed and a shipment of rails from Britain was unloaded at Esquimalt. But political debate in Ottawa over who should pay for the line—and whether the "Seaboard of British Columbia" meant Vancouver Island or the mainland—prevented track from being laid. The rails were shipped to Yale on the mainland in 1878 and used by the CPR. An "Island Railway or Secession" protest in Victoria in 1880 kept the issue alive, but no one, least of all the CPR, was willing to actually build the line until Victoria's politicians and coal baron Robert Dunsmuir agreed to do so.

Macdonald, whose bronze statue stands outside Victoria City Hall, was a Member of Parliament for Victoria riding in the House of Commons from 1878 to 1882, having been given the safe seat—so safe that he never visited it—after losing a by-election in Kingston. In 1886, when he finally appeared in Victoria, he quipped that he had been waiting for the CPR to open so that he could cross the continent on a Canadian, not an American, train. Ironically, Dunsmuir's syndicate, which underwrote construction of the E&N, included a cabal of American financiers. The message "Long Looked For—Come at Last" that greeted the first train into Esquimalt may have cheekily referred to Macdonald as well as the railway, but it was Robert Dunsmuir's image that beamed down from the banner—as well it might. The *Times* and the *Colonist* suggested Vancouver Island should be renamed "Dunsmuir Island" in his honour, a not inappropriate accolade since he already owned a considerable amount of it, in land grants given to him at public expense as an inducement to build the line.

The E&N was extended into town to terminate at a station on Store Street at the foot of Pandora Avenue in 1888. Attracted by land grants, the railway's Royal Mail contract and freight traffic from the Dunsmuir mines, the CPR bought the line from James Dunsmuir in 1905. A locomotive roundhouse was built at Songhees Point in 1913 and a huge steel bridge, which had formerly crossed the Fraser Canyon, was re-erected to replace a wooden trestle north of the city. But this was the last significant investment in the line that nobody wanted to build.

In 1990 the sleepy railway, which many thought had been closed for years, steamed onto the nation's front pages when Ottawa proposed closing the passenger service despite an agreement, enshrined in 1871 and upheld by BC courts, to maintain it "in perpetuity." The issue went to the Supreme Court which ruled that Ottawa did not have an obligation to maintain the passenger service. While construction of the railway was "an act of nation building," it was "an historical, not a constitutional, fact." Provincial politicians, interviewed on the steps of the Parliament Buildings, retorted that Robert Dunsmuir and the CPR had benefitted from the lavish land grants and Ottawa and the CPR were accused of "still living off the wealth of British Columbia that was granted to them at the time." Forgotten in this exchange was the fact that it was provincial politicians who had been responsible for the great Dunsmuir giveaway in the first place.

·◁ CAPTAIN JACOBSEN HOUSE ▷·
5o1 Head Street, Esquimalt

Finnish seaman and shipwright Victor Jacobsen jumped ship in Victoria in 1881, after discovering he could earn more ashore, and hid in the woods on Mount Douglas until his vessel, the *City of Quebec*, sailed. He worked on a farm before shipping out as a crewman on sealing schooners. His own ships, the *Minnie McLean* and the *Eve Marie*, named after his wife and daughter, became well known in the Inner Harbour. After the *Minnie* was wrecked on the Aleutian Islands, while Jacobsen was confined below with an infected eye (which he later lost), he added the *Casco* and other vessels to his flotilla. The *Casco* had previously been chartered in San Francisco by Robert Louis Stevenson—a fitting coincidence, for Jacobsen could have been a character from one of the writer's books.

Victoria was home port for a fleet of over fifty sealing schooners that followed fur seal migrations on the coast between Mexico and Alaska and across the Bering Sea to Japan. In its heyday in the early 1890s, Victoria's sealing fleet employed 1,500 sailors and skinners, many of them Natives. Each schooner carried half a dozen sailing skiffs or Indian canoes that were launched in the hunting grounds. Three-man, harpoon-armed crews, straight from the pages of *Moby Dick*, slaughtered the seals and skinned them, heaving bloody carcasses overboard. Many hunters vanished in the north Pacific fogs despite the mother ships' sporadic gunfire to give them bearings. Schooners were sunk by storms or wrecked on the coast. Crews drowned after encounters with killer whales.

Jacobsen's ships were not the only ones to employ Indian crew members. Native seafaring tradition predated the first Europeans to explore the coast in the late eighteenth century. Working on the schooners was nothing to Haida and Nootka deckhands, compared to paddling their thirty-five-foot dugout canoes on whale hunts out of sight of land. Around five hundred Indian men and women sailed with Victoria's sealing fleet each season, a fact that partly dispels the notion that Natives failed to adapt to the white man's way. Some of the schooners were brought around Cape Horn by sealing captains from the Maritimes. During the boom years from 1884 to 1911, sealing ships from as far away as Antwerp and Adelaide swept the hunting waters of the Bering Sea.

Finnish seaman and shipwright Victor Jacobsen, shown here c. 1890, jumped ship in Victoria in 1881 and made a swashbuckling career in the city's sealing trade. The dashing Finn's exploits could have leapt off the pages of a Melville, Conrad, or Stevenson story. BCARS B–00601

HISTORIC ESQUIMALT

507 Head Street

Victoria's shipbuilding and ship repair industries, not to mention the city's many bars, were kept afloat by the trade, a mainstay of the local economy. At its high tide, 75,000 seal pelts were shipped to London auction houses every year.

Buccaneering skippers like "Flying Dutchman" Gustav Hansen and "Sea Wolf" Alexander McLean risked arrest, and confiscation of their vessels, while poaching seal colonies on Alaskan and Russian shores. Hansen and his crew were jailed in Vladivostok for six months. Captain Cutler of the *Agnes Macdonald* became the talk of Wharf Street's saloons after outpacing a Russian cruiser. Jacobsen too hunted the disputed waters off Alaska, always looking to the horizon to avoid Russian or American warships. Sometimes, in the fog and squalls, even he would be taken by surprise, and his Nelson touch would be required to escape where others would have surrendered. Ordered to heave-to by an American coast guard cutter, Jacobsen turned to his mate. "What is she signalling?" "Can't see, sir." "Good man, set sail."

Sealers spent summers on the north coast and returned to Victoria in the autumn to sell their haul. The schooners were refitted in Victoria during the winter. Crewmen mended sails, amused children by carving seal and whale bone trinkets on the dockside, and sang accordion-accompanied shanties that echoed down the Old Town's cobbled alleys. Seal tooth brooches, bracelets, ivory picture frames and whale tooth ornaments became as popular in city curio shops as Indian souvenirs. Sealers who could, temporarily exchanged ships' winches, oilskins and Wellington boots for their wives' warm kitchens, gingham tablecloths and wood stoves. But after 1911, when treaties between Japan, Russia and the United States banned Victoria's fleet from their waters, the hunting

Most of Esquimalt's significant historic buildings are military structures but the municipality has several notable nineteenth-century homes. The most eccentric is the 1893 "Steamboat Gothic" style Captain Jacobsen House. RW

stopped. Canada received 10 percent of the other nations' catches in compensation, a share negotiated by Britain. Victoria's sealers were scuppered and their schooners sold or scrapped. There were hardly any seals left to catch anyway.

When he built a pattern book house in 1893, to which he later retired, Jacobsen personalized the design with shingles patterned like fish scales and decorated with floral trim, seabirds, anchors and nautical knots and ropework. The home's blustery Steamboat Gothic style, an eclectic mix of Victorian Italianate and French Second Empire, was popular in New England and Nova Scotia in the late nineteenth century. Jacobsen's house was copied from the A. J. Bicknell and Company's *Detail, Cottage, and Constructive Architecture*, published in New York in 1873. Bicknell's book, for "Architects, Builders, Carpenters, and all who contemplate building," was an example of nineteenth-century architectural novelty and enterprise. Its "75 Large Lithographic Plates Showing a Great Variety of Designs . . . for Cottages, Summer Houses, Villas, Sea-Side Cottages and Country Houses" were a boon to local builders, and to architects who had lost their muse.

From his rooftop belvedere overlooking West Bay, the one-eyed Jacobsen could tinker with his telescope and watch his sealing captains set sail. In 1901 he might have spied another Victoria mariner he knew crossing Brotchie Ledge from Oak Bay to sail around the world. Captain John C. Voss began his career as a deckhand in Germany and settled in Victoria. He rebuilt an Indian dugout canoe, adding a cabin, masts and sails. Voss claimed to have encountered cannibals on South Pacific islands, perhaps the reason why his shipmate, a journalist, deserted him at Fiji and returned to Victoria. Voss arrived in England three years later. His saga, *The Venturesome Voyages of Captain Voss*, was published in 1913. Voss's vessel *Tilikum*, stranded on the Thames, was rescued by the Victoria and Island Publicity Bureau. It was displayed among the totem poles of Thunderbird Park and then restored, for display in the Maritime Museum, by the elderly Jacobsen and fellow old salts.

·⇐ ESQUIMALT HARBOUR ⇒·

Lieutenant Manuel Quimper, a Spanish sailor, was the first European to sail into Esquimalt Harbour while venturing up the coast in 1790. He named the inlet Puerto de Cordova, after the Viceroy of Mexico. His fellow countryman, Captain Dionisio Alcala Galiano, who anchored at Esquimalt in 1792, noted in his log that the harbour was "beautiful, and affords good shelter for sailors; but the water is shallow . . . [the Indian chief] informed us: the land is very irregular." The Indian name "Is-whoy-malth"—Place of Shoaling Waters—describes the head of the harbour but, as the British later found, the body of water was deep enough for their largest vessels. James Douglas, on board the Hudson's Bay Company's ship *Beaver*, nosed his way into the anchorage in the spring of 1842 searching for a site to build Fort Victoria. Had his report been more positive, Esquimalt, not Victoria, would have eventually become British Columbia's provincial capital.

Douglas took the Indian name as a hopeful sign. He described the inlet as "one of the best harbours on the coast, being perfectly safe and of easy Access, but in other respects it possesses no attractions." The shores were "rugged and precipitous, and I did not see One level Spot clear of Trees of sufficient Extent to build a large Fort upon; . . . Another serious Objection to this Place is the Scarcity of fresh Water." Douglas sailed on to Victoria's Inner Harbour whose landscape was, he judged, better defended and better suited for a fort and farming. The choice, however, proved to be a bane for mariners. Admiralty charts of Victoria Harbour warned: "The Channel is buoyed but it is necessary to take a pilot and the space is so confined and tortuous that a long ship has considerable difficulty in making the necessary turns; a large percentage of the vessels entering the port, small as well as large, constantly run aground from these causes, or from trying to enter at an improper time of tide." When the Canadian Pacific Railway's Empress liners began to call in the 1890s they had to dock at specially built wharves at Ogden Point.

The superiority of Esquimalt, "commodious and accessible at all times," was not lost on the British Admiralty in London. Its secluded anchorage and coves, three miles west of Victoria, were a safe haven from winter storms blowing off the Strait of Juan de Fuca. Out to sea, between Esquimalt and Albert Head, Royal Roads anchorage (named by the British in 1846 but first used by Spanish navigators) was used when winds and tides prevented access to Esquimalt or Victoria's Inner Harbour. But even on a placid day, salt and seaweed on the wind tell that Royal Roads is not a place to linger in bad weather. West of Fisgard Lighthouse, not far from the wooden trestle that bridges the entrance to Esquimalt Lagoon, an anchor and cairn erected by the Thermopylae Club marks April Fool's Day 1883, when a southeasterly gale swept four unsuspecting sailing ships ashore.

Esquimalt Harbour was explored by Captain John Alexander Duntze on the frigate HMS *Fisgard* in 1844 and charted by Lieutenant Commander James Wood on HMS *Pandora* in 1846. Wood named the islands and points around the harbour after Duntze and his crew. The *Fisgard* and *Pandora* had sailed to Esquimalt from Valparaiso, where the Royal Navy's Pacific Squadron had been based since 1837. Warships were increasingly dispatched to Esquimalt to maintain an aggressive British presence in the area, whose boundary was being negotiated with the United States. The navy also deterred Natives from attacking the weakly defended Fort Victoria. In 1848, Captain George Courtenay's marines from the Esquimalt-based frigate HMS *Constance* put on a salutary show of force after Indians fired shots at the fort.

During the Crimean War, Rear Admiral Henry William Bruce, Commander in Chief, Pacific Squadron, wrote to Governor Douglas requesting temporary hospital facilities after raids on Russia's Pacific coast. A temporary hospital was built at Duntze Head and three warships, with a handful of wounded men, arrived at Esquimalt after the bombardment. A barracks was later built at Skinner's Cove for a detachment of Royal Engineers sent to survey the boundary between British

Columbia and the United States between 1858 and 1862. During the gold rush in 1858, the Royal Navy helped Douglas maintain his authority. In 1865, the Admiralty established a permanent base at Constance Cove to protect the colony from American expansion. Douglas's resolve ensured that British rule prevailed, but he was aided by the British government's deployment of a handful of warships, an example of the over-the-horizon imperial influence that naval power—"The manifestation of Her Majesty's ability to enforce obedience to her laws"—achieved for the British Empire at the time.

"Send a gunboat!" was the Colonial Office's cry when any crisis broke out abroad. But the uncharted inlets of the west coast were a known hazard that Rear Admiral Robert Lambert Baynes, Commander in Chief, Pacific Station, 1857–60, preferred to avoid. Shipwrecks were easy prey for plundering Natives. Lucky crews escaped with their lives. A handful of incidents in the 1850s gave the coast a gruesome reputation. In the early 1860s, thanks to surveys by Captain George Henry Richards and the arrival of steam-powered warships, Douglas was able to persuade the navy to send gunboats to suppress piracy and punish the Natives. He also enlisted the navy to hunt down white whisky traders and confiscate their vessels. Commander John W. Pike of the sloop HMS *Devastation* was singularly effective in 1862–63, capturing a floating distillery at the Nass River and putting whisky traders at Fort Rupert out of business.

Warship captains and crews trained for sea battles with enemy fleets found themselves acting as a colonial police force. Pugilistic vessels from Esquimalt—HMS *Forward*, *Grappler*, *Boxer* and *Rocket*—cruised the coast in the 1860s, their captains heaving-to offshore to bombard Indian villages and teach their inhabitants a lesson. But some were disturbed by their duties. John Moresby, gunnery lieutenant on HMS *Thetis*, wearily recalled the 1853 murder investigation and subsequent punitive expedition against the Cowichan Indians as "one of the myriad tragedies of the red man's collision with civilisation." In a report to Rear Admiral Baynes, Captain Richards of HMS *Hecate* wrote: "It appears to me that in the present relations existing between our people and the Indians, it cannot be a matter of surprise if many wrongs are committed on both sides, and my opinion is that the Natives in most instances are the oppressed and injured parties."

Richards's successor on the *Hecate*, Captain Daniel Pender, surveying Barkley Sound on the west coast of Vancouver Island in 1861, was less charitable. He thought the local Indians were a "most treacherous, thievish lot of rascals." In 1864 the *Kingfisher*, trading for seal oil, was attacked in Matilda Creek, Clayoquot Sound. The captain and crew were murdered, mutilated, weighed with stones and dumped in the creek. Rear Admiral Joseph Denman, a veteran of colonial skirmishes and anti-slaving patrols off the coast of West Africa, sailed up the coast in his flagship HMS *Sutlej*, accompanied by Commander Pike on the *Devastation*. Under covering fire from the *Sutlej*, shore parties landed and, despite being sniped at by Indians hiding in the trees, seized several war canoes. In all, nine Native villages were shelled and burned, and sixty war canoes destroyed or captured to avenge the *Kingfisher* murders. The suspected ringleader, the Ahousaht Chief Chapchah, who had lured the crew of the

Captain George Henry Richards, c. 1860. Richards was a veteran of the Chinese opium wars and the search for the Franklin expedition in the Northwest Passage. While stationed at Esquimalt in 1857–63, he surveyed Vancouver Island's coastal waters and, like his predecessors who made the first surveys in the 1840s, put naval names—Nelson Island, for example—to features on his charts. Esquimalt Harbour's secluded anchorage was explored in 1844 by Captain John Alexander Duntze on the frigate HMS Fisgard and charted by Lieutenant Commander James Wood on HMS Pandora in 1846. Wood named the islands and points around the harbour after Duntze and his crew. The names of the two ships survive as street names in Chinatown. BCARS A–03352

HMS Malacca *and* Sutlej *anchored in Esquimalt Harbour. In 1864 the Royal Navy's Pacific Squadron had fourteen ships under the command of Rear Admiral Joseph Denman, a veteran of colonial skirmishes and anti-slaving patrols off the coast of West Africa. After the crew of a*

trading ship were murdered by Indians at Clayoquot Sound, Denman sailed up the coast in his flagship Sutlej *to punish the Natives. Shore parties landed under covering fire from the warship to burn Indian villages where it was thought the culprits were hiding.* BCARS E–01355

Kingfisher to their doom, escaped. Other Indians were captured and tried in Victoria, but the navy's success was followed by judicial fiasco. The cases were heard by Douglas's brother-in-law, Judge David Cameron, who refused to accept the testimony of Native witnesses that might have resulted in convictions. The prisoners were released. Cameron resigned the next year. Indian Agent Gilbert Malcolm Sproat ruefully remarked that the Ahousahts "had gained a victory over the ships . . . Chapchah has added to his reputation; he is the great chief who defied and baffled the English on King-George war vessels." In London, the Admiralty's response to the Pacific Squadron's activities was concern that its noble ships were being used by the Colonial Office to burn women and children out of their homes.

Apart from these belligerent excursions, navy life at Esquimalt could seem rather like home—a sort of Portsmouth with pine trees—an aspect that the base retains. There is an "Admiral's House" complete with croquet lawn, and there are relics of rum and salt meat stores that suggest the tougher life of the ordinary seaman. Esquimalt Road was built by sailors from HMS *Thetis* past the site (now Memorial Park) of the small Roman Catholic St. Joseph's Mission, built by Bishop Demers in 1858. By the time Esquimalt was incorporated as a municipality in 1912, the road was lined with pubs: the Esquimalt Hotel, the Coach and Horses, the Halfway House (built in 1860, halfway between the naval base and Victoria), and the Sailor's Rest. Turning a blind eye to jolly jack tars on Esquimalt Road, one resident recalled: "In these halcyon days of the old Port a beautiful wooden road led from Esquimalt to Victoria and it was

By the 1890s, Victoria's sealing fleet employed 1,500 sailors and skinners, many of them Indians—whose seafaring tradition pre-dated European contact. Working on the schooners was nothing to Haida and Nootka (left) deckhands compared to paddling their thirty-five-foot dugout canoes on whale hunts out of sight of land.
BCARS A–06920

311

always busy . . . officers riding into the city to some function or to watch cricket . . . there was always something interesting to see . . . for besides the men-of-war, liners were constantly coming and going with hundreds of men on their way to the gold fields or returning with small fortunes." Before the docks at Ogden Point were opened, ocean-going vessels anchored offshore at Royal Roads before entering Esquimalt Harbour, from where passengers were taken by road or ferried to Victoria—the more privileged courtesy of naval launches.

Esquimalt's cultured, cricket-playing, mainly English naval officers fitted seamlessly into the colonial hierarchy established by the HBC, and brought gaiety and some sophistication to the rude settlement. The first naval balls were held in a "most dismal-looking" local marketplace in 1859. Lietenant C. W. Wilson wrote: "we got all the flags we could from the ships & turned in 30 or 40 sailors, & in a short time a fairy palace of flags was erected, so that not a particle of the building was visible; we then rigged up some large chandeliers & sconces of bayonets and ram-rods wreathed in evergreens . . . got up a large supper room in the same style & managed to provide a first-rate supper. Everybody came to the ball from the governor downwards nearly 200 in all & we kept the danc-ing up with great spirit till ½ past 3 in the morning . . . nobody says ball in this part of the world, it is always party. The ladies were very nicely dressed, & some of them danced very well, though they would look much better if they would only learn to wear their crinolines properly."

·⮜ HER MAJESTY'S CANADIAN DOCKYARD ⮞·
CFB Esquimalt, Esquimalt Road

Until recently, the old Royal Navy station, now Canadian Forces Base, Esquimalt, was accessible only to authorized personnel, but in 1994 the public gained limited access to the historic site on bus tours run by navy guides. No one need now experience the reception given to Lieutenant Adrian Keyes RN, a submarine officer who arrived at Esquimalt with a group of sailors after a rapid train journey from Toronto in 1914. German spies were rumoured to be in Victoria, and the naval dry dock was guarded after an intelligence report warned of possible sabotage. Lieutenant Keyes and his companions were wearing blue suits, not uniforms. One of his fellows recalled the episode that followed: "We took a Train to Esquimalt . . . Keyes borrowed some of the Train Conductors' Gold Braid which we adjusted to his coat sleeves. We were met at Esquimalt by various people with revolvers & were placed under close arrest. To be shot seemed hardly a fitting end to our Enterprise." Keyes eventually persuaded the base commander that they really had come to sail the navy's submarines, not to sink them.

Keyes had been sent to train the crews of "McBride's Navy," two submarines bought by Premier Sir Richard McBride on the eve of the war. "Glad-Hand Dick," a staunch imperialist throughout his reign from 1903 to 1915, was approached by a group of Union Club members concerned that the one-ship navy, the cruiser HMCS *Rainbow*, at Esquimalt was not a sufficient deterrent to the German Pacific fleet. The base had de- clined after the British left in 1906—Kipling described it as "a marine junk-store . . . reached through winding roads, lovelier than English lanes." The group met with J. V. Patterson, a Seattle shipbuilder, who had two submarines, originally ordered by Chile, for sale. McBride suggested the Commander in Chief, Esquimalt should buy them before American neutrality prevented their purchase. Impatient with the navy's bureaucratic response, McBride bought the boats and made secret delivery arrangements—so secret that the submarines were almost fired upon by Esquimalt's gunners when they approached the harbour. Being shot at while entering its home port was the only hazard British Columbia's own navy experienced in its short war. Three days later Ottawa footed the $1-million bill and the boats were transferred to the Royal Canadian Navy. Fort Rodd's gun crews became used to seeing the two submarines submerging like seals offshore as Keyes's crews struggled with the American shipyard's manuals and the boats' Spanish dials and controls.

When the First World War began, the Admiralty in London cabled Esquimalt to "expect immediate attack" from the German East Asiatic Squadron, which had vanished from its base at Tsingtao. Apart from McBride's navy, the only warship on the coast was the *Rainbow*, an elderly cruiser built for the Royal Navy in 1893 and bought by the RCN in 1910. In 1914 the *Rainbow* played a brief role in the hunt to destroy the German squadron, by sailing south hoping to find the German cruiser *Leipzig*. Fortunately, the *Rainbow* never found its quarry, a superior ship with a more experienced crew.

The *Rainbow* is remembered among the ships' bells, builders' nameplates, and medals from the Crimea to Korea in the Naval and Military Museum at Admirals Road and Colville. Here are the images and artifacts from the heyday of the Senior Service: the Royal Navy Flying Squadron from 1870; the sternplate of HMS *Cormorant*, the first ship to enter the naval dry dock in 1887; photographs of the *Rainbow* and HMCS *Ontario*, "Pride of the Pacific Squadron," and a recruiting poster rallying "Strong, Healthy, and Well Educated Men and Boys . . . must have good character, God Save the King." In the library there are ships' logs, seafaring lore, and *The Grand Fleet, 1914–1916*, by Admiral Viscount Jellicoe of Scapa Flow. Names from Jellicoe's era are also present outside. Esquimalt's streets are signalled by gold-braided names from naval engagements of the First World War and earlier: Grenville, Anson, Beatty, Sturdee, and Craddock.

Navigating the workaday clutter of today's activity it is possible to turn a corner and suddenly glimpse a scene from the past—the rocky, pine-fringed headlands are much like old photographs show them to have been when HMS *Fisgard* cautiously nosed her way in past Duntze Head in 1844. The museum's bungalow was built in 1891 as an officers' hospital and later became pleasant quarters for the commander of HMCS *Naden* torpedo training school. The officers' ward, and barracks built around a parade ground, look like dozens built by the British from Suez to Singapore in the nineteenth century. Their bricks, slates, window and door frames were shipped from Britain round Cape Horn in 1888–92. English architect John Teague designed several buildings on the base, including the bungalow and Admiral's House, an Italianate villa built at Duntze Head in 1885, his most conspicuous. Other historic buildings, like the security block for "deranged patients," are camouflaged among the accumulations and alterations of what is a working, not a static historic site. At the harbour entrance, frigates designed for the twenty-first century slip past two iron cannons cast in the nineteenth century at Woolwich Arsenal, London, and the redundant Bickford Tower, erected so the admiral could exchange semaphore signals with his ships at anchor. Other Royal Navy relics include the Commodore's Residence, built in 1879 (the oldest building at the base); Married Quarters, a two-storey English terrace; Chief of Staff's residence, built in Georgian Colonial style; a grim jail; and the "Stone Frigate," a barrack block built in 1901.

The most impressive structures at Esquimalt are two titanic dry docks. The 400-foot-long graving dock, completed in 1886 and opened the following year, was one of the most ambitious construction feats attempted in the empire at the time, and in its setting one of the most extraordinary. This image from the Industrial Revolution, with its stepped stonework, pumping house and chimney, is still in use. Excavated on a site owned by former Hudson's Bay Company men Finlayson and Tolmie, the dock was a Confederation promise from Ottawa, along with the Canadian Pacific Railway. But, like the railway, it took years to build and was bedevilled by financial wrangling and construction delays. When it did open for HMS *Constance* in 1887, the Admiralty was finally spared the embarrassing hospitality of the United States' navy yard at San Francisco or the need to direct its warships to Hong Kong, where a similar dock had been constructed.

The second dry dock was a spectacular excavation engineered by the Department of Public Works in 1921–27, and remains the largest graving dock on the Pacific coast. The 1,186-foot dock's most famous but most secret visitor was the Cunard White Star liner *Queen Elizabeth*, the world's largest liner. The 1,031-foot ship squeezed into the dry dock in February 1942, her main mast higher than the dock's hammerhead crane. Thousands of workers toiled round the clock to refit the Clydebuilt liner as a troop ship capable of carrying 15,000 men. The vessel was so big that workmen were given maps to find their bearings below decks. Wartime security officers told those who saw her not to speak of the event— "loose lips sink ships." After twelve days, the *Queen Elizabeth*, coated with ten tons of grey camouflage paint, slipped silently away, reappearing on the North Atlantic ferrying Canadian and American soldiers to Britain.

> *HMS* Cormorant, *the first ship to enter the newly completed naval dry dock at Esquimalt in 1887. Esquimalt was one of twelve strategic coaling stations from Cape Town to the Falkland Islands that allowed the Royal Navy to patrol the oceans protecting British ships and imperial outposts. The Royal Canadian Navy took over the base in 1910.* BCARS F–08452

·⟸ ST. PAUL'S NAVAL & GARRISON CHURCH ⟹·
1379 Esquimalt Road

Partly paid for by a parsimonious Admiralty, but only after the chaplain sent letters to Queen Victoria, St. Paul's Naval & Garrison Church was consecrated in 1866 in the old village of Esquimalt. Only the church survives from the scattering of clapboard houses, picket fences, false-fronted hotels and stores, and a school, built below Signal Hill to serve the Royal Navy station that was established in 1865. The remains of the village were bulldozed during the Second World War when the naval base was enlarged. The Garrison Church, built in the rustic Picturesque Gothic style of the mid-nineteenth century, survived because it had already been moved up the road in 1904. The church, built on a windy

site below Signal Hill, was pounded less by the weather than by a coastal artillery battery mounted on Deadman's Island in 1887. Every time the guns were test-fired the concussion caused alarming vibrations, and the church was hauled on rollers to its present site to spare it further damage. Two English stained glass windows flanking the altar survive from 1879 along with the church organ, shipped round Cape Horn. Leaded windows in the vestry are still bowed from the gunners' nineteenth-century target practice.

Inside the intimate sanctuary, poignant tidings of parish history and struggles at sea hang from the rafters and decorate the walls. Glinting brass plaques and tattered regimental flags loyally embroidered "God, King, and Country" recall Esquimalt's ships and seafarers. This sobering encounter with the past is summed up by "witness to one of the most impenetrable silences of the sea"—the memorial to "the Commander and Men of HMS *Condor* . . . lost with all hands in December 1901 off the coast of Vancouver Island. From that day to this, nothing has been heard of her or her helpless crew. No rockets were seen, no messages came over the air. Vanished into the ocean's vastness. Only a short time after there was washed ashore a seaman's cap and the ship life buoy, now on the wall." When the church was built in the village, the naval cemetery was put on Deadman's Island, a rocky outcrop offshore. It was replaced in 1868 when the Admiralty bought part of the Hudson's Bay Company's nearby Constance Cove Farm. The Garrison Cemetery, tucked away behind a ridge off Colville Road, and now oddly secluded between the

Fort Rodd's gunners waited in vain for enemy ships to sail into their sights. At the start of the First World War they were so nervous from rumours of attack from German raiders that they almost sank two of their own submarines. The first coastal artillery battery, mounted on Deadman's Island in 1887, caused the Garrison Church to be moved—every time the guns were test-fired the concussion caused alarming vibrations. RW

twelfth and seventeenth holes of Gorge Vale Golf Course, was opened in 1869. Nineteen sailors were exhumed from Deadman's Island and reburied in the new location, where a tiny Gothic Revival chapel was opened in remembrance.

The graveyard, with its toy-like white chapel deep in an evergreen grove, exudes an inescapable and silent sadness. On stone and wooden cross after cross "erected by fellow shipmates" are the names of stokers, sergeants-at-arms, signalmen and seamen—mostly drowned or, like Edwin Butland of HMS *Zealous*, "Fell from Aloft." Among the carved anchors and ropes is a more ostentatious memorial: "Sacred to the Memory of Frederick Seymour ESQ. Governor and Commander in Chief of BC ... died at sea on board HMS *Sparrowhawk* while in the discharge of an important official duty"—a euphemistic epitaph, for the unfortunate alcoholic Seymour's last duty had been to deal with a scrappy vendetta among the Indians on the north coast.

·⇐ FORT RODD ⇒·
Fort Rodd Hill Road, off Ocean Boulevard

At first sight, Fort Rodd Hill National Historic Site seems to be a country park laced, as it is, with trails and picnic grounds. But down toward the shore its more serious purpose is excavated and exposed. Fort Rodd was once the centrepiece of Victoria and Esquimalt's coastal defence fortifications and, a short distance from the car park, their incongruous remains can be found.

How odd to find these antiquated gun emplacements so remote from the imagery of the Crimean and First World Wars that they evoke. Here is the upper battery with its forbidding gateway, riflemen's slits in the concrete perimeter, and a ghostly guardhouse whose rudimentary accommodation would have been familiar to red-coated British soldiers from Pretoria to Peshawar. Here are the sunken passageways, trenches and cool damp chambers designed to protect the garrison and its equipment. Here too are smooth earthwork mounds angled to deflect incoming shells, emplacements for searchlights expected to expose enemy ships 5,000 yards out at sea, and a "disappearing gun" sprung to lower with its recoil for reloading and to appear swiftly erect above the earthwork to fire again. On top of the emplacement, officers, binoculars tight to the eyes, once scanned the far horizon while below, earmuffed gunners humphed heavy shells from the magazines. All waited with hopeful trepidation for enemy warships that never came.

Warships from Russia's Pacific Fleet caused mild alarm in 1862 and 1878 with unexpected calls at Esquimalt. In 1881 the defences were observed by the commander of a visiting Russian cruiser. Curious citizens hired a steamer from Victoria to sail around the tsar's anchored vessel, but below the surface of officers' mutual courtesies, naval strategists wondered what calamity would befall the province if Russia, or any other power, sent warships to bombard the base. Strengthening the batteries along the coast to thwart surprise attack from the sea became an urgent enterprise. Begun in 1878, Fort Rodd was the most extensive fortification of several constructed to defend Victoria and Esquimalt harbours in the nineteenth century. The fortifications, from Royal Roads to Beacon Hill Park, were manned initially by British gunners and then by the Royal Canadian 5th BC Field Regiment, Garrison Artillery. But no real threat arrived until 1914, when the German cruiser *Leipzig* was thought to be lurking off the coast. Fort Rodd's gunners cheered HMCS *Rainbow*, the only warship defending the coast, when she steamed out past Fisgard Lighthouse to protect merchant shipping from the suspected raider.

How effective a surprise attack could be was demonstrated at the time by another ship of the German East Asiatic Squadron when the *Emden* made a dawn foray into Georgetown, Penang, disguised as a British cruiser and sank a dozing Russian warship. Fort Rodd's jumpy gunners nearly shelled two unidentified submarines offshore that had been bought from a Seattle shipyard by Premier Richard McBride to bolster the home fleet. Fort Rodd was again on alert in 1942, after a Japanese submarine was reported to have shelled Estevan Point Lighthouse farther up the coast. These alarms aside, the strongest impression of the now-deserted upper and lower batteries is of the unremitting ennui of garrison life. One permanent garrison family, living in the Married Quarters, a red brick reminder of provincial England built in 1897 to Royal Engineers' stock plans, managed to produce ten children while based at the battery. Along with information about the disappearing guns, a sign notes that in summer beer could be kept at a drinkable temperature in the cellar, a small mercy for off-duty gunners enviously watching Royal Navy warships slipping into harbour, knowing that by suppertime their officers would be feted and entertained at the Union Club or the Empress Hotel. War games and discipline were required to keep the gunners sufficiently alert to quickly straddle an enemy ship with well-placed salvos. But the descriptive diagrams placed around the site explaining the operation of the "depression range finder" and the disappearing guns' quick-firing sequence are the closest the garrison ever came to sinking the *Leipzig*. The hopeful training routine—"enemy vessel sighted . . . take post command issued . . . gunfire opened . . . enemy vessel sunk, rendered harmless, or retired out of range"—was never put to the test, and the lonely never-fired-a-shot-in-anger relic of imperial defence closed in 1956.

·⇐ FISGARD LIGHTHOUSE ⇒·
Fort Rodd Hill Road, off Ocean Boulevard

The cliffs and gun emplacements of Fort Rodd overlook the Strait of Juan de Fuca and the causeway to Fisgard Lighthouse. The lighthouse, completed in 1860 to mark the entrance to Esquimalt Harbour, was the first built on the coast. After reverberations from Fort Rodd's guns shattered the glass lantern in 1898, the lightkeeper was given a warning shot in time for him to close shutters on the glass. Architects John Wright, with Hermann Otto Tiedemann, designed Fisgard Lighthouse under the supervision of Colonial Surveyor and Engineer J. D. Pemberton. Wright also designed the adjoining red brick residence in the then fashionable Picturesque Gothic style. Fisgard was the first light station erected on the British Columbia coast, and the first of five built around Victoria's shores in the nineteenth century. Built on a granite foundation, the walls are four feet thick at the base. Brick imported from England was used to build the tower, a classic British design—although after twelve years the brick was plastered with cement and three coats of white paint to protect the structure from the fierce winter weather. The house, designated along with the light tower as a historic site in 1960, is open to the public, but because the lighthouse is still in use, the iron spiral staircase that allowed keepers to light the light at the top of the tower every night, can be seen but not climbed.

It is possible to walk across a causeway to Fisgard Lighthouse today, but the early lightkeepers knew no such ease; the causeway was built in 1951. From 1860, when it was built to mark the entrance to Esquimalt Harbour, until 1929 when it was automated, the lighthouse could only be reached by dinghy. In winter storms and tides, despite the short distance from shore, George Davis, the first lightkeeper, and his wife and three children were often cut off for days on end. Davis oversaw the fitting of the English-made light to the tower. Every night the light had to be lit and the outside of the glass wiped clean. A clockwork system of counterweights and gears revolved the light apparatus, which needed to be rewound and have its wick trimmed every three or four hours. Davis's wife Rosina was paid a stipend since she often shared these duties and kept watch.

James Douglas petitioned the Colonial Office to build the light, writing that Esquimalt was "a harbour whose growing importance can scarcely be over-estimated . . . During the day the entrance is difficult enough to find to those possessing no previous knowledge of the locality, but at night the difficulties of distinguishing it are so great that the attempt to enter the harbour is never made except by those whose long acquaintance with the coast has rendered them familiar with every peculiarity." Captain George Henry Richards, in command of the Royal Navy survey ship HMS *Plumper* before he was captain of the *Hecate* from 1857 to 1860, sent a report to the Admiralty supporting Douglas's assessment. Richards chose the site for Fisgard Light, one of the first public works projects undertaken by the colonial government, and a second at Race Rocks at the tip of Vancouver Island. London agreed to pay the construction costs for two "Imperial lights" and to supply the materials, Scottish granite at Race Rocks and English brick at Fisgard.

Fisgard's name comes from Richards's ship, the frigate HMS *Fisgard*, built at Pembroke Dockyard, Wales in 1819 (the ship was named after Fishguard in Wales—coincidentally lightkeeper Davis's native land). Davis later manned Race Rocks lighthouse, also built in 1860. It was a more daunting posting: Race Rocks had been named by Hudson's Bay Company mariners in 1842 who learned to steer clear of the swirling tides. Davis painted black and white hoops on the tower's granite blocks—which had been cut and numbered by quarrymen in Scotland and shipped via Cape Horn—to make the structure more visible. From his vantage point the gas lights of Victoria could be seen but, as one keeper lamented, the point was so isolated that "my wife and family have been at Race Rocks for two years and nine months and during that time have never been able to visit Victoria." At Fisgard, the keeper could row to the harbour shop.

Construction at Race Rocks began in 1859 but came too late to save the *Nanette*, from London, which was driven ashore by the tide while lighthouse construction workers watched aghast. HMS *Grappler* took the crew off the beached and disintegrating vessel the next day and the wreck was plundered by locals. Three days later the light that would have saved the *Nanette* was lit for the first time. In December 1865 keeper Davis and his wife, who were posted to Race Rocks after Fisgard, watched in horror as a boat bringing her brother, sister-in-law and three friends on a Christmas visit capsized within twenty feet of shore. Davis couldn't save them: the station dinghy had been withdrawn as a cost-saving measure. A year later George Davis fell ill. For over a week his wife waved at passing ships and flew the Union Jack at half-mast to signal for help. No one came. After he died the *Colonist* campaigned for a system of signals that would alert the town to lightkeepers' distress. But ships continued to pile up on Race Rocks in bad weather. Foghorns were installed in 1892 but losses continued—leading to the belief, given credence by ships' masters who claimed they didn't hear the hooting horns, that somewhere offshore there was a "silent zone" where the horns could not be heard. Some thought they were not sounded at all, especially after keeper Thomas Argyle began to pay Victoria shopkeepers in gold sovereigns of which he seemed to have a constant supply. It was rumoured he had a secret treasure trove that he had discovered on a wreck while diving on Race Rocks.

Fisgard Light's location seems innocuous compared to the treacherous Race Rocks. But the eerie isolation and ghosts of the past are soon felt. Outside, west of the causeway, the beach is strewn with bleached, washed-up logs that look, from a distance, like the splintered timbers of wrecked ships. Softly illuminated from Gothic windows in the two empty rooms downstairs, the exhibits at Fisgard take on a sepulchral air. There are photographs of the impressively buttressed Estevan Point and other lights, and a display of antique lenses. The sitting room's floorboards are patterned with a faded checkerboard "poor man's marble" painted by an unrecorded keeper (of the twelve men stationed here not one photograph has been found). Photographs of heaving seas and spectacular wrecks, ominous sounding hazards like Brotchie Ledge and Scrogg Rocks show why such structures were needed on the coast; "21 instructions for lightkeepers," and a map showing the fifty light stations up the ragged shore— and another with scores of anchors marking shipwrecks recorded up to 1921— evoke the ennui and sudden fright of the keepers' routine. There were so many wrecks on the reefs and rocks of the west coast's dismal shore that the coast was given the sonorous sobriquet "the Graveyard of the Pacific."

The cliffs and gun emplacements of Fort Rodd overlook the causeway to Fisgard Lighthouse. The lighthouse, completed in 1860 to mark the entrance to Esquimalt Harbour, was the first built on the coast. After reverberations from Fort Rodd's guns shattered the glass lantern in 1898, the lightkeeper was given a warning shot in time for him to close the shutters before target practice commenced. RW

·⇐ CRAIGFLOWER FARMHOUSE ⇒·
Island Highway at Admirals Road

Craigflower Farmhouse and the nearby Craigflower Schoolhouse offer a glimpse of life in one of the first pioneer agricultural communities in British Columbia. The farmhouse is the only survivor of four Hudson's Bay Company farms that were established in the Victoria area in the mid-nineteenth century. Seventy or so Scottish, and some English colonists with their families, led by Kenneth Mackenzie and his wife Agnes, were employed by the Hudson's Bay Company to clear the land and settle the area in 1853. Each settler was promised an allowance of seventeen pounds of meat per annum and a land grant of 25 to 50 acres in return for five years' service. Mackenzie was charged with recruiting volunteers in Scotland. He hired those with useful skills—artisans, labourers and farmers. Eighteen men and their families sailed with him in 1852.

The Mackenzies boarded the HBC's annual supply ship *Norman Morrison* at Granton, near Edinburgh. Other settlers and HBC staff were picked up at the East India Docks in London, among them Thomas Skinner and family, also hired by the HBC, who ran Constance Cove Farm at Esquimalt. They arrived after a six-month voyage around Cape Horn to Vancouver Island. Robert Melrose, who was on the *Norman Morrison* with his wife, recorded the erratic approach to Esquimalt in January 1853: "Very rainy, brisk gale, sailing under close-reefed top sails . . . espied Cape Flattery and Vancouver Island. Nearly struck reefs . . .

driven out to sea . . . wet day. . . driven out to sea again . . .Came close to the mouth of the Sound . . . evening, all hands on deck to guard against the rocks . . . fine day, sailed up the Sound very slow. Cast anchor in the Royal Bay. Saw the Indians in their canoes." Little provision had been made for the settlers and they had to accept overcrowded accommodation at Fort Victoria. The Skinners found themselves in a shack on Kanaka Row. One of their maids promptly accepted a marriage proposal from one of the sailors on the *Norman Morrison* and returned to England. But in two years, those who stayed transformed the wilderness. Craigflower became a community of twenty-one dwellings including barns, a sawmill, brick kiln, blacksmith's shop, bakery, slaughterhouse and general store. The manor house was completed in 1856 in Georgian Colonial style. The schoolhouse, directly across a bridge over Gorge Inlet, was built in similar style in 1855. They are the only buildings to survive from the settlement.

The Mackenzies were relatively well off when they moved into Craigflower Manor. Even when they arrived, they were not exactly refugees from the Highland Clearances: Mackenzie was the HBC's bailiff, in charge of the four farms established by the Puget Sound Agricultural Company, an HBC subsidiary. Mackenzie's house, a well-proportioned Georgian Revival building that plays quirky notes with Greek pediments framing a Gothic front door, was architecturally the most elegant in the Victoria area at the time. But its urbane facade was literally studded with

Craigflower Farmhouse's Georgian style was given frontier functionality with a pedimented Neo-classical entrance and Gothic Revival front door designed for more than decoration. Studded with hand-forged iron nails it was thick enough to withstand Indian attack. Kenneth Mackenzie, bailiff at Craigflower, one of four Hudson's Bay Company farms in the Victoria area, named it after a farm in Scotland owned by Alexander Colville, then Governor of the HBC. RW

frontier necessity—hammered with hand-forged iron nails, it was built thick enough to withstand Indian attack. Inside, it is as plush as any British country manor of the time with a chaise longue in the drawing room, antimacassars on the chairs, engravings of Queen Victoria and Prince Albert on the walls, and leather-bound volumes of Byron's complete works and *Chambers Biographical Dictionary* in Mackenzie's bookcases. Prints of the Crystal Palace, London, site of the Great Exhibition of 1851, decorate the walls.

The Mackenzies had actually seen the Great Exhibition where, in the vast, glazed halls of the Crystal Palace, among the displays of aspidistras, steam engines and Victorian gadgets, they spied a cast-iron "Kitchener" range, a novel oven which they brought with their possessions on the long voyage round Cape Horn. A replica of the original is built into the kitchen wall. The Mackenzies entertained HBC staff from Fort Victoria and officers from Royal Navy ships that called at Esquimalt. Admiral's House, a residence for the naval commander in chief built by Mackenzie down Admirals Road (originally a trail that ran from the farm to the harbour), was the reciprocal setting for garden parties and croquet games (Mackenzie and the other farmers also supplied the fleet with food). The house burned down in 1910 but something of the languid leisure of officers and gentlemen and navy wives on colonial stations still exists at the present Admiral's House, built at Duntze Head in 1885.

Mackenzie's work was essential to the success of the HBC's trading enterprise at the fort, and ultimately left its mark on the character of the colony. The HBC's traders saw the land's potential, and liking the idea of living like the gentry, they soon amassed substantial estates for themselves. The British government insisted the HBC encourage settlement in the region as a condition of granting control of Vancouver Island to the company—the intention being to introduce the social hierarchy of England to the new colony, re-creating a world of gentleman farmers and loyal yeomen. The HBC maintained control of its Fur Trade Reserve around Victoria, and reluctantly oversaw settlement on behalf of the

Colonial Office. A handful of independent settlers who trickled in were forced to farm on the edges of the HBC's fiefdom. Many prospective immigrants preferred South Africa, Australia or New Zealand to the long voyage round Cape Horn or a railway journey across the malarial Panama isthmus to reach Victoria. Many would-be settlers elected to stay in San Francisco. Colonial surveyor Joseph Pemberton described the Panama isthmus in 1851: "Who that crossed it then can forget the heat and filth . . . the packs of curs and flocks of buzzards . . . the scenes of riot and debauchery at the villages, jungle fever, and the bones that marked the mule tracks through the plains." Land regulations discouraged individual settlers and squatters but encouraged would-be gentleman farmers, like Captain Walter Colquhoun Grant, to make the trip and to re-create the British agricultural system of estates run by landed gentry.

Grant's career speaks for countless British adventurers for whom the colonies presented a second chance. "A splendid fellow, every inch an officer and a gentleman," according to Dr. Helmcken, Captain Grant was a cavalry officer and the colony's first independent settler. He resigned his commission in the Scots Greys and, with money from an uncle—one senses his family were happy to see him set sail—landed in Victoria in 1849. Grant was in debt when he left England and sold his army commission. But he convinced the HBC he was a surveyor and was hired by the company in London. His passage was advanced by the HBC but had to be repaid by installment—a practice still in force in the 1970s, the last decade of the company's annual recruitment of staff from Britain to man its trading posts. By the time he arrived, with eight workmen, he had spent most of his money in Panama and San Francisco but he did have his baggage; in typical upper-crust fashion its contents included a library, brass cannons, engraved shotguns and a bag of cricket gear.

The laird of Sooke, where he farmed, didn't last long as either the company surveyor or the local squire. He lost his way in the forest while attempting surveys and made a fruitless effort to farm his estate. He also built a sawmill from where he planned to export logs. When he could he socialized at the fort, where his demonstrations of swordplay caused mirth in the officers' mess. James Anderson, who was a schoolboy at the time, remembered with affection: "Our amusements consisted of marbles, cricket, rounders, shinny, horse-riding, fighting Indian boys, worrying Indian dogs, some surreptitious shooting with our antiquated flintlock muskets . . . Captain Grant, late of the Scots Greys, God bless him, was our patron as regards cricket, having presented us with a full set, which enabled us to indulge the game which was usually played on the ground where the Burns Memorial now stands." Teaching cricket to the fort's schoolboys was one of Grant's few lighter moments. He wrote: "I have been living a totally solitary existence . . . I soon got tired of my own society & except when a stray ship came along the coast, never saw a creature save my own men and a few rascally Indians." His men, a disgruntled bunch, threatened to desert for the California gold fields. His surveys were incomplete—he claimed his instruments had been damaged in transit from England—and he resigned as colonial surveyor in 1850 (he was replaced by J. D. Pemberton).

Grant took an HBC ship to Hawaii, still promising London his long-awaited maps, but returned to sell his property to the HBC to clear his debts at the company store. He secured a homeward passage and left Victoria in 1852 for England. He rejoined his regiment, fought with gallantry in the Crimean War and even presented a paper, "Description of Vancouver Island," at the Royal Geographical Society in 1857. He died while serving in India in 1861. Grant may not have succeeded as a cartographer or farmer but he left his mark across the local landscape—Scotch broom, which he is said to have planted after being given seeds by the British Consul in Hawaii (his Sooke neighbour, former HBC miner Andrew Muir, is thought to have brought the first seeds from Scotland).

The colony's second gentleman farmer, Captain Edward Edwards Langford, who named his property Colwood after his home in Sussex, had more staying power—but even he left in 1861, mainly because he found the HBC's regime intolerably oppressive. Langford crossed swords with Governor Douglas after being given a log shack in the fort as a temporary billet when he landed. The relationship never improved. He repeatedly clashed with Douglas on the issue of a colonial assembly, to which Douglas was opposed. But when he sailed back to England (where he continued to complain to the Colonial Office about Douglas) the *Colonist* said he had "done much to soften the rude features of pioneer life" and introduced "the tone of modern English society to the colony."

The HBC farmers, however, stuck to their five-year contracts. In 1858, the *Victoria Gazette* noted "the settlement of Craigflower consists of some 30 or 40 families, and an extensive and well-cultivated farm, a saw mill, flour mill etc. The settlement is principally Scotch, who we should judge, still retain their national characteristics as a people—energy, perseverance, shrewdness and unconquerable industry. One or two of the children we saw were dressed in the highland costume—knee breeches, loose coats, kilts, etc., with legs bare. None but the best breed of cattle and horses and sheep, and the most improved machinery, is ever imported. All the buildings erected by the Puget Sound Agricultural Company are exceedingly substantial and well built, and if they do not possess great architectural beauty, certainly are massive. The most profitable part of the business is stock and wool raising—large quantities of the wool are annually shipped to the Mother Country." But, showing their characteristic shrewdness and unconquerable industry, most of the original *Norman Morrison* settlers, being released from their contracts, planned to farm land they had saved for. The Mackenzies did the same in 1866.

·⇐ HATLEY PARK ⇒·
2006–2050 Sooke Road

Stained glass mottos at Hatley Park read "East, West, Home's Best." No wonder: Edwardian colonial ostentation and aristocratic ambition reached its west coast apogee at Hatley Park, a romantic sandstone pile built in 1908 for James Dunsmuir, the eldest son of Robert Dunsmuir, the coal mining, shipping, political and business baron of Craigdarroch fame. Set on an 800-acre estate at Colwood, west of Esquimalt, Hatley Park is even grander than Craigdarroch, the Dunsmuirs' Scottish Baronial mansion in Victoria. James Dunsmuir succeeded his wealthy father as president of the family firm and became premier of British Columbia from 1900 to 1902 and lieutenant governor from 1906 to 1909, positions that he held more by social status than ability. His taste of the high life at Government House led him to commission architect Samuel Maclure to design a castellated stately home in sixteenth-century English style, where he retired to live like a feudal potentate.

Maclure's clients often returned from visits to Britain with grand ideas—and pictures of houses they had seen and wanted Maclure to copy. Hatley Park was said to have been based on an Elizabethan manor house in Warwickshire. When it opened in 1910, the *Colonist* swooned that the Dunsmuir dwelling was comparable to Blenheim Palace. Maclure, with Boston landscape architects Brett and Hull, also planned the garden's curving driveways, croquet lawn and ornamental features all in the Olmsted oeuvre. The Neptune Steps, facing the castle's porte-cochère, were designed as a water cascade in eighteenth-century European landscape manner. The formal Italian Garden was laid out with rigid pathways, but softened with wisteria-clad pavilions and a curving arbour—a landscape studded Florentine-style with classical urns and statuary of the four seasons. The Japanese Garden, hidden in a glen, was planted with cherry trees, maples, umbrella pines and rhododendrons; its island teahouses were linked by bridges on ornamental lakes. Indigenous Western red cedars and arbutus trees contrast with the castle's imported horticultural and architectural innovations: a banana tree in an iron and glass conservatory was not only a decorative centrepiece beneath the central dome, it allowed the Dunsmuirs to provide their dinner guests with an unexpected tropical dessert, courtesy of the Chinese stokers who fed the conservatory's coal-fired boilers.

The estate had six miles of roads, a village for the Dunsmuirs' 120

Chinese workers, stables, a dairy, a laundry and a slaughterhouse. The castle's interior contained a dining room, billiard room, library and other salons on the ground floor, and a ballroom, twenty-two bedrooms and nine bathrooms upstairs. Such opulence required twelve servants and numerous maids, supervised by an English butler who attended to the building's maintenance and the Dunsmuirs' desires. There was a chauffeur and a crew for Dunsmuir's 218-foot Clydebuilt steam yacht which was moored offshore. James Dunsmuir's American wife Laura kept the servants occupied preparing for visiting royalty, governors general and her husband's political cronies. The cellars were well stocked with port and claret, and the grounds flush with game for the benefit of Dunsmuir and his hunting and shooting pals.

Hatley Park was built at a time when even the smallest details received creative attention. Douglas James, brother of Rattenbury's associate Percy Leonard James, produced 250 working drawings detailing everything from the Art Nouveau bell-push styled as a nymph in beaten copper, the monogram with the owner's initials and leaves interwoven on the porte-cochère, and the positions of the dozens of cast-iron monogrammed drainpipes ordered from Glasgow. There are hand-crafted heraldic stained glass and acres of specially selected Australian mahogany and Canadian red oak crafted by a platoon of twenty-five British carpenters. The castle far exceeded Dunsmuir's previous home Burleith, designed by John Teague in romantic Queen Anne style in 1892 overlooking the Gorge. In 1910 the Dunsmuirs sent Maclure and his wife Daisy to Paris and London to select fittings and furnishings for the castle, after Maclure advised his client that the three stags' heads above the fireplace in the two-storey galleried Gothic Revival entrance hall were insufficient, and a somewhat passé decoration in such a palatial dwelling: Hatley Park's architecture was, Maclure considered, a cut above the average bogus baronial hunting lodge home.

Inside Hatley Park's oak-panelled halls and winding stairways the Dunsmuir ghosts wander in unhappy limbo: the Prince of Wales, later the Duke of Windsor, is said to have left a bullet hole in the billiard room wall; in the smoking room James Dunsmuir reputedly sat listening to "Where, Oh Where, Is My Wandering Boy Tonight?" until the record wore thin, after learning that his favourite son, a cavalry officer, had gone down with the *Lusitania* at the beginning of the First World War, the crumpled front page of the *Colonist* that annouced the loss of the liner by his feet. His brother Alexander Dunsmuir died in San Francisco of stress and drink; his mother Joan was an implacable matriarch. Despite promises to James and Alexander that they would inherit the family empire, Robert Dunsmuir left his assets to his wife. The sons managed the business, but their mother retained control. In 1886 one of their sisters, Emily, married the foppish Northington Pinkney Snowdon and built a lavish Jacobean manor, Ashnola—evidence, the brothers thought, that their mother would continue to fritter away the family fortune seeking eligible husbands for her other daughters. It was ten years before they wangled a transfer of the assets in 1899.

When Alex Dunsmuir died in 1900 he left his company stocks to his brother, although he had pledged them to his mother. Joan Dunsmuir then sued James for the loot, a case that even caught the attention of the *New York Times*, whose headline writers splashed "Premier of British Columbia Sued by His Mother" across their pages in November 1901. After four years in the courts, James won the case. When his mother died in 1908 she left him not a penny. Her estate went to the five surviving daughters. James Dunsmuir's fortune was left to his wife Laura with the instruction that it be divided equally among his nine children. Today, the relics of the Dunsmuir empire are tourist attractions. The family's decline traced a route taken by many of the great patriarchal nineteenth-

Hatley Park's Italian Garden was laid out with formal pathways studded with classical urns and statuary symbolizing the four seasons. Wisteria-clad pavilions and a curving arbour add a dreamy unreality to this Pacific coast Renaissance garden. RW

century industrial dynasties from Clydeside to California: the patriarch built the empire, the sons inherited and then sold it, the grandchildren frittered away the proceeds in Los Angeles, London and Monte Carlo.

Erstwhile and ineffective Premier of British Columbia and Lieutenant Governor James Dunsmuir, squire of Hatley Park, was more comfortable lounging on the deck of his Clydebuilt steam yacht than fielding questions in the legislative chamber. This snapshot was taken c. 1900. In 1940 Hatley Park was converted to a naval training school, HMCS Royal Roads Military College (closed in 1995). BCARS H–02818

·⇐ BUTCHART GARDENS ⇒·
800 Benvenuto Avenue, Saanich

Butchart Gardens, a floral and arboreal spectacle north of Victoria, was begun as a hobby in 1904 by Jennie Butchart, and subsequently expanded to camouflage her husband's derelict quarry, a wilderness ravaged by cement workings that she reclaimed and beautified with picturesque and avid planting. She was born to an Irish family in Toronto in 1868; her husband Robert Pim Butchart was of Scottish stock. He founded a cement business at Owen Sound, Ontario in the 1880s. After a visit to England, where he learnt the secret of Portland cement, a white limestone material, the Butcharts moved to Vancouver Island where he founded the Vancouver Portland Cement Company in 1904 at Tod Inlet on Brentwood Bay, fourteen miles north of Victoria. At its deepest excavation, before the First World War, the quarry employed four hundred Chinese, East Indian and white workers who lived in barracks nearby. Butchart's workmen quarried limestone to feed a plant from which cement was barged to building sites in Victoria and on the mainland. The quarry closed after the First World War and production was moved to Bamberton across the inlet.

While Robert Butchart ran the company from an office in Victoria's Board of Trade Building, his wife Jennie was planning an ambitious garden on the 130-acre family estate next to the quarry. The English, Italian and Japanese gardens she laid out were a bold beginning for any amateur gardener. Books from her library, *The Ideal Garden and Rock Gardening for Amateurs, Japanese Gardens, English Flower Garden and Home Grounds* and *Gardening for Beginners*, were among her sources of inspiration as she sat waiting for her Japanese butler to hand her the latest publication or seed packet arrived by Royal Mail from London. She also had practical help from the Empress Hotel's gardener, Arthur Robillard, who had worked on a French country estate and many in Victoria—and from Samuel Maclure (Hatley Park was one of her models).

Few books could have guided her on her most imaginative task, an idiosyncratic plan for the site's most dramatic topographical feature, the disused quarry. From 1920, with help from her husband's Chinese quarry labourers who were supervised by William Henry Westby, an English landscape designer and horticulturist, she created the Sunken Garden. Seeing this feature for the first time is an absolutely stunning experience. From the Butcharts' house, a rambling piece of English Edwardiana designed by Maclure and the main architectural feature of the estate, a wooded path leads quickly and abruptly to a giddy vantage point from which the fruit of Jennie Butchart's imagination and labour is unveiled. Almost every person who ventures onto the precipitous lookout stops and gasps at the sudden vista, punctuated in the distance by a tall chimney, a relic of the quarry, that stands like a Neo-classical folly behind a screen of Lombardy poplars planted in 1910. Jennie Butchart did not attempt to restore the natural landscape, destroyed by the quarry, to its original state. Instead she transformed it—planting ivy to the sheer walls while suspended in a bosun's chair—into a sublime eighteenth-century romantic landscape. The scene, in its picturesque harmony, is reminiscent of the Buttes-Chaumont, a romantically pinnacled park in Paris, also a former quarry and abundant with twisting pathways, creeping foliage, Neo-classical gazebos and grottos. Jennie Butchart may have known of the Buttes-Chaumont; she won a scholarship to study art in Paris but marriage postponed the trip. Paris or not, her landscaping, free and painterly in the Sunken Garden and delicately formal in the English, Italian and Japanese gardens, is in a class of its own.

The Butcharts wintered in Victoria and roamed around the world in search of new flower and plant specimens and ornaments (several Italian bronzes adorn the site). They retained Maclure to extend their villa, Benvenuto, with an indoor salt water swimming pool. They formed the Benvenuto Seed Company in 1920 in part to encourage visitors to the popular gardens to grow their own plants rather than surreptitiously snipping cuttings to take home. Jennie Butchart hoped that the public would experience the gardens and tea rooms as she planned them—primarily for pleasure—and her wish is still honoured. There is a "plant identification centre" at the house but outside the exhibits are not identified, because she felt that to label every item would turn the place into a botanical garden full of species for study rather than enjoyment. She hoped that the gardens would retain their highly personal, almost private charm. She also wished that entry to the gardens, first opened to the public in 1904, would remain free. But financial crisis forced the family to start charging for admission during the Second World War (the gardens had been offered to the provincial government for $1 in 1939 but this was turned down). Uniformed military personnel, however, did not have to pay. Brochures publicizing the 50-acre gardens still refer to the founders as "Mr & Mrs Butchart," as if their era of genteel teatime conversation and lazy garden parties has not quite been erased. Fans write gushing comments in the visitors' books in the loggia by the lily pond: "a Garden of Eden" and "Paradise" are the most frequent observations. ✌

The crater left by Robert Butchart's limestone quarry—the most dramatic
topographical feature at Butchart Gardens—was once a hellish pit full of
dust, drills, dynamite and donkey engines. Jennie Butchart visualized the
scarred landscape as the centrepiece of a picturesque garden and set about

creating her horticultural heaven in 1904. The quarry was transformed into a Sunken Garden with a fifty-foot-deep artificial lake, winding walkways, alpine rockeries, plunging cliffs—and a screen of Lombardy poplars to camouflage the derelict quarry plant. RW

Hatley Park's castle and gardens—now Royal Roads University —are the epitome of Edwardian country house style. They remain Victoria's most ambitious interpretation of European aristocratic splendour. RW

Epilogue

GARDENS OF EDEN have pervaded Victoria's consciousness ever since James Douglas, founder of Fort Victoria, wrote in 1843: "The place itself appears a perfect Eden, in the midst of the dreary wilderness of the North West Coast, and so different . . . from the wooded, rugged regions around, that one might be pardoned for supposing it had dropped from the clouds into its present position." Princess Louise thought the setting was "halfway between Balmoral and Heaven." Francis Rattenbury spent his career decorating the Inner Harbour as an architectural Eden. British settlers who brought roses, heather, gorse and other seedlings—elm, beech, hawthorn, holly, yew, and rowan trees—created Victoria's garden city colouring. The monkey puzzle trees native to Chile that were planted at Rockland and James Bay, and the name of the indigenous Douglas fir, were the result of nineteenth-century British botanical exploration and fashion. Samuel Maclure was subtly sensitive to the temperate west coast setting and British pretension when he designed Hatley Park and introduced the nostalgic Tudor Revival style to Rockland. His landscape design, as much as the villas themselves, gave wistful form to an idealized past as much as it was a symptom of wealthy Edwardians' desire to escape from the industry and commerce that made such indulgence possible.

If one could be pardoned for supposing, like Douglas, that Victoria had dropped from the clouds into its present position, the same lenience could be given to the enthusiastic script in the Butchart Gardens visitors' books. Not only are the Butchart Gardens an idealized vision of the Garden of Eden that Douglas saw—and the ultimate garden in a "City of Gardens"—but also, in their sentimental reinterpretation and remaking of the past for display, a revealing expression of Victoria's compulsions, contradictions and cultural nostalgia. ✍

Bibliography

*In addition to source material at the British Columbia Archives
and Records Service, Victoria, and the Vancouver Public Library,
the following publications were consulted:*

ADAMS, JOHN. *Historic Guide to Ross Bay Cemetery.* Victoria:
British Columbia Heritage Trust, 1983

BARMAN, JEAN. *The West Beyond the West: A History of British
Columbia.* Toronto: University of Toronto Press, 1991

BARRETT, ANTHONY and LISCOMBE, RHODRI WINDSOR. *Francis
Rattenbury and British Columbia: Architecture and Challenge in
the Imperial Age.* Vancouver: University of British Columbia
Press, 1983

The Beaver: Magazine of the North. Winnipeg: Hudson's Bay
Company, 1970

BERTON, PIERRE. *Klondike: The Last Great Gold Rush 1896–1899.*
Toronto: McClelland & Stewart, 1958

BINGHAM, JANET. *Samuel Maclure, Architect.* Ganges BC: Horsdal
& Schubart, 1985

BISSLEY, PAUL L. *The Union Club of British Columbia, 100 Years
1879–1979.* Victoria: Union Club 1979

British Columbia; Pictorial and Biographical. Vancouver: The S. J.
Clarke Publishing Co., 1914

British Columbia; A Centennial Anthology. Toronto: McClelland
& Stewart, 1958

CARR, EMILY. *The Emily Carr Omnibus.* Vancouver: Douglas &
McIntyre, 1993

CHITTENDEN, NEWTON H. *Travels in British Columbia,* Victoria
1882

COLE, DOUGLAS. *Captured Heritage: The Scramble for North-west Coast Artifacts.* Vancouver: Douglas & McIntyre, 1985

The Colonist. *Victoria Illustrated.* Victoria: Ellis & Co., 1891

COTTON, PETER NEIVE. *Vice Regal Mansions of British Columbia.* Victoria: British Columbia Heritage Trust, 1981

DOWN, SISTER MARY MARGARET. *A Century of Service 1858–1958.* Victoria: The Sisters of St. Ann, 1966

EWERT, HENRY. *Victoria's Streetcar Era.* Victoria: Sono Nis Press, 1992

FRANCIS, DANIEL. *The Imaginary Indian, The Image of the Indian in Canadian Culture.* Vancouver: Arsenal Pulp Press, 1992

GOWANS, ALLAN. *Building Canada: An Architectural History of Canadian Life.* Toronto: Oxford University Press, 1966

GOUGH, BARRY M. *British Maritime Authority and Northwest Coast Indians 1846–1890.* Vancouver: University of British Columbia Press, 1984

GRAHAM, DONALD. *Keepers of the Light: A History of British Columbia's Lighthouses and their Keepers.* Madeira Park BC: Harbour Publishing, 1985

HART, E. J. *The Selling of Canada: The CPR and the Beginnings of Canadian Tourism.* Banff: Altitude, 1983

JUPP, URSULA, ed. *Home Port Victoria.* Victoria: Ursula Jupp, 1967

HOWAY, F. W. and SCHOLEFIELD, E. O. S. *British Columbia; From the Earliest Times to the Present.* Vancouver: The S. J. Clarke Publishing Co. 1914

KALMAN, HAROLD. *A History of Canadian Architecture.* Toronto: Oxford University Press, 1994

KIPLING, RUDYARD. *Letters of Travel (1892–1913).* London: MacMillan and Co., 1920

KLUCKNER, MICHAEL. *Victoria, the Way it Was.* Vancouver: Whitecap, 1986

LAI, DAVID CHUENYAN. *The Forbidden City within Victoria.*
Victoria: Orca Book Publishers, 1991

NESBITT, JAMES K. *Victoria, Historical Review.* Victoria: Victoria
Centennial Society, 1962

NEWMAN, PETER C. *Company of Adventurers: The Story of the
Hudson's Bay Company.* Toronto: Penguin Canada, 1991

ORMSBY, MARGARET A. *British Columbia: A History.* Toronto:
Macmillan of Canada, 1958

PETHICK, DEREK. *Victoria: The Fort.* Vancouver: Mitchell Press,
1968.

_____. *James Douglas: Servant of Two Empires.* Vancouver:
Mitchell Press, 1969

REKSTEN, TERRY. *The Dunsmuir Saga.* Vancouver: Douglas &
McIntyre, 1991.

_____. *Rattenbury.* Victoria: Sono Nis Press, 1978.

_____. *More English Than the English: A Very Social History of
Victoria.* Victoria: Orca Book Pubishers, 1986

ROBINSON, LEIGH BURPEE. *Esquimalt "Place of Shoaling
Waters."* Victoria: Quality Press, 1948

SANFORD, BARRIE. *The Pictorial History of Railroading in British
Columbia.* Vancouver: Whitecap, 1981

SEGGER, MARTIN. *The Buildings of Samuel Maclure: In Search
of an Appropriate Form.* Victoria: Sono Nis Press, 1986.

_____. *The Parliament Buildings of British Columbia.* North
Vancouver: Associated Resource Consultants Ltd., 1979.

_____. *Victoria: A Primer for Regional History in Architecture
1843–1929.* Watkins Glen, NY: Pilgrim, 1979.

STARK, STUART. *Oak Bay's Heritage Buildings.* Victoria: The
Hallmark Society, 1988

STURSBERG, PETER. *Those Were the Days, Victoria in the 1930s.*
Victoria: Horsdal & Schubart, 1993

SCOTT CHARLES H. gallery. *The Photographs of Hannah Maynard.*

Vancouver 1992

SMITH, DOROTHY B., ed. *The Reminiscences of Doctor John Sebastian Helmcken.* Vancouver: University of British Columbia Press, 1975

TAYLOR, G. W. *Shipyards of British Columbia.* Victoria: Morriss Publishing, 1986

TURNER, ROBERT D. *The Pacific Empresses: An Illustrated History of Canadian Pacific Railway's Empress Liners on the Pacific Ocean.* Victoria: Sono Nis Press, 1981.

_____ . *The Pacific Princesses: An Illustrated History of Canadian Pacific Railway's Princess Fleet on the Northwest Coast.* Victoria: Sono Nis Press, 1977.

Victoria, City of. *A Brief History of Beacon Hill Park 1882–1982.* Victoria: City of Victoria Parks Department, 1982

_____ . Victoria, City of. *This Old House. An Inventory of Residential Heritage.* Victoria, 1979.

_____ . Victoria, City of. *This Old Town. City of Victoria Central Area Heritage Conservation Report.* Victoria, 1977

WADDINGTON, ALFRED. *The Fraser Mines Vindicated.* Victoria: P. de Garro, 1858

WALBRAN, CAPTAIN JOHN T. *British Columbia Coast Names: Their Origin and History.* Ottawa: Government Printing Bureau, 1909

WILLIAMS, DAVID R. *The Man for a New Country: Sir Matthew Baillie Begbie.* Sidney BC: Gray's Publishing, 1977

WOODCOCK, GEORGE. *Amor de Cosmos: Journalist and Reformer.* Toronto: Oxford University Press, 1975

_____ . *British Columbia: A History of the Province.* Vancouver: Douglas & McIntyre, 1990

Index

Africa Rifles, 141, 224-25

Agnes Macdonald, 301

Ahousat, 306, 311

Albion Iron Works, 127, 133, 152, 158, 179, 236

Alexandra Club, 27

All Red Route, 74, 132, 172

America, HMS, 93

American annexation, 65–66

American Civil War, 104, 140

American Museum of Natural History, 54, 58

Anderson, Alexander Caulfield, 88

Anderson, James, 38–39, 94, 117, 126, 332

Anderson, William P., 128, 131

Andrews & Co., 262

Angela College, 233

Anglican Church Missionary Society, 227

Angus, James Alexander, 234, 246

Anti-German riots 1915, 25

Argyle, Thomas, 325

Armadale, 77

Art Gallery of Greater Victoria, 249–54

Ashmore, Peter, 167

Ashnola, 336

Ballantine, James, 242

Balmoral Castle, 15, 114, 162

Bamberton, 339

Banff Springs Hotel, 16

Bank of British Columbia, 160–61, 168–69, 176–80

Bank of Montreal, 180–82

Barclay, Archibald, 97

Barkerville, 212

Barkley Sound, 306

Barnard, Francis, 273

Barnard, George Henry, 186

Bastion Square, 107–08, 125, 220

Battle of Omdurman, 226

Bay Street Armoury, 222, 225–26

Bayley, Charles, 281

Baynes, Robert Lambert, 305

Beacon Hill Park, 58, 62, 83–89, 97, 135, 206, 274, 282

Beaver, Rev. Herbert, 29, 32

Beaver, 12, 92, 96, 102–03, 118–19, 125–27, 303

Begbie, Matthew Baillie; arrival in BC, 12; biography, 111–14; and Chinese, 200; court cases, 33, 63, 88, 125, 143, 207; death, 114, 290; and Native Indians, 53, 112–13, 121, 228; painting of, 8; statues of, 7, 26, 68–69

Belmont Building, 162

Benvenuto Seed Co., 341

Bering Sea, 298

Bickford Tower, 315

Bicknell, A. J., 302

Birkenhead Park, 89

Blacks, 140–41

Blair, John, 89

Blanchet, Norbert, 34

Blanshard, Richard, 104, 112

Bligh, Capt. William, 15

Bloomfield, Henry, 7

Bloomfield, James, 7, 268

Board of Trade Building, 107, 177

Boas, Franz, 54, 78

Bodega y Quadra, Juan Francisco de la, 8

Boer War, 225

Bolduc, Jean Baptiste, 45, 92

Bonnifield, Sam, 152

Boomerang Inn, 107–08

Bossi, Carlo, 189, 292–93

Bossi, Giocomo, 189

Bottineau, Pierre Versailles Baptiste, 95

Boxer, HMS, 212, 258, 305

Bradford Town Hall, 2, 10

Brentwood Bay, 339

British American Paint Works, 71

British Colonist, 143–46, 149, 154–55

British Columbia & Victoria Soap Works, 70–71, 133

British Columbia Electric Railway, 276–77

British Columbia Emigration Society, 137, 233

British Columbian, 63, 114

British Columbia Natural History Society, 55

British Columbia Pottery & Terracotta Co., 173

British Columbia Society of Fine Arts, 252

British Museum, 49, 58–59

Brooklyn Institute of Arts & Sciences, 79

Brotchie, Capt. William, 83–84

Brotchie Ledge, 83–84, 302, 325

Brother Jonathan, 144

Brown, Eric, 253

Brown Jug Saloon, 189

Bruce, Henry William, 304

Burdett-Coutts, Angela, 29, 230, 233

Burke, Edmund, 220–22

Burleith, 335

Burns, Robert, 84, 87

Burns Building, 108

Butchart, Jennie, 339–43

Butchart, Robert Pim, 339–43

Butchart Gardens, 339–43, 345

Butland, Edwin, 320

Buttes-Chaumont, 340–341

Byng, Baron, 23

Cadboro, 83, 92

Cairns, Hugh, 111

California & Hawaii Sugar Refining Co., 133

California Steam Navigation Co., 137

Cameron, David, 145, 236–37, 311

Canadian Pacific Lawn Bowling Club, 48

Canadian Pacific Navigation Co., 73, 128, 133, 153

Canadian Pacific Railway, 3, 10–22, 24, 73–74, 132, 166, 186, 193–94, 213, 284–85, 295–97

Canadian Pacific Railway Steamship Terminal, 10–13, 22, 286

Capital Iron Co., 133

Carey, J. W., 207

Carnarvon, Lord, 296

Carnegie, Andrew, 217–18

Carnegie Library, 216–18

Carr, Alice, 252

Carr, Emily, 34, 62–63, 76–77, 79–83, 89, 186, 250–57, 289

Carr, Richard, 80–83

Carr House, 76–77, 80–83

Carroll, Ellen, 238

Cary, George Hunter, 206, 266

Cary Castle, 245, 250, 266–69

Casco, 298

Cause Célèbre, 288

Centennial Square, 211

Central Park, N.Y., 89, 282

Chapchah, 306, 311

Charbonneau, Joseph, 95

Charybdis, HMS, 134

Château Frontenac, 16–17

Chateau Lake Louise, 22–23

Chicago World's Fair, 58

Chilcotin "War", 113, 188

Chilkoot Pass, 152–53, 179–80, 284

Chinatown, 189–203

Chinese Consolidated Benevolent
    Association, 194, 197–98

Chinese Exclusion Act, 203

Chinese immigration, 192–94, 199–200, 203

Chinese Imperial School, 190–91, 194,
    198–200

Chinese Point, 278

Chinese Public School, *see* Chinese
    Imperial School

Chittenden, Newton Henry, 55, 214–15, 295

Christ Church Cathedral, 30–31, 33, 98–99,
    226, 238–43

Churchill, Winston, 21, 243

Church of Our Lord, 28–34

City of Kingston, 128–29

City of Quebec, 297

Cizek, Albert Frank, 9

Clayburn, 248

Clayoquot Sound, 306

Cleopatra's Needle, 54

Clyde shipyards, 133

Coleman, D. C., 22

Collins, John, 87

Colonial Administration Buildings
    ("The Birdcages"), 53, 62–65,
    68–69, 172

Colonist Hotel, 82

Colville, Alexander, 329

Colwood, 98, 332–33, 334

Commodore, 135–36, 140–41

Commonwealth Games, 123

Compagnie Franco-Canadienne, 282

Condor, HMS, 319

Confederation, 45, 48, 66, 69, 295

Constance, HMS, 93, 96, 117, 304, 315–17

Constance Cove, 98, 305, 319, 326

Cook, Capt. James, 12, 15

Cormorant, HMS, 314

Courtenay, Capt. George W., 93, 117, 304

Cowichan Indians, 102–03, 116

Cowichan River, 103

Craigdarroch Castle, 70, 245, 256–65

Craigflower, 46, 58, 106, 326, 328–33

Crease, Henry Pering Pellew, 200

cricket, 84, 87, 97, 275, 332

Cridge, Rev. Edward, 28, 32–34, 230,
    233, 290

Crosby, Thomas, 228–29

Crystal Garden, 21–24, 286

Crystal Palace, 23, 171, 330

Customs House, 138–39, 151–54, 168–71

Dallas, Alexander Grant, 106

Dallas Hotel, 77

Davis, George, 128, 323–25

Davis, Rosina, 323–25

Dawson City, 152–54, 179

Deadman's Island, 319–20

Dean, John, 293

de Cosmos, Amor, 69, 105, 114, 143–51, 289

de Garro, Paul, 144–45

Delta Cannery, 135

Demers, Modeste, 34–41, 50, 144, 227,
    235, 311

Denman, Joseph, 306, 308–09

Devastation, HMS, 305–06

Dorsey, George A., 54, 58–59, 78, 229

Douglas, Amelia, 32, 44, 97, 101–02

Douglas, David, 87–88

Douglas, James; actions as governor, 28, 38, 63, 65, 94–95, 97–98, 103, 105–06, 134, 145–46, 172, 220, 225, 237, 304–05, 323; and the *Beaver*, 127; biography, 98–106; creating Beacon Hill Park, 62, 84; and E. E. Langford, 332–33; family life, 39, 43–44, 97, 101, 140; founding Fort Victoria, 45, 91–92, 101, 303, 345; funeral, 30–31, 34, 289–90; gold rush, 136–37, 142–43; obelisk, 2; painting of, 8; personal residence, 47, 62, 66–67, 246; and Peter O'Reilly, 157–58; relations with Bishop Demers, 35–36, 40; relations with Blacks, 140–41; relations with Native Indians, 47–48, 102–03, 116, 118, 121, 281, 305; relations with Richard Blanshard, 104

Douglas treaties, 48, 118, 121

Downing, Andrew Jackson, 246–47, 249

Driard, Sosthenes, 186

Driard Hotel, 186–87

Driver, HMS, 104

Duchess of San Lorenzo, 32

duelling, 87

Dufferin, Lord, 122, 267

Duncan, William, 227–28, 230

Dunsmuir, Alexander, 336

Dunsmuir, Emily, 234, 336

Dunsmuir, James, 225, 264–65, 268, 272, 297, 333–39

Dunsmuir, Jessie Sophia, 262

Dunsmuir, Joan, 257, 260, 262–63, 336

Dunsmuir, Laura, 335–36

Dunsmuir, Robert, 70, 150, 178, 199, 207, 246, 256–65, 289–90, 297, 333, 336

Duntze, Capt. John A., 304, 306

Duntze Head, 330

Eaton Centre, 162, 187

Ella, Capt. Henry Bailey, 245

Ellesmere, 246

Ellis, Charles Ezekiel, 28

Emden, 321

Empire Hotel and Restaurant, 188

Empress Hotel, 2, 4, 10–11, 14–22, 28, 62, 77, 181, 186, 274, 284

Empress of India, 73

Empress of Japan, 74–75, 132, 198

Empress of Scotland, 132

Enterprise, 106

epidemics, 58, 78, 116, 198

Esquimalt, 69, 72, 93, 95, 97, 118, 123, 125, 137, 157, 208, 220, 227, 238, 258, 296, 303–20, 330

Esquimalt & Nanaimo Railway, 174, 186, 199, 208, 263, 294–97

Esquimalt Road, 311

Estevan Point lighthouse, 131–32, 322

Eve Marie, 297

Fannin, John, 53–56, 58–59, 78

Fan Tan Alley, 191–94, 197, 202–03

Fan Tan Cafe, 203

Fergusson, John Duncan, 252

Field Museum, 54, 58, 78–79

Finlayson, Roderick, 32, 43–45, 92–95, 115–18, 122, 150, 192, 207, 289–90

Finlayson Point Battery, 84

First Presbyterian Church, 241

Fisgard, HMS, 304, 306, 324

Fisgard lighthouse, 64, 80, 128, 172, 304, 322–27

Fisher, Elmer H., 250

Five Sisters Block, 166, 177

Foote, Capt. Hamilton, 153

Fort Kamloops, 136

Fort Langley, 91, 142

Fort McLoughlin, 92

Fort Nisqually, 93
Fort Rodd, 225, 313, 318–22
Fort Rupert, 104, 305
Fort St. James, 101–02
Fort Simpson, 93, 227–28
Fort Vancouver, 32, 34, 87, 91–92, 101
Fort Victoria, 8, 32, 35, 38, 43, 45, 47, 50,
    61, 90–99, 101, 103, 106, 115–23, 133, 135,
    140, 220, 288, 344
Forward, HMS, 137, 305
Fox, Cecil Crocker, 173
Franklin, Lumley, 237
Franklin, Semlin, 237
Fraser Mines Vindicated, The, 105, 188
Fraser River gold rush, 103, 105, 111, 112,
    121–22, 133, 135–37, 140, 142–43, 146–47,
    192, 237, 305

Galiano, Dionisio Alcala, 303
Garrison Artillery, 224-25, 321
Garrison cemetery, 319–20
Garry, Nicholas, 87
Garry oaks, 87
Geological Survey of Canada, 79
German Club, 25
Gibbs, Mifflin, 141
Gibson, George, 9
Gibson, William Wallace, 63
Glad Tidings, 228
Glasgow City Chambers, 3
Glenlyon School, 281, 287
gold rush, *see* Fraser River gold rush
Gonzales, 172
Goodacre, Lawrence, 186
Gordon, Capt. John, 93
Gorge Vale Golf Course, 320
Government House, 17, 23, 28, 241, 246,
    265–75
Government Street, 16, 80–83, 160–73

Gowans, Alan, 287
Grand Pacific Hotel, 189
Grand Trunk Pacific Railway, 18, 21,
    274, 285
Grant, Walter Colquhoun, 331–32
Grappler, HMS, 305, 324
Great Eastern, 134
Green, Alexander Arthur, 250
Grey, Earl, 91, 104, 118
Group of Seven, 253

Haddington Island, 9
Haida, 56–58, 78, 117
Hansen, Gustav, 301
Hardy Island, 73
Harris, Thomas, 205–07
Hastings, George F., 134
Hastings Mill, 134
Hatherleigh, 72
Hatley Park, 274, 333–39, 344–345
Hays, Charles Melville, 285
Hayward, Charles, 84
head tax, 199–200
Hecate, HMS, 305, 324
Helmcken, Cecilia Douglas, 44, 47
Helmcken, J. S., 32, 35, 42–47, 50, 66, 78,
    93–95, 97–98, 126, 141, 143, 146, 150–51,
    238, 266, 331
Helmcken House, 40, 43–47
Herald, HMS, 220
Higgins, David William, 144–45, 246
Hills, Rev. George, 29, 33–34, 230–33, 237
Hollybank, 47, 77
Hooper, Thomas, 36, 71–72, 167–68, 173,
    182–85, 187, 218, 235, 272
Hotel Canada, 182–83
Hotel Vancouver, 166
Howe, Joseph, 144
Howe, S. L., 254

Hudson's Bay Company, 8, 29, 32, 43–47,
    58, 61, 73, 77, 83–84, 91–106, 115–18,
    120–21, 125–27, 133, 135–36, 142, 145,
    171–72, 192, 219–23, 258, 275, 281, 326,
    329–33
Hughes, William, 12

Illahie, 246
Imperial War Graves Commission, 289
Ingram, Arthur Foley Winnington, 243
Inverness Museum, 54
Irish Linen Stores, 162
"Iron Chink," 135
Isabel, 12
Islander, 153

Jacobsen, Victor, 297–99, 301–02
James, Douglas, 335
James, Percy Leonard, 22–23, 286, 335
James Bay, 28, 44, 60–89, 141
James Bay Bridge, 74–75
Jellicoe, Viscount, 314
Jewish cemetery, 237, 288
Jewish community, 236–37
Joly de Lotbinière, Henri-Gustave, 84, 272
Jonckau, John, 235
Judge, William, 152–53
Julien, Philip, 282

Kaiserhof Hotel, 25
Kanakas, 95, 96
Keen, Rev. J. H., 229
Keith, John Charles Malcolm, 241–42
Kennedy, Arthur, 266–67
Kew Gardens, 23, 78
Keyes, Lt. Adrian, 312–13
Kingfisher, 306
Kipling, Rudyard, 17, 278
Klee Wyck, 254

Klondike gold rush, 133, 151–54, 179–80
Kwong Lee & Co., 192, 197

Ladysmith, 225
Lally, Robert, 131
Lam, David, 272
Langford, Edward Edwards, 332–33
Larkin, Pegleg, 145
Laurel Point, 71
Le Courrier de la Nouvelle Caledonie, 144
Lee's Benevolent Association, 194–95
Legislative Assembly, 45–46
Leipzig, 314, 321–22
Leiser, Simon, 246
Lemmens, John Nicholas, 234
Lester, Peter, 141
Lester & Gibbs, 141
Lockwood, Henry Francis, 4, 10
Lockwood & Mawson, 2–4
Lorne, 262
Lorne, Marquis of, 39
Loudon, John Claudius, 288–89
Lusitania, 25, 273, 336
Lush, Henrietta, 82
Lush, William, 82
Lytton, Edward Bulwer, 47–48, 106

Macauley, William James, 71–72
McBride, Richard, 123, 313, 321
McCausland, Joseph, 8
McCreight, John, 149
Macdonald, Alexander Davidson, 178
McDonald, Alexander, 152
Macdonald, John A., 45, 149, 158, 186,
    295–96
Macdonald, W. J., 77, 133, 192
Macfie, Rev. Matthew, 123, 140
McGregor, J. Herrick, 26
Mackenzie, Agnes, 326

Mackenzie, Kenneth, 289, 326, 329–30

McLean, Alexander, 301

McLean, Donald, 136

McLean, G. K., 272

McLoughlin, John, 32, 101

Maclure, John Cunningham, 173

Maclure, Margaret Catherine Simpson, 174

Maclure, Samuel, 166, 173–77, 234,
    244–49, 268–69, 274, 277, 286–87,
    334–36, 340–41, 345

McNeill, William Henry, 126

McPherson Playhouse, 212

Malacca, HMS, 308–09

Man Yuck Tong, 203

Marega, Charles, 9

Maritime Museum, 125–32, 302

Market Square, 184–85, 189

Marquis of Bute, 28

Martin, Mungo, 48, 53

Mary Dare, 126

Mawson, Richard, 2

Mawson, William, 2

Maxwell, Edward S., 285

Maynard, Hannah, 121, 128–29, 210–17

Maynard, Richard, 211–17

Meadows, "Arizona Charlie", 152

Melrose, Robert, 326

Menzies Street drill hall, 222

Merchants Bank, 161–62

Metlakatla, 227–28, 230

Metropolitan Methodist Church, 235–36

Michaud, Charles, 37

militia, 224–25

Milne, Alexander Roland, 188

Milne Block, 187

Minnie McLean, 297

Moody, Sewell, 84

Moresby, John, 93, 97, 101–03, 305

Morley, Alfred James, 277

Morris, E. A., 167–71

Morris, William, 87

Morris & Co., 7, 273

Mount Baker Hotel, 276

Mount Royal Rice Milling &
    Manufacturing Co., 133

Mount Royal Park, 282

Muir, Andrew Maxwell, 108, 208, 272, 332

Muir, John, 153

Munro, Alexander, 73

Munro's Books, 171, 182, 185

Murchie, John, 162

Musgrave, Anthony, 265–66

Musgrave, Richard John, 262

Naden, HMCS, 314

Nanaimo, 220

Nanette, 324

National Gallery of Canada, 253

Natural History Museum, 3, 287

Nass River, 305

Native–non-Native relations, 29, 34, 36,
    47–50, 54, 58, 113, 115–23, 227–30, 305–06

Naval and Military Museum, 314

Nelson Island, 9, 306

Neues Museum, 54

Newcombe, Charles Frederic, 58–59,
    77–79, 253

Newcombe, William, 79

New Zealand, HMS, 27

Nisga'a, 230

Norman Morrison, 43, 245, 326, 329, 333

North West Company, 98, 221

North-West Mounted Police, 153

Nuttgens, J.E., 242

Oak Bay, 62, 275–81

Oak Bay Hotel, 276

Oak Bay Land & Improvement Co., 276

Oblates of Mary Immaculate, 227

Occidental Hotel, 189

Ogden, Peter Skene, 77, 221

Ogden Point, 72–79, 127, 131, 133, 303, 312

Ogilvie, William, 153

Oliver, William, 228–29

Olmsted, Frederick Law, 89

Olmsted, John Charles, 282–83

Olympian, 138–39

opium factories, 192–93, 203

O'Reilly, Caroline Trutch, 158

O'Reilly, Charlotte Kathleen, 154, 156–58

O'Reilly, F. J., 26

O'Reilly, Peter, 154, 156–59, 289

Oriental Hotel, 189

Otter, 90–91, 96, 136

Pacific, 84

Pacific Mail Steamship Co., 258

Pacific Swift, 125

Painter, Walter S., 18

Pakenham, Alma, 21, 286, 288

Pamir, 130–31

Panama, 12

Pandora, HMS, 304, 306

Pantages, Alexander, 212

Paper Box Arcade, 188

Parliamentary Library, 9–10, 22

Parliament Buildings, 1–10, 21, 55, 61, 68–69, 236, 254, 273, 277, 287

Paterson, Thomas Wilson, 272–73

Patterson, J. V., 313

Paxton, Joseph, 89

Pearkes, George, 272

Pelly, John Henry, 91, 102, 104

Pemberton, Frederick Bernard, 172

Pemberton, J. D., 98, 171–72, 323, 331

Pemberton Holmes Building, 168–69, 171–73

Pender, Capt. Daniel, 306

Pendray, William J., 70–71, 289

Pendray House, 70–72

Perrault & Mesnard architects, 232–34

Phillips, Andrew, 238

Pig War, 104

Pike, John W., 305–06

Pinehurst, 71–72

Pioneer Shaving Saloon and Bath House, 141

Plumper, HMS, 96, 118, 324

Point Ellice House, 154–59

Poole, Charles Edward, 289–90

potlatch, 58, 113

Powell, Israel W., 54

Powell Bros., 7

Price, Bruce, 16

Prince of Wales, 17

Prince Rupert, 21

Princess Alice, 132

Princess Joan, 127

Princess Kathleen, 12

Princess Louise, 39–40, 345

Princess Louise, 213

Princess Marguerite, 12–13, 132, 273

Pritchard, Thomas, 238

Providence, Sister Mary, 39

Provincial Court House (Vancouver), 166

Puget Sound Agricultural Co., 220, 329, 333

Puget Sound & Alaska Steamship Co., 128

Quadra Street burial ground, 237–38, 288

Queen Charlotte Islands, 56–58, 117, 213, 252–54

Queen Elizabeth, 315–16

Queen Elizabeth 11, 49, 241

Quimper, Manuel, 303

Race Rocks, 324–25
railway hotels, 14–16
Rainbow, HMCS, 313–14, 321
Rattenbury, Florence, 284-86
Rattenbury, Francis Mawson; and Bastion
    Square, 107; design for Crystal Gardens,
    21–23, 286; design for Empress Hotel,
    10, 15–21; design for Government
    House, 246, 268–72; design for Parlia-
    ment Buildings, 3–4, 7–10, 21, 69, 71,
    236, 287; early life, 2–3; Klondike busi-
    ness venture, 152, 284; married life,
    284–86; miscellaneous buildings, 161–62,
    166, 170, 180–82, 198, 218, 249, 276–78,
    282, 284–85; murder, 288; personal resi-
    dence, 277, 280–81, 284–88; relationship
    with Alma Pakenham, 21, 286, 288; and
    Union Club, 24; working for CPR, 10,
    18, 22, 284; working for Grand Trunk
    Pacific, 18, 21, 285
Rattigan, Terence, 288
Redon, Louis, 186
Reed, Kate, 18
Reformed Episcopal Church, 290
Regent's Park, 88
Regent's Place, 246
Reksten, Terry, 263
residential schools, 227
responsible government, 149
Rexford, Loring P., 25
Richards, Capt. George Henry, 118,
    305–07, 324
Richardson, H. H., 177, 235–36
Ridley, William, 226, 228
Riffington, 282
Rithet, Robert Paterson, 47, 73–75, 77, 133,
    135, 150, 206, 289
Robertson II, 125
Robillard, Arthur, 340

Robson, John, 63, 114
Rocket, HMS, 54, 290, 305
Rockland, 62, 70, 245–75
Rogers, Charles W., 162–63, 167
Rogers, Mrs. Charles W., 162–63, 167
Rogers' Chocolates, 162–63, 167–68
Ross, Charles, 45, 92, 95, 97, 237, 288
Ross, Frank M., 17, 274
Ross Bay cemetery, 34, 107, 115, 150, 237,
    264, 288–93
Royal Academy, 242
Royal Bank of Canada, 171, 182–83, 185
Royal Bavarian Art Institute, 235
Royal British Columbia Museum, 47–48,
    52–59, 79
Royal Canadian 5th BC Field Regiment,
    273, 315
Royal Canadian Navy, 313
Royal Engineers, 14, 136, 271–72, 304–05
Royal Geographic Society, 115, 332
Royal Institute of British Architects, 242
Royal London Waxworks, 11
Royal Navy, 69, 104, 117–18, 133, 158,
    208, 220, 238, 258, 304–09, 312–15,
    321–22
Royal Ontario Museum, 79
Royal Roads, 304, 312
Royal Roads Military College, 338–39
Royal Roads University, 344
Royal Scottish Museum, 79
Royal tour 1939, 273–74
Royal Victoria Yacht Club, 275
Russell, G. Horne, 274
Russian American Co., 102

St. Andrew's Cathedral, 232–35
St. Andrew's Presbyterian Church, 24,
    205, 234
St. Ann's Academy, 34–40

St. Ann's Chapel, 37

St. Ann's Convent, 288

St. John the Divine Church, 222, 233–34

St. Joseph's Hospital, 36, 40

St. Joseph's Mission, 311

St. Louis College, 36

St. Mary's Priory, 257

St. Paul's Anglican Church, 230

St. Paul's Naval and Garrison Church, 316, 319–20

salmon canning, 135

San Juan Islands, 104

San Pedro, 83

Satellite, HMS, 142

Scott, George Gilbert, 243

Scott, Robert Falcon, 158

Scott, Thomas Seaton, 151

Scott, Premier Walter, 284–85

Scrogg Rocks, 325

Sea Bird, 12, 35

sealing, 298, 301–02, 310–11

Seeman, Berthold, 220

Seghers, Charles John, 25, 235

Selfridges Department Store, 220, 222

Service, Robert, 154, 179–80

Seymour, Frederick, 267, 320

Shaughnessy, Thomas, 16, 186

Shawnigan Lake, 295

Signal Hill, 316

Simpson, George, 91–92, 101, 103, 106, 126–27, 221

Sisters of St. Ann, 35–40, 137, 227, 233

Skagway, 153–54

Skidegate, 56–57

Skinner, Thomas, 326, 329

Skinner's Cove, 304

Smith, Arthur L., 261

Smith, Donald, 219

Snowdon, Northington Pinkney, 336

Society for the Propagation of the Gospel, 227

Songhees, 50, 78, 92, 115–23

Sooke, 331

Sorby, Thomas, 165–66

Southwell, George H., 8, 254

Sparrowhawk, HMS, 320

Spencer, David, 187, 250

Spencer House, 249–50

Spode Shop, 162

Spratt, Capt. Joseph, 127

Sproat, Gilbert, 73, 311

Staines, Rev. Robert, 32, 38–39, 44, 94

Stamp, Edward, 12, 134–35

Star shipyards, 133

Steele, Sam, 153

Stevenson, Robert Louis, 298

Stewart, Alexander, 25

Straith, George, 162

submarines, 313, 321–22

Sullivan, Louis, 177

Sutlej, HMS, 306, 308–09

Tate Gallery, 254

Teague, John, 33, 36–37, 108, 159, 186, 189, 197, 207–08, 289, 315, 335

Temple Building, 166, 173–77

Temple Emanuel, 236–37

Thames City, 12

Thermopylae, 127, 133

Thetis, HMS, 93, 97, 101, 103, 305

Thunderbird Park, 47–53

Tiedemann, Hermann Otto, 64, 107–08, 111, 322

Tiffany Studios, 273

Tilikum, 302

Titania, 134

Titanic, 285

Tod, John, 97, 275–76

Tod Inlet, 339
Todd, Charles Fox, 246
Tolmie, William Fraser, 46, 54
Topaz, HMS, 236
totem poles, 48–53, 79, 123, 253
Trial Island, 131
Triangle Island, 131
Trimen, Leonard Buttress, 234
Troup, Capt. J. W., 289, 292–93
Trutch, Joseph, 66, 122, 149, 158
Tsimshians, 227–29
Turner, J. H., 78
Tynemouth, 137, 233
Tyrwhitt-Drake, M., 26

Union Club, 24–28, 115, 313
Union shipyards, 133
Upland, John, 281
Uplands, 278–79, 281–83
Uplands Farm, 98, 281–82
urban parks, 88–89

Valencia, 127–28
Vancouver, Capt. George, 1, 7–8, 15, 69
Vancouver Art Gallery, 254
Vancouver Coal Mining and Land
    Co., 258
Vancouver Hotel, 10
Vancouver Portland Cement Co., 339–40
Van Horne, William Cornelius, 15, 17–18
Vaux, Calvert, 282
Vereydhen, Charles, 36
Vernon, C. H., 173
Victoria, Queen, 1–2, 15, 102, 252
Victoria & Sidney Railway, 211
Victoria City Hall, 33, 135, 206–09, 296
Victoria Daily Chronicle, 145
Victoria Electric Light Co., 186
Victoria Electric Railway Co., 276

Victoria Golf Club, 276
Victoria Horticultural Society, 23
Victoria Law Courts, 64, 108–09, 111,
    125, 172
Victoria Machinery Depot, 72, 127, 189
Victoria Philharmonic Society, 115
Victoria Phoenix Brewery, 248
Victoria Pioneer Rifle Corps, 224–25
Victoria Public Market, 208, 211–12
Victoria Roller Flour and Rice Mills, 133
Viewfield, 98
Voss, John C., 302
Voysey, C. F. A., 173

Waddington, Alfred, 105, 113, 135, 144, 188
Waddington Alley, 188
Wallace, Hubert, 282
Wallis, Christopher, 241
Walpole, Spencer, 111
Ward, Robert, 166, 173–74
Wark, John, 46–47, 95, 97, 159, 237, 289
Warspite, HMS, 262
Weiler family, 165
Weiler Building, 162, 164–66, 168–69
Weissmuller, Johnny, 23–24
Welch Rithet & Co., 135
Wells, W. C., 268
Wentworth Villa, 245–46
Westby, William Henry, 340
Whitechapel Bell Foundry, 241
White Pass, 153
William and Ann, 126
Williams, Warren Heywood, 178–79,
    257, 261
Williams & Co., 154–55
Willows Farm, 275–76
Wilson, Biggerstaff, 244–45, 247–49
Wilson, Lt. C. W., 96
Wilson, W. & J., 162

Wilson, William, 248

Wilson, William Ridgeway, 222,
   233–34, 250

Windsor Park, 275–77

Windsor Station, 3, 16

Wood, Lt. James, 304, 306

Woodcock, George, 150

Work, John, *see* Wark, John

Workingman's Protection Society, 199

World's Columbian Exposition, 283

Wright, John, 80, 159, 233, 236, 245, 267,
   322–23

Yale, 103, 136

Yarrows shipyard, 72, 127, 241, 282

Yat-Sen, Sun, 199

Zealous, HMS, 320